DINING IN GRAND STYLE

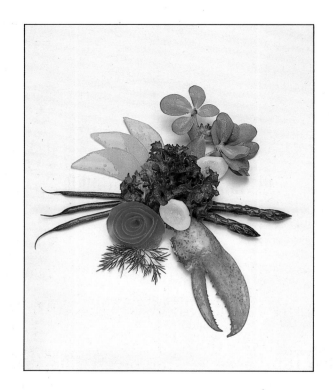

PHOTOGRAPHY BY MICHAEL GRIMALDI

DINING IN GRAND STYLE

BY ELIZABETH SCHNEIDER

◆

WITH DIETER HANNIG

AND THE CHEFS OF HILTON INTERNATIONAL

THORSONS PUBLISHERS, INC.
Rochester, Vermont

DESIGN BY ANA ROGERS
PHOTOGRAPHS STYLED BY DIETER HANNIG

It is with much pride in their accomplishments that we dedicate this book to all the Hilton International chefs and their kitchen brigades.

John Jarvis
Chairman
Hilton International Co.

The publisher would like to acknowledge the tremendous support and cooperation of all the individuals whose contributions helped to realize this project. Of special note are Alan Gould and Maddy Cohen of Hilton International; Thorsons Publishers, Inc., staff members Leslie Colket, Estella Arias, and Jeanie Levitan; and the staff members of Thorsons Publishing Group in the United Kingdom.

Ehud C. Sperling, Publisher

Thorsons Publishers, Inc., One Park Street, Rochester, Vermont 05767

Text and photography copyright © 1988 by Thorsons Publishers, Incorporated

Library of Congress Cataloging in Publication Data
Schneider, Elizabeth.
Dining in grand style / by Elizabeth Schneider with Dieter Hannig and the chefs of Hilton International; photography by Michael Grimaldi.
p.   cm. Includes index.
ISBN 0-7225-1003-9
1. Cookery, International.   2. Hilton International (Firm)
I. Hannig, Dieter.   II. Grimaldi, Michael.   III. Hilton
International (Firm)   IV. Title.
TX725.A1S4217   1988
641.509-dc19   87-18938

Composed by NK Graphics in Times Roman with Latin Elongated display type
Printed by New Interlitho in Milan, Italy

10 9 8 7 6 5 4 3 2 1

Distributed to the book trade in the United States by Harper & Row Publishers, Inc.
Distributed to the book trade in Canada by Book Center, Inc., Montreal, Quebec.

PAGES 2–3: Stuffed Tofu with Shrimp (see page 264 for recipe) on an ornamental carrot net
PAGES 4–5: A fleet of canapes from the Hilton International Wien
PAGES 6–7: Braised and Grilled Chicken in Coconut and Javanese Spices (see page 312 for recipe) surrounded by chili-peppers, cones of palm sugar, lemon grass stalks, candlenuts (kemiri), fresh turmeric, and wild lime leaves
PAGES 8–9: Executive chef Albert Schnell (holding silver *cloche*) with his precision team in Toronto

CONTENTS

THE AMERICAS

EUROPE

ASIA AND AUSTRALIA

Dining in Grand Style...

O nce upon a time the good life revolved around hotels. At the heart of each great hotel were its dining rooms and ballroom, where fashionable society gathered. When chef Auguste Escoffier reigned at the Grand Hotel in Monte Carlo, then the Savoy, and the Carlton, the *haut monde* followed—taking their steamer trunks bursting with morning dresses, smoking jackets, tea gowns, and sundry supper finery. The days of a "year abroad" would commence beneath down coverlets with a silver service of hot chocolate, discreetly delivered, and finish with a champagne soiree in the ballroom.

Dining in grand style is not simply a dream of yesteryear, for the old-style service and spacious and tranquil dining rooms of Hilton International are more in tune with Escoffier's era than the business bustle of the jet-age. The array of crystal and cutlery, the decorative napkin folds, the dazzling (not fussy) garnishes, and the low-key formality all suggest a past few have known—with all the modern conveniences. Today's luxury hotel is a haven from the speed of our times, whether it serves as an oasis for the accomplishment of business negotiations or for romantic idylls.

Worldwide...

The term "hotel dining" has quite different meanings from one continent to another. In the Americas, particularly the United States, the words "fine food" and "hotel" have until recently been just about mutually exclusive; but a resurgence of quality dining in hotels is refreshingly apparent. In particular, local ingredients and cooking styles have come into their own, and restaurants that celebrate regional specialties have burgeoned. In the mid-seventies European-trained Albert Schnell, area chef for Hilton Canada, began featuring superb local produce—Manitoba wild rice, Alberta beef, Canadian apples and maple syrup—in elegant dinner menus in the hotels he supervised. At the outset of the '80s, a team at the American Harvest Restaurant in the Vista International Hotel in New York City pioneered the fine-dining-room presentation of simplified traditional dishes, such as Martha's Vineyard Green Corn Pudding and Shaker Lemon Pie.

In contrast, fine dining has long been considered a province of hotels throughout Europe, which are *expected* to prepare the best food—even when measured against small restaurants run by big-name chefs—whether in Strasbourg, Brussels, or Vienna and whether they serve 20 or 2,000 meals a day. Europe is the best known jousting ground for proving culinary prowess. Critics lie in wait to applaud, downgrade, bemoan, enshrine, and otherwise point out the virtues and vices of every morsel of food that enters a luxury dining room. And the European audience, parochial or cosmopolitan, amateur or professional, is composed of indefatigable judges. In this competitive atmosphere Hilton International hotels have flourished, winning kudos (and stars) from such travel arbiters as *Michelin* recommendations of the highest order in restaurant handbooks, and a devoted local clientele wherever Hilton chefs hang their toques.

In Asia, food presentation in hotels is, simply, without equal. Every diner is visiting royalty. Graceful men and women attend. Roses and jasmine perfume the air. Drink

Messieurs Bergeret (left) and Dupont of the Hilton International Genève in the hotel's dining room, Le Cygne

and food preferences, and the names of each member of the party are recorded by the staff, it appears, from the moment of arrival. Torrents of carved fruit greet the early morning breakfaster or all-night discoer at the hotel's coffee shop. Ice sculptures and sprays of orchids vie for attention with the overflowing desserts displayed at even the simplest lunch buffet. The choice of cuisines is considerable throughout the Orient, and European-trained chefs and American cultural exports have recently expanded the repertoire. Businessmen zip between Tokyo and San Francisco, London and Hong Kong, and bring with them their East-West tastes and appetites. Yet traditional Oriental cuisines are still the focus in most Asian hotels. Venerable local dishes, exquisitely prepared, star in the Hilton International restaurants in Tokyo and Jakarta, Bangkok, Kuala Lumpur, Singapore and Taipei, among others, even as those same kitchens are transforming the riches of the East into a powerful new hybrid vocabulary.

To meet the multicultural requirements of contemporary guests (represented by as many local residents as worldly voyagers), each Hilton International hotel includes several restaurants—from coffee-shop casual to sparkling fine dining room. These proffer both internationally known classics and, most intriguing for the adventurous traveler, dishes that reflect the cooking of the country in which the hotel is located—both scrupulously researched authentic fare and chefs' original creations. The interpolation of local ingredients and use of regional handicrafts in the decor are key policies of the company, which educates staff members in the culture and cuisine of an area through an extensive culinary heritage program. Whether the subject is speedily stir-fried noodles with Oriental vegetables in the Jakarta Hilton International's informal Peacock Cafe, or a complex chef's invention such as spiced smoked duck breast with a palette of sweet-hot Eastern vegetable salads in the elaborate Taman Sari Grill Room in the same hotel, aesthetics and flavors are sure to be Indonesian.

With the Chefs of Hilton International

It takes a special kind of executive chef to supervise the scope of these large hotels, to oversee the banquet and room service operations and as many as a half-dozen restaurants. For not only must he be superbly organized, able to direct others, imaginative, cost-conscious, healthy as a horse, and have the physical and emotional energy to keep up such a balancing act; he must be willing and able to assimilate the culture and customs of a foreign country in order to appreciate and understand his staff, the food, and the local guests. He usually does this without the personal celebrity allotted to chefs whose names are synonymous with their own small restaurants. He is what might be called a chef of the old school, who apprentices in his early teens, works through the ranks, and whose life *becomes* the hotel kitchen. It is not unusual, for example, to find a 35-year-old chef who has spent 22 years in the business, working a strenuous 14 or so hours per day, six days per week. The drive and dedication needed to sustain such a role might be compared to that of a ballet dancer or competitive athlete—always in training, always ready to perform. Yet the chef's performance takes place backstage; it is the food that stars.

A chef's work is reinforced by every member of the food staff, maintained by kitchen teams that often work together for decades. He relies on his sous-chef(s) to handle the grand-scale fulfillment of each day's assignments and on his maître d' to report responses to a new dish on the menu; the waiter depends upon the maître d's familiarity with the clientele to guide him through the maze of personalities and individual preferences. Dining rooms and kitchens of this calibre are no place for transient actors, college students, or other part-timers, as is often the case in more casual restaurants. The roles are reserved for professionals who are devoted to the task. As in a fine theater troupe, all parts, no matter how small, are pivotal to the performance.

About the Recipes

Although each of Hilton International's hotels offers unique dishes in its dining rooms, the recipes in this volume represent about one-quarter of its hotel kitchens in the Americas, Europe, and Asia. In order to create a broad and balanced selection of flavors—and to produce a book that is portable—a number of noteworthy restaurants have necessarily been left aside.

While this may be a geographical simplification, it nevertheless describes much of the scope of the food produced in the Hilton International kitchens, where culinary cross-fertilization is a fact of life: Oriental presentation deeply affected all of European Nouvelle Cuisine; European chefs working in Asia applied their Western techniques to the stimulating array of unfamiliar ingredients; concurrently, other European-trained cooks traveled westward and were captivated by the bounty of North America; while at the same time, the American Melting Pot was boiling over with newly found regional self-expression. The recipe for a dish created in the United States by a Swiss chef who has spent years in the Caribbean will be found in the Americas section, because that is where the chef, restaurant, and diners for whom the dish has been developed are located. Thus the recipes do not usually reflect any single national cuisine, but rather a multicultural approach to restaurant dining.

A meal in the fine dining room of a deluxe hotel is a special event. There, one celebrates—a fiftieth anniversary, a success in business, Christmas, the beginning of a new career, or falling in love. The atmosphere is far from the ordinary, but not so demanding that attention focuses on the surroundings, rather than the occasion. Diners dress up in order to feel festive and formal, to create an aura of timelessness, a magic landscape. Thus, for the most part, people come to enjoy "non-home" cooking, to be pampered, to linger—to eat more and drink more than they do other evenings. Although dishes may appear simple, more often than not they will be intricate and rich. It is in a fine dining room that a chef can let his creative fancy run free, where exotic and unfamiliar ingredients are explored, where luxury reigns. This is party food.

Naturally, no one eats party food every night, nor would a home cook attempt to duplicate some of the specialties served in a Vista or Hilton International dining room—unless he/she had a kitchen staff of 15. Selected here are a range of particularly delicious and unusual recipes of varying degrees of simplicity and difficulty of preparation, all of which have been tested and adapted for successful reproduction by the home cook. Some are quickly made and inexpensive, some are time-consuming to prepare, many are gloriously rich, and some undeniably luxurious. All are to be enjoyed in a party mood, for that is what fine dining is about.

RECIPES BY CATEGORY

APPETIZERS

SALADS

SOUPS

VEGETABLES, GRAINS, AND PASTA

SEAFOOD

MEAT AND POULTRY

DESSERTS

RECIPES

APPETIZERS

SALADS

SOUPS

VEGETABLE AND GRAIN DISHES

PREVIOUS PAGE: **Executive chef Walter Plendner with members of the kitchen staff of the Vista Hotel in New York**

SEAFOOD

MEAT AND POULTRY

DESSERTS

The Food Research Center:
The Heart of the Story

When a delegation of Indonesian businessmen at the Vista International Hotel in Washington, D.C., wishes to treat their American associates to an authentic *rijstaffel,* the chef needs little time to find out how to prepare and serve the many parts of this traditional meal. The Texas businessmen staying at the Jakarta Hilton International and pining for a homestyle American barbecue can have their desire fulfilled easily. A Hilton chef in Nairobi who wishes to learn about the latest developments in vacuum-pouch cooking can become *au courant* at a moment's notice. Before a chef garde-manger (cold kitchen chef) moves from Strasbourg to the Caribbean, he can acquaint himself with the fruits and spices of the area, while a barman transferring from Chicago to Sydney can familiarize himself with Australian specialty drinks in no time flat. And the banquet for 4,000 that requires the same number of starched napkins to be folded artichoke-style will run more smoothly if the new employees study up on the intricate creases with the help of Napkin Folding II.

What gives the Hilton International kitchen staff immediate access to these topics are the microfiches created by the Food Research Center in New York City. Through the magic of a tiny color transparency, the Center has made it possible for all members of the food and beverage staff of Hilton International to obtain information about the subjects above and some 150 others. Each of the hotels is equipped with a microfiche reader (comparable to a small slide projector) that allows the operator to view the film at his own speed, either on a small personal-size screen or a large one, for class instruction. The goal of this microfiche system is not to create a uniform style or to dictate what is correct or incorrect, but to offer springboards off which kitchen teams can perform in ways that best suit them, given the limitations of each geographical/ cultural region. The recipes included in such films are points of departure for the chef, for Hilton International encourages the personal expression of its cooks, and even flights of fancy (a German chef constructed an entire Bavarian gingerbread village for Christmas at the Mayaguez Hilton in Puerto Rico, for example—to the delight of the staff, guests, and locals).

The tiny Food Research Center quietly ticks along in an unglamorous subterranean maze beneath the shining silver towers of Three World Trade Center at the Vista International Hotel. The microfiches, as well as an award-winning in-house quarterly trade magazine, are generated from this modest office. Begun in 1976 at the Queen Elizabeth Hotel in Montreal, the Center has since completed some 290 microfiches. Foremost is the collection of over 4,200 recipes from 43 countries—the result of Hilton International's 39 years in the hotel business, and a clear expression of the willingness of its chefs to share their wisdom and experience.

The microfiches are conceived, written, and photographed through the Food Research Center. Subjects are determined by the proposals of company chefs and food and beverage managers, who submit annual suggestions for their preferences. About two-thirds of these are fulfilled on location (worldwide) by the director of the Food Research Center assisted by the individual hotel staffs; one-third is executed completely

Dieter Hannig of the Food Research Center—en route, as usual

at the Center, in its shining test kitchen. It takes a unique combination of culinary, photographic, teaching, and diplomatic skills to be able to handle the job of director of the Food Research Center for Hilton International; but if anyone can live up to the challenge, it is energetic, experienced, charming Dieter Hannig, whose considerable stamina and organizational abilities have earned him medals both in hotel kitchens and on ski slopes worldwide.

Consider a morning in the life of the Food Research Center: As chambermaids who tend to the 829 rooms of the Vista New York chat and change in locker rooms alongside, as the remains of a wine-tasting for 500 are wheeled by for disposal and a group of new employees are guided through the corridor on a tour of the hotel's underpinnings, Hannig (the same fanciful chef responsible for the Caribbean cookie town) pulls out the microfiche on Atlantic Salmon Farming. With the film in the microfiche reader to check a fact for a press release to be used by the American Harvest Restaurant upstairs, he casts an eye over the supply of oranges needed to demonstrate a giant new juicer to the visiting food and beverage managers of 25 hotels attending a course at the Career Development Institute of Hilton International, farther down the hall. He hurries into the kitchen adjacent to his office to lower the heat on the duck stock that will be part of tomorrow's lunch for a departing executive, sets aside the muffins he is testing and will later photograph for a microfiche on American breakfast items, and smiles to welcome a cheesemaker from New Jersey who has arrived with samples of her excellent goat cheese. He then reviews the schedule for London, where he will be presenting a workshop on vacuum-pouch cooking that weekend, questioning a few points. His utterly unflappable secretary notes the changes, accepts a delivery of electrically heated copper chafing dishes to be evaluated, puts off a manufacturer of instant sauces who has just telephoned, and greets the troupe that squeezes into the kitchen for the juicer demonstration.

As is the case for most European chefs, training for Mr. Hannig began early, away from home. From an apprenticeship begun at 13, he moved among fine hotels in

The Magical Microfiche: A 6x4-inch plastic-coated film containing 49 photos and 49 recipes or training lessons is Hilton International's primary communicating medium

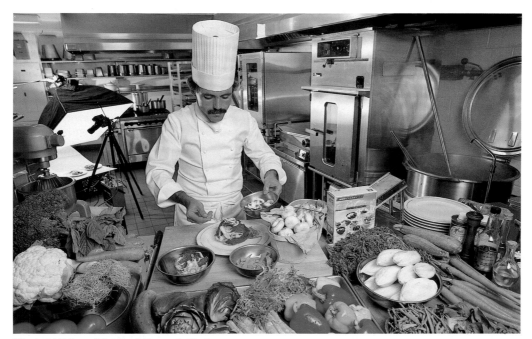

The test kitchen of the Food Research Center

Germany and Switzerland. Divided between a career in the kitchen or on the ski slopes, the cooking side won out—although the athletic outlets are still numerous. Hannig became sous-chef of the Hilton International Kensington in 1974, then held various positions of authority throughout the company. It was during assignments in locales with little access to up-to-date culinary magazines and books that he became acutely aware of the need for transmitting information throughout the whole system on a regular basis. "Many of our chefs do not have the opportunity to stay abreast of the new food trends and technical developments because of their geographical location," he explains. "In certain regions of the globe professional literature is rare or nonexistent. Microfiche projects judged superfluous by some constitute a precious work tool for others."

Even on a small scale, Mr. Hannig is a hands-on learner and educator, enthused by the challenge of the new. Faced with the unfamiliar task of testing recipes for a cook-book, he plunged in with gusto, so thoroughly adapting to the needs of a home cook that his colleagues at Vista suggested he exchange his chef's garb for a ruffled apron with roses. Teased continually about tiny whisks and spoonlets, he cheerfully continued to acquire a *batterie* of home-size utensils, the cup and teaspoon measures dwarfed to ridiculousness by the professional-scale equipment that surrounds the testing area. He became the part, rearranging sliced meat on platters to serve family-style, avoiding last-minute preparations, finding compromises that would not alter the integrity of a dish; in short, raising questions that simply do not enter into the vocabulary of a professional chef. What he does, he does wholeheartedly. He has visited almost all the hotels to under-stand the workings of the kitchens, staff, and surroundings. His natural curiosity and in-tuition have given him a keen awareness of the strengths and weaknesses of the vast human network that makes up the Hilton International family—which has in him an effective, sympathetic central transmitter for its food and beverage communications system.

SMOKED SALMON AND GOLDEN CAVIAR CRÊPES WITH SALAD GREENS

CANADA

This is the work of Albert Schnell (executive chef of the Hilton International Toronto), who pays particular attention to the acquisition of the finest local ingredients. While he calls for both Canadian smoked salmon and Canadian golden caviar, fish from other waters would not be out of order. The luxurious appetizer is generously endowed with silky salmon in a cream mosaic twirled into pale crêpes. The spiral slices are embellished with a flurry of fashionable (and striking) salad leaves.

1 whole egg
1 egg yolk
Salt
½ cup half-&-half
⅓ cup (1½ ounces) all-purpose flour
1 tablespoon melted butter, plus additional melted butter for the pan
4 ounces (about ½ cup) golden (whitefish) caviar (or substitute red lumpfish eggs)
1 cup sour cream
1 teaspoon minced onion

About 1 teaspoon lemon juice
9–10 ounces smoked salmon, cut into paper-thin slices
1 teaspoon minced shallot
1 tablespoon red wine vinegar
Pepper
¼ cup walnut oil
Minced tarragon and chives (or other herbs to suit)
32 assorted salad leaves, rinsed and dried (see Options)

1. Blend together the whole egg, egg yolk, a pinch of salt, and half-&-half in a mixing bowl. Mix in the flour. Add the butter. Strain through a fine sieve. Cover and let stand for 1 hour or longer.

2. Heat a 6-inch crêpe pan over moderate heat. Brush lightly with butter. In portions of 3 scant tablespoons each, ladle the batter into the pan; quickly tilt and shake to cover the bottom of the pan completely. Cook the crêpe for 30–45 seconds, until the top is dry; turn and cook for 15 seconds, until barely colored. Set aside. When all of the batter is used, you should have 7 crêpes—one as security, or to eat.

3. Place the caviar in a small strainer and tap firmly until no more liquid drips off. Combine in a small bowl with ¾ cup sour cream. Add the onion and about ½ teaspoon lemon juice, or to taste. Spread the cooled crêpes with the remaining ¼ cup sour cream, smoothing with a flexible spatula. Top each with a neat layer of smoked salmon to cover completely. Spread the caviar-cream over this, leaving a margin around the rim. Gently and slowly roll into neat cylinders.

4. Place the crêpes on a platter, wrap tightly, and refrigerate for 2–6 hours.

5. At serving time, cut each roll into 4 pieces on the diagonal, slicing slowly and carefully. Arrange 3 slices on each of 8 plates.

6. Combine the shallot, vinegar, ½ teaspoon lemon juice, and salt and pepper to taste in a small bowl. Whisk in the oil. Gently toss with the minced herbs and salad leaves. Distribute on the plates.

Serving/Presentation: *Do not crowd the rolls. Serve on wide plates that play off the color and drama of the arrangement.*
Advance preparation: *The crêpes can be made up to a day before serving. The salmon rolls can be prepared and refrigerated up to 6 hours ahead. If tightly covered, they even can be sliced in advance.*
Options: *Bibb, radicchio, Belgian endive,* mâche *(corn salad), and Boston lettuce are colorful and tasty companions—choose all or some.*

8 SERVINGS AS AN APPETIZER

SNAILS IN BLACK BEAN SAUCE ON TOFU
(Escargots Dau See)
HAWAII, UNITED STATES

A striking departure from traditional snails in garlic butter—both in appearance and flavor: dark snails and salty black beans are spooned over white tofu rectangles accompanied with shining snow pea pods and cherry-red bell pepper strips. This unusual opener is a regular (in a restaurant filled with devoted regulars) at the deliciously gaudy Maile restaurant of the Kahala Hilton in Honolulu. Gold-trimmed presentation plates, the heaviest cut crystal, an ochre carpet studded with red Japanese medallions, and mammoth displays of bamboo, ginger flowers, cerise anthurium, and polished maile leaves ("to Hawaii, what the laurel was to Rome") set the scene in what is among the most beautiful properties in the company.

Two 7-ounce cans snails (about 36), preferably from France
1 pound medium tofu (also called regular or Japanese tofu)
2 medium scallions
3 tablespoons peanut oil
1 teaspoon minced garlic
1 tablespoon minced fresh ginger
2 tablespoons fermented (salted) black beans, chopped (see Note)
½ cup homemade (unsalted) chicken stock
¼ cup oyster sauce (see Note)

About 2 teaspoons minced fresh hot chili-pepper (such as jalapeño or Cayenne, seeds removed)
¾ teaspoon sugar
1½ tablespoons Chinese rice wine (or substitute dry sherry)
1 teaspoon cornstarch
36 snow peas (about ¼ pound), strings removed
1 large red bell pepper, seeds and ribs removed, cut into 2 × ¼-inch strips
Cilantro leaves

---

1. Preheat the oven to 400°. Drain the snails, reserving the liquid. Cut the tofu crosswise into 6 pieces. Place on a towel to drain. Cut the scallions in fine slices, separating the white and green parts.

2. Heat 1 tablespoon of the oil in a medium saucepan over moderate heat. Stir in the garlic, ginger, and the white part of the scallions. Stir for 1 minute to soften, but not color.

3. Add the black beans, chicken stock, oyster sauce, 1 teaspoon chili-pepper, and sugar; bring to a simmer. Blend together the rice wine and cornstarch. Stir into the sauce and bring to a boil. Add the snails, 2 tablespoons of the reserved liquid, and the green part of the scallions; remove from the heat.

4. Heat an ovenproof nonstick skillet with 1 tablespoon of the oil. Place the tofu in the pan in a single layer, leaving some extra space. Set in the center of the oven for 10 minutes.

5. Meanwhile, heat the remaining 1 tablespoon oil in a wide skillet. Add the snow peas and red bell peppers and toss over moderate heat for 4–5 minutes, until they lose their raw crunch, but are still crisp. At the same time, warm the snails over low heat.

6. Arrange the tofu on 6 dishes; over this, spoon the snails and sauce. Arrange the vegetables alongside. Sprinkle with the remaining chili-pepper and cilantro to taste.

Note: *Salty, dried fermented black beans are available in plastic packs or cans in all Oriental markets, as is oyster sauce. Both will keep indefinitely in the refrigerator.*

6 SERVINGS AS A FIRST COURSE

GRAVLAX (SALMON MARINATED WITH DILL AND PEPPER)
CANADA

While this version of the classic Scandinavian salt-cured salmon was developed by Albert Schnell, executive chef of the Hilton International Toronto, many variations are best-sellers in Hilton International hotels worldwide.

The firm, translucent slices of salmon are counterpoised by a sharp-sweet, herb-flecked sauce that is quite light in texture and holds its shape softly. This popular appetizer is appropriate year-round, particularly with iced aquavit and pumpernickel fingers.

1½-pound salmon fillet (with skin)
⅓ cup coarse kosher salt
½ cup sugar
1 tablespoon white peppercorns, crushed

1 small bunch fresh dill (reserve some for garnish)
1 tablespoon brandy
1 tablespoon light vegetable oil

1. With tweezers or fine pliers, pull out any small bones that may remain in the salmon fillet. Place the fish, skin side down, in a heavy plastic bag.

2. Combine the salt, sugar, and peppercorns; rub over the fish. Turn over the fillet. Bruise the dill to release its aroma; spread over the fish. Drizzle the brandy and oil over this. Close the bag tightly and set it in a pan; place another pan on top and set a 3-pound weight in this to press down the fish. Let stand at room temperature for 6 hours or so, turning occasionally. *(continued)*

3. Refrigerate the *gravlax* for about 2 days, turning as convenient—preferably every 6–8 hours, then replacing the weight.

4. Shortly before serving, remove the fish from the bag and reserve the marinade. Scrape the seasoning mixture from the fish, and set the salmon on a work surface. Working at an extreme angle, cut into very thin, even slices, freeing each slice from the skin with a firm cut.

5. Arrange the slices petal-fashion on individual serving dishes. Place about 2 tablespoons Mustard-Dill Sauce (recipe follows) alongside and garnish with dill sprigs.

8–10 SERVINGS AS AN APPETIZER

Mustard-Dill Sauce for Gravlax

3 tablespoons sugar
1½ teaspoons dry mustard
3 tablespoons distilled white vinegar
1 tablespoon strained marinade from
   Gravlax (preceding recipe)
6 tablespoons mild prepared mustard

2 teaspoons sharp or Dijon-style
   mustard
1 scant cup sunflower oil (or another
   light vegetable oil)
2–3 tablespoons minced dill leaves

1. Combine the sugar, dry mustard, vinegar, and reserved marinade in a small non-aluminum bowl. Stir to blend. Add the mild and sharp prepared mustards.

2. Gradually whisk in the sunflower oil. Add the dill. Cover and refrigerate for 1 hour or longer.

8–10 SERVINGS (ABOUT 1⅓ CUPS)

Swordfish and Grapefruit Escabeche

PUERTO RICO, UNITED STATES

This sunny yellow appetizer is perfect for parties, as it mellows and improves with keeping. Sweetly oniony, gently spiced, the modicum of olive oil and refreshing addition of grapefruit make this updated version of a traditional Caribbean recipe considerably lighter than its forebears. Its concentrated flavors and close textures are more attractive in small portions, as a first course, than as a main course, but escabeche *is customarily offered in large servings.*

1¼ pounds swordfish
About ¾ teaspoon salt
White pepper
5–6 tablespoons olive oil
¼ teaspoon turmeric
3 medium onions, halved and
   sliced thin
2 medium yellow bell peppers, cut
   lengthwise into thin slices
1 medium garlic clove, sliced thin
1 teaspoon mixed pickling spices

½ teaspoon minced thyme or
   lemon thyme
1 bay leaf, crumbled
3 medium-large grapefruits
3–4 tablespoons white wine vinegar
3 small heads of Bibb lettuce, rinsed
   and dried
1 red bell pepper, cut into fine julienne, *or* 4-ounce package Oriental radish sprouts *(kaiware)*

---

1. Trim away the skin and dark center area from the fish. Cut the flesh on the diagonal into 1½-inch-square slices, each about ½ inch thick. Sprinkle with ½ teaspoon salt and white pepper to taste.

2. Heat 1½ tablespoons oil over moderate heat in a wide nonaluminum skillet. Add half the fish and color on both sides, just to cook through—about 2 minutes. Transfer to a wide dish. Heat 1 tablespoon oil and cook the remaining fish; add to the dish.

3. Blend 2 tablespoons oil with the turmeric. Add to the skillet and reduce heat to low. Add the onions, peppers, garlic, pickling spices, thyme, and bay leaf. Cook for 5 minutes, until the vegetables are no longer raw, but still crisp.

4. Squeeze enough grapefruit to make ¾ cup juice. Add to the vegetables, along with 3 tablespoons vinegar; simmer for 3 minutes. Pour over the fish, distributing evenly.

5. Let cool, then cover and refrigerate for at least 24 hours, or up to 3 days, turning occasionally. Season with salt, oil, and vinegar to taste.

6. To serve, let the *escabeche* reach room temperature. Arrange the lettuce on 6 plates. Cut all the rind, pith, and membrane from the 2 remaining grapefruits. Cut between the membranes to release the sections. Arrange them with the *escabeche* on the lettuce. Top with the red pepper julienne or radish sprouts.

6 SERVINGS AS A FIRST COURSE

TERRINE OF GRAVLAX

UNITED STATES

Originated in European kitchens, this fine appetizer has been adapted by Leo Waldmeier, executive chef of The Drake hotel in Chicago. Opalescent strips of leek and rosy salmon meld in a mosaic of shining aspic. When cut, the colorful checkerboard design is as charming and unpretentious as the straightforward flavors: salty salmon and fresh-sweet vegetables in a light, briny aspic.

2½–3 quarts fish stock (see recipe, page 326)
4 large leeks (about 3 pounds)
1 envelope unflavored gelatine
8 long, narrow carrots (about 1¼ pounds)

Gravlax (see recipe on page 35, but do not slice)
Mustard-Dill Sauce (see recipe on page 36)

1. Boil the stock until reduced to 1¾ cups.

2. Meanwhile, have ready a 1-quart narrow terrine mold (about 11 × 3½ × 3½ inches). Trim the roots from the leeks. Remove several layers by cutting a lengthwise slit in each and unpeeling; when you have a smooth central core of leek about ¾ inch in diameter, stop removing the layers. Trim this core to the length of the mold. Discard dry or damaged outer layers of leek; trim the green from the remaining peeled-off layers. Place these and the 4 cores to soak in cold water.

3. When the stock has reduced, sprinkle the gelatine over it and stir to dissolve. Peel and trim the carrots. Drop them into a large kettle of boiling salted water. Cook until tender (*no* crunch remaining or the terrine cannot be cut smoothly), about 8 minutes. Fish them out of the water and place in ice water to chill; drain and dry on towels.

4. Drop the 4 leek cores into the water; poach gently until tender, 4–5 minutes. Lift these out, then refresh in ice water. Drain and dry thoroughly on towels, pressing to remove liquid. Turn the heat to high, drop the leek layers into the boiling water and boil until pliable, a minute or two. Refresh, drain, and dry.

5. Set the pot of stock in a pan of ice and water. Stir the aspic now and then until syrupy-thick.

6. Line one side of the terrine with the leek layers, arranging them so that they overlap slightly and one narrow edge is centered in the bottom of the terrine while the other hangs over the side. Continue around the terrine, overlapping the bottom slices slightly as you place them in the other side of the terrine. Trim the carrots as necessary to form a single band along each long side of the terrine.

7. Cut the skin from the *gravlax*. Slice the fillet lengthwise to form 4 equal strips, which should be more or less the same length as the terrine. Set one of these between the carrots. Ladle in enough almost-jelled aspic to just cover this layer. Set the terrine in ice water until the aspic gels.

8. Place a whole leek core lengthwise on top of each carrot band. Cover the salmon strip in the center with trimmed lengths of carrot. Place a strip of salmon on top of each leek. Pour in chilled aspic to barely cover this layer, then set in ice water.

9. When the aspic has firmed, place another trimmed band of carrot along each side, a leek next to this, and a salmon strip in the center. Pour in aspic to barely coat. Fold the leek ends over the top, trimming to meet neatly in the center. Finish with a thin coat of aspic.

10. Chill for at least 6 hours, or up to 24. To unmold, dip in hot water, then run a knife gently around the edge to release the aspic. Invert onto a cutting board, rapping sharply. Immediately return to the refrigerator for a few minutes to fix any melting exterior aspic.

11. Cut gently into serving slices, sawing rather than pressing down on the loaf. Serve with Mustard-Dill Sauce alongside each slice.

Serving: *As an appetizer, offer one slice per person. For a cool, summer lunch, serve 2 slices, along with boiled red potatoes (with skins)—set at a distance from the cold aspic, or they'll melt it.*

14–16 SERVINGS AS AN APPETIZER; 8 AS A LUNCH MAIN COURSE

BARLEY "RISOTTO" WITH BLUE CHEESE

UNITED STATES

Dieter Hannig, director of the Food Research Center, developed this unusual multi-national first course in the style of the Italian rice specialty risotto when he was working on a microfiche about French cheeses. In the southern part of Germany, where he has lived, grains (particularly barley) are used with almost daily regularity. In this rather sumptuous treatment of an ingredient usually considered rustic, the chewy barley is enriched by the fermented flavor of the blue cheese, the undertone of wine, and a generous butter liaison. The pearly, cream-slicked grains are far too dense and rich to serve as anything but a first course, perhaps with a red wine from the Rhône Valley. Follow up with a main course of ham or cold veal roast and salad.

1⅓ cups barley
8 tablespoons butter
⅓ cup minced shallots
1¼ teaspoons minced garlic
½ cup dry white wine
¼ cup heavy (or whipping) cream

4 ounces mild blue cheese, such as
   Bleu d'Auvergne (see Options),
   crumbled (about ¾ cup)
Pepper
Watercress

---

1. Pour the barley into a generous amount of boiling salted water, stirring until it returns to a boil. Boil gently until tender to taste, about ½ hour. Drain, rinse lightly.

2. Heat 6 tablespoons butter in a wide, deep skillet or casserole over moderate heat. Add the shallots and garlic and cook until softened, but not browned.

3. Add the barley and toss over high heat until the grains are coated. Add the wine and stir for a few minutes until most has evaporated. Add the cream and bring to a boil, stirring. Remove from the heat.

4. Stir in the cheese, then the remaining 2 tablespoons butter; add pepper to taste. Spoon into heated plates, garnish with watercress, and serve immediately (or the dish becomes gluey).

Options: *Any mild blue-veined cheese can be substituted for the* Bleu d'Auvergne, *if it is difficult to obtain:* Fourme d'Ambert, Pipo Crem', *Gorgonzola. The stronger blues—such as Roquefort and Danish blue—are too sharp.*

4 SERVINGS AS A FIRST COURSE

Avocado and Grapefruit Salad with Honey Vinaigrette

CANADA

When Albert Schnell, area chef for Hilton Canada, Inc., introduced this salad on the appetizer menu of the Beaver Club at the Queen Elizabeth hotel in 1976, it was a novelty. Now, similar recipes are popular throughout North America, but few have the delicate balance of this simple classic: the creamy dressing (both light textured and colored— thanks to the sunflower oil) clings to the smooth avocado and juicy grapefruit without hiding the natural, low-key flavors.

1 tablespoon honey
¼ teaspoon salt
¼ teaspoon white pepper
3 tablespoons lemon juice
⅓ cup sunflower oil

2 medium grapefruits
2 medium avocados (preferably the dark, pebbly-skinned Haas variety)

1. In a blender or processor, mix the honey, salt, pepper, and lemon juice to blend. With the motor running, gradually add the oil, whizzing until pale and creamy. Refrigerate until serving time.

2. Cut all rind, pith, and membrane from the grapefruits. With a sharp knife cut between the interior membranes to free each section. Halve, pit, and peel the avocados; cut each half into 5 lengthwise slices.

3. Alternate overlapping slices of the avocado and grapefruit over 4 salad plates. Spoon dressing over each slice.

Note: *Although the dressing can be made in advance, do not cut the grapefruit much before serving, or it will liquefy the dressing. If you find it inconvenient to prepare this way, place the sliced fruit in a strainer until serving time.*

4 SERVINGS AS A SIDE DISH OR FIRST COURSE

Spinach, Quail Eggs, and Livers in Raspberry-Walnut Vinaigrette

CANADA

Like all of Albert Schnell's recipes, this one is a thoughtful balance of color, texture, temperature, and taste. A mound of spinach ribbons crowned with white mushroom

(continued)

Spinach, Quail Eggs, and Livers in Raspberry-Walnut Vinaigrette

confetti, red-orange tomato dice, and glistening walnut bits is accented by halved ovals of quail egg. The walnut flavor blends with the gamy liver and earthy vegetables for a salad that is at once fresh and rich. The dish is suitable for light supper or lunch, perhaps preceded by a delicate cream soup; or served as a first course.

---

2 tablespoons raspberry vinegar
About ¼ teaspoon salt
White pepper
1 teaspoon finely minced shallot
1 teaspoon lemon juice
½ teaspoon minced fresh tarragon leaves, or ¼ teaspoon dried, crumbled
8 tablespoons walnut oil
¾ pound small-leaf spinach

6 quail eggs (see Note)
¼ pound medium button mushrooms, chopped (see Note)
2 medium tomatoes, peeled, seeded, and diced (about ¾ cup)
⅓ cup walnut halves, coarsely chopped
¾ pound (about 12 medium) chicken livers, cleaned and halved

---

1. In a small bowl, combine the vinegar, ¼ teaspoon salt, pepper to taste, shallot, lemon juice, and tarragon: stir to blend. Gradually whisk in 7 tablespoons of the walnut oil.

2. Dunk the spinach into a sink filled with cool water. Swish around, then lift out so the soil falls to bottom. Repeat as necessary. Strip the stems from the leaves and discard them. Dry the leaves completely, preferably in a spin-dryer. Set aside 24 of the smallest; cut the remainder into thin strips.

3. Place the quail eggs in a small pan of simmering water and cook for 1½ minutes. Refresh momentarily in cold water, then peel carefully (their centers will be soft).

4. Mix the mushrooms and tomatoes with 2 tablespoons of dressing. Combine the spinach strips and walnuts; toss with ¼ cup of the dressing. In another bowl, combine the whole leaves with 2 tablespoons of the dressing.

5. Arrange the whole leaves around 4 plates. Divide the strips into the center of each, then top with mushrooms and tomatoes.

6. Sprinkle the livers with salt and pepper. Heat the remaining 1 tablespoon walnut oil over moderate heat in a small skillet. Sear the livers to brown lightly on each side. Add the remaining dressing; toss the livers to just cook through.

7. Arrange the livers on the plates; garnish with the quail eggs, carefully halved. Serve warm.

Note: *If you cannot obtain quail eggs, substitute 2 hard-cooked chicken eggs (these larger eggs cannot be neatly cut if soft-cooked), each sliced into 6 wedges.*
  If you prefer to have palest white mushrooms, peel them.

4 SERVINGS AS A MAIN COURSE; 6–8 AS A FIRST COURSE

Snow Pea-Cucumber Salad

UNITED STATES

Low-calorie, nutritionally balanced recipes, such as the following, are the subject of a microfiche put out by the Food Research Center. Summery ribbons of snow peas and yellow bell pepper, cucumber crescents, and sweet rounds of water chestnuts are refreshingly dressed with lemon and ginger. Appealing crunchiness and simplicity make this a fine foil for barbecued and fried meat, fish, or poultry.

About 9 ounces fresh water
   chestnuts (see Note)
6 ounces snow peas
3 medium cucumbers (about 1½
   pounds), peeled
1 yellow bell pepper, seeds and ribs
   removed, cut into fine julienne

2 tablespoons chopped onion
1 tablespoon grated fresh ginger
3 tablespoons safflower oil or
   another light vegetable oil
¼ cup rice vinegar
Salt

1. Scrub the water chestnuts under running water. Peel as closely as possible, then drop into boiling salted water and boil for 7–8 minutes, until cooked through. Meanwhile, zip the strings from the snow peas; cut the pods diagonally in half. Lift the water chestnuts from the pot with a sieve and drop into ice water. Toss the snow peas into the water; boil until they just lose their raw crunch—a minute or so. Drain and add to the ice water.

2. When the vegetables are cooled, drain them. Cut the water chestnuts into thin coins. Pat the peas dry on paper towels. Quarter the cucumbers lengthwise, then scoop out the seeds. Slice crosswise into thin crescents. Combine in a bowl with the water chestnuts, snow peas, and bell pepper.

3. Combine the onion, ginger, oil, vinegar, and salt to taste. Toss together with the vegetables. Season to taste. Chill thoroughly, but no longer than 6–7 hours, or the cucumbers will give off too much liquid and the snow peas will discolor.

Note: *Fresh water chestnuts, available in Oriental groceries and some supermarkets, are sweet, crisp, and altogether delightful. In comparison, canned chestnuts are crunchy—and that's about it. However, if you cannot obtain the fresh, an 8-ounce can of whole peeled water chestnuts will do.*

4 SERVINGS AS A FIRST COURSE OR SIDE DISH

Pepper Slaw

UNITED STATES

When the American Harvest Restaurant at the Vista International New York was planned, 1,500 well-loved typical American recipes competed for inclusion in the seasonally-adjusted menu. Among the final selections was this version of a recipe from James Beard, whose readers frequently requested that it be reprinted in his newspaper columns.

It is a pleasant change from more traditional cole slaws, with its larger pieces, big crunch, and vivid color. Serve it with hamburgers, steak sandwiches, ham, and all kinds of barbecue.

⅓ cup distilled white vinegar
½ teaspoon salt
Pepper
1 tablespoon Dijon-style mustard
2 teaspoons mustard seeds
2 teaspoons celery seeds
2 teaspoons sugar
½ cup light vegetable oil
1 very small white cabbage (about 1¼ pounds)

1 pound green bell peppers (about 4 medium), seeds and ribs removed
2 small carrots, cut into paper-thin slices
1 medium onion, halved and cut in paper-thin slices
1 celery rib, cut into ½-inch dice

---

1. Combine the vinegar, salt, pepper to taste, mustard, mustard seeds, celery seeds, and sugar in a bowl; whisk to blend. Slowly add the vegetable oil, whisking.

2. Trim the cabbage; cut into ¾-inch slices, then cut these again to form squares; separate the layers. Cut the peppers into ¾-inch squares. Combine in a bowl with the carrots, onion and celery.

3. Pour the dressing over the vegetables; toss. Add seasoning to taste. Refrigerate for 3–6 hours. Season again before serving.

6 SERVINGS AS A SIDE DISH

Scallops, Cucumbers, and Mushrooms in Basil-Peppercorn Vinaigrette

UNITED STATES

Crunchy cucumbers, soft scallops, zesty cress, and fleshy raw mushrooms contrast and complement in a pale-hued salad touched with the keen pungency of green and pink peppercorns—the work of Franz Kranzfelder, award-winning senior sous-chef at The Drake hotel in Chicago.

¼ **cup white wine vinegar (preferably basil-flavored)**
½ **teaspoon salt**
¾ **cup olive oil**
About 1½ teaspoons drained, water-packed green peppercorns, chopped
About 1 teaspoon dried pink peppercorns, crushed with a knife blade
1 hard-cooked egg, chopped
2 tablespoons very finely slivered basil leaves

1½ **teaspoons minced shallot**
2 pounds sea scallops
1 cup boiling water mixed with ½ teaspoon salt
1 large hothouse (English, burpless, gourmet) cucumber
¾ **pound small-medium mushrooms, peeled**
1 bunch watercress (about ¼ pound), trimmed, rinsed, and dried
8 cherry tomatoes, halved

1. Make the dressing: Blend together the vinegar and salt; slowly add the oil, whisk in. Stir in 1½ teaspoons green peppercorns, 1 teaspoon pink peppercorns, the egg, basil, and shallot. Mix well and set aside for at least 2 hours so that flavors blend.

2. Place the scallops in a saucepan in a single layer; pour over the boiling salted water; cover and return to a simmer. Remove from the heat, uncover, and let cool.

3. Cut the cucumber into fine julienne (do not peel); arrange in the center of 4 large plates to make a circular bed in each.

4. Drain the scallops. Slice into ⅛–¼-inch rounds. Arrange over the cucumbers.

5. Trim the mushroom stems, slice the mushrooms and arrange in 4 heaps on each plate, around the cucumber.

6. Place heaps of watercress between the mushrooms. Decorate with cherry tomatoes. Divide the dressing evenly among the salads, stirring frequently and spooning slowly to coat all ingredients.

Advance preparation: *The salads can be arranged up to an hour in advance, as the scallops are particularly tasty at room temperature.*

4 SERVINGS AS A MAIN COURSE; 6–8 AS A FIRST COURSE

TOP: **Terrine of Gravlax (see page 38 for recipe) with Mustard-Dill Sauce (see page 36 for recipe)** BOTTOM: **A slightly modified version of Scallops, Cucumbers, and Mushrooms in Basil-Peppercorn Vinaigrette**

BLACK BEAN AND SEAFOOD SALAD

PUERTO RICO, UNITED STATES

When Dieter Hannig was executive chef at the Hilton International Mayaguez, he served special dinners in a dining room off the kitchen called The Chef's Table. There, local products were the focus and culinary invention the expected mode. An example of such an approach is this salad based on the ubiquitous black beans—in a new guise.

---

1 cup dried black beans (turtle beans)

1 medium onion

1 bay leaf

2 cloves

1 pound cleaned squid (or 1¼ pounds uncleaned; see page 324)

8 very large shrimp in the shell (about 1 pound)

3 medium plum tomatoes, peeled and chopped (about 1 cup)

1 large green bell pepper, seeded and cut into small dice

1 tender celery rib, minced

1 small onion, chopped

2 tablespoons chopped cilantro

¼ teaspoon salt

½ teaspoon black pepper

1 tablespoon lime juice

2 tablespoons sherry vinegar

1 tablespoon minced garlic

2 tablespoons olive oil

4 cilantro sprigs

---

1. Rinse and pick over the beans. Soak overnight in cold water, covered.

2. Drain the beans and combine with 4 cups water in a saucepan. Bring to a boil; lower the heat, then return to a boil, skimming. Make an incision in the onion and insert the cloves and bay leaf. Add to the beans; cook, covered, over low heat until just tender. (Timing can vary considerably, but 45–60 minutes is usual. Check often after 30 minutes of cooking.) Cool, uncovered, then strain off any liquid.

3. Meanwhile, slice the squid mantles into thin rings. Divide the tentacles into manageable mouthfuls, if necessary. Drop into a pan of boiling salted water. Barely simmer for 2 minutes, or until just cooked through. Drop the shrimp into another pan of boiling salted water; return to a simmer and remove from the heat. Drain, then peel and devein.

4. Combine the beans, squid, tomatoes, bell pepper, celery, chopped onion, and cilantro in a large bowl and blend gently.

5. Combine the salt, pepper, lime juice, sherry vinegar, garlic, and olive oil in a small bowl; mix well. Pour over the salad and toss gently. Marinate for 1 hour or so. Taste for seasoning. Divide the salad onto serving plates. Slice the shrimp lengthwise and set around the salad. Garnish with cilantro sprigs.

Advance preparation: *The salad can be refrigerated for 24 hours, but the flavors will be more pronounced.*
Options: *At the Hilton International Mayaguez broiled shrimp were served instead of the cold poached ones, and the dish was served with deep-fried plantain slices (tostones) and corn sticks (surullitos).*

4 SERVINGS AS A MAIN COURSE; 6–8 AS A FIRST COURSE

Mussel Salad with Leeks

CANADA

Lightly cooked leek strips and full-flavored mussels are bound here with a pale yellow mayonnaise-like dressing made from reduced cooking juices. Shreds of celery and acid tomato slivers balance harmoniously, thanks to chef Albert Schnell. The portions suggested will do nicely as a main course for lunch. Gauge about 20 medium-large mussels per person, or 25 smaller ones.

2 large shallots, minced
¾ cup dry white wine
About 5 pounds (3 quarts) cultivated mussels (see page 324)
2 medium leeks (about 1 pound), trimmed, halved lengthwise, and well washed
2 tablespoons olive oil
¼ teaspoon saffron threads

½ cup heavy (or whipping) cream
Salt and pepper
Lemon juice
2 heads of Bibb lettuce, cleaned
1 tomato, peeled
½ cup thin julienne of tender celery ribs
1 teaspoon minced fresh tarragon (see Options)

1. Combine the shallots and wine in a wide nonaluminum pot and bring to a boil. Add the mussels, cover, and cook, shaking the pot occasionally, over moderately high heat just until opened, about 2 minutes. Lift out the mussels and let them cool briefly, then remove from the shells, placing mussels in a large bowl.

2. Strain the cooking liquor through doubled, dampened cheesecloth, pouring slowly to avoid sand that may lurk in the bottom. Pour into a skillet or saucepan.

3. Cut the leeks into fine julienne about 2½ inches long (you should have about 4 cups). Add to the pan. Bring to a full boil, reduce the heat, and cook on low for 5 minutes, or until just tender.

4. With a slotted spoon, transfer the leeks to the bowl with the mussels. Add the olive oil, saffron, and cream to the poaching liquid in the pan; boil, stirring, until reduced to 1 cup.

5. Pour over the mussels and leeks, mix, and leave to cool. Cover and refrigerate for several hours or up to 1 day.

6. Arrange the lettuce leaves on a large serving platter. Season the mussel mixture, adding salt (taste carefully: mussels can be very salty), pepper, and lemon juice to taste. Arrange over the lettuce leaves. Quarter the tomato; cut out and discard the interior. Slice the tomato shell into thin julienne. Arrange these and the celery over the mussels. Sprinkle with tarragon; serve.

Options: If fresh tarragon is difficult to find, substitute thyme, basil, or parsley. A dash of Pernod or Ricard adds a lively Mediterranean lift.

4 SERVINGS AS A MAIN COURSE; 6–8 AS A FIRST COURSE

MANOLO DÍAZ

Conquistadores con Canapés, Bar Mitzvahs con Brio at the Caribe Hilton International— Where It All Began

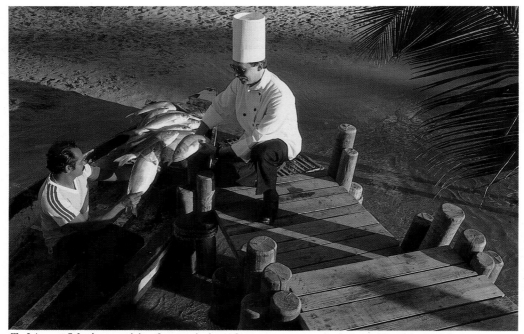

Chef August Schreiner receiving the morning's catch PREVIOUS PAGE: **A photographic session on location**

D ifficult as it may be to believe, there was little tourism in Puerto Rico until relatively recently. The 18 acres of Atlantic oceanfront that embrace the complex of buildings that make up the Caribe Hilton International (and include the only virtually private beach in Puerto Rico) went begging for years. When local businessmen could not be encouraged to build a first-class tourist hotel in the area, the president of the Puerto Rican Industrial Development Company turned to the United States for investors. There was just one interested party, who replied in Spanish: Conrad N. Hilton. The rest, as they say, is history, for thus began the operation of the first hotel by the company that has since become Hilton International. A resounding success since its first day in 1949, it has remained the foremost resort on the island, attended by a devoted following of local residents and mainland guests who are moving into their third generation.

The staff and much of the menu are doing the same. Foods favored in the fine dining room, La Rotisserie, have not changed dramatically since the opening: roast prime ribs or rack of lamb, spit-roasted poultry, and broiled steaks and lamb chops are in the forefront. Warm, chatty Miguel Marquez, the maître d', has greeted diners there for 35 years (as have five of the waiters). Handsome Roberto Pagan, red-kerchiefed and dressed in starched white, has manned the open broilers of the dining room for 21 years (a relatively short time for a member of this staff), keeping up with the demands of a regular audience ("Roberto, remember that I want the end-cut," or "I'll be in for dinner at 8 o'clock tomorrow with company; 12 kosher chickens, nice and dark, with crispy potatoes—you know, the way I like them)." Daily, William Otero has confected 13 types of pastry for 29 years—with Napoleons, rum balls, and *coquitos* (toasty, supersweet coconut squares with a fudgelike texture) the most popular items. Hector Torres, the affable bar manager, heads a staff of 35, whose members represent over 700 years of service to the hotel. Seventy-year-old Ramon (Monchito) Marrero, who invented the celebrated piña colada at the Caribe, has supervised the assembly of what is now a daily average of at least 300 of the rum, coconut cream, and pineapple juice drinks. Expressive Epifanio Rivera (Riverita), who began in 1949, explained, gesticulating, that "if you don't feel it, you can't work in a hotel. It involves your family, your mind, everyone. New boys coming in—they don't love the life the way we do." In fact, about 35 percent of the food and beverage staff has been on board for at least 20 years, giving the large and ever-growing Caribe a surprisingly homey quality.

Francisco (Pancho) Gonzales, the methodical, dignified chef garde-manger (cold kitchen chef) "began as a cold meat man when the hotel opened and is still the absolute best and fastest in the business," praised August Schreiner (Augusto to all), the electrically charged, much-loved executive chef, who works at lightning pace himself (and speaks at the same, alternating English, Spanish, and German). "Just last week Pancho prepared 10,000 canapés in eight hours; someone else would need two days for the job," praises Chef Augusto. The party for which Pancho set up the canapés was for 3,000 guests (who polished off 6,000 piña coladas). Riverita was responsible, among other things, for the preparation of 10,000 *empanadillas de carne* (fried meat-filled turnovers), 1,000 pounds of blood sausage, and a farm-full of pigs for barbecue.

Every event seems larger than life in this buzzing extension of the San Juan social community. The day's activity calendar in the lobby lists seminars for Citibank, cooking classes, a local dance troupe's show, a lecture on chromosome abnormality, junior executives' society cocktails, a bar mitzvah—and more. Doctors in grey suits brush past bikini-garbed sun-worshipers en route to poolside; beruffled wedding parties pour into a banquet room recently vacated by the manufacturers of a new soft drink. An average year tallies 50 weddings; 125 cocktail parties, 75 dinners, and 80 lunches (all for more than 400); 70 poolside barbecues; 150 grand-scale birthday parties; 85 theme events (Caribbean Night, Conquistador Night, and such); 75 food society gourmet dinners; 16 mammoth bar mitzvahs; and 200-plus miscellaneous events, including conventions of 1,200 for a week at a time. (Among the more complex, a 10-day kosher convention required a total overhaul of equipment, replacement of all cooking and cleaning utensils, removal of all existing foodstuffs, new chinaware, and the fulfillment of 40 more requirements, plus a grocery list of near-200 kosher items).

For a recent party, the garden, usually studded with sleepy peacocks, was transformed into a Taino (local Indian) village. Thatched huts overflowed with salads of conch, squid, corn and pepper, and green bananas; chilled shellfish displays; Caribbean lamb stew with root vegetables and coconut; fried plantains with *chorizo* (spicy sausage), mini corn sticks, and crab turnovers. Accompanied by the omnipresent *chir-up* sound of tiny *coquis* (tree frogs), guests crossed a torch-lined causeway to San Jeronimo, the small fort adjoining the grounds. With surf pounding and an escort of *conquistadores*

A traditional country-style feast at the Caribe Hilton International

playing a trumpet fanfare, they entered the 350-year-old structure, where they perched on cannons and turrets to consume *paella,* spicy shrimps and crayfish (heaped in an old fishing boat), barbecued sausages, kebabs, and on and on. For the finale, a large ballroom inside the hotel had been transformed into an 18th-century version of the Port of San Juan, so that guests could plunder the cargo wagons of pastries, fruits, cheeses, and breads. (Of course, the whole affair could have fallen on the same day as a Wine Society dinner for 12, consisting of three autumn terrines, duck consommé perfumed with tarragon, scallops in orange butter, saddle of rabbit with mustard, spiced granita, noisettes of venison in port, cèpe-stuffed crêpes, Alpine cheeses, chestnut charlottes, coffee and petits fours, with eight noteworthy wines and spirits.)

This type of hoopla is, naturally, additional to the routine of La Rotisserie, where à la carte lunch and dinner are served daily; the Caribe Terrace, a large, open-air restaurant, where breakfast, lunch, and dinner buffets (a different theme and decor each night) are offered; El Cafe, where you can snack anytime; the Caribar Cocktail Lounge; Juliana Discotheque; the Club Caribe; the vast bar; and of course, room service. A romantic, octangular restaurant, El Batey del Pescador, has recently opened among the palms at beachside to serve broiled Caribbean lobster, grilled scallops and their roe, buttery soft-shell crabs, and fish and more fish. Cooking classes, private dinners at the Chef's Table, and various outside catering jobs help keep Chef Augusto and his brigade from sitting idle and twiddling their fingers between courses.

PUREED SQUASH-*APIO* SOUP WITH CRABMEAT

PUERTO RICO, UNITED STATES

A favorite of August Schreiner, executive chef of the Caribe Hilton International, the delicacy of this golden puree is punctuated by a blast of minced fresh ginger added at the last moment. Although the tuber known as apio *(or* arracacha*) is used in Puerto Rico, celeriac (also called celery knob and celery root) is an excellent substitute if there is no Latin market in your vicinity. This very popular first course is served with alternative garnishes, most frequently lobster medallions, though for a simple meal, a sprinkle of cilantro will do. The light soup can also be enjoyed chilled (you may want to thin it with a bit of half-&-half or stock) or reheated.*

3 tablespoons butter
1¾ pounds *calabaza* or butternut squash, peeled, seeded, and cut into 1½-inch chunks (see Note)
2 medium-large carrots (about 6 ounces), peeled and cut thin
1 pound *apio* or celeriac, peeled and thin-sliced
1 bay leaf
About 5 cups chicken stock

About ½ cup heavy (or whipping) cream
1½ teaspoons very finely minced peeled fresh ginger
About ¾ teaspoon Worcestershire sauce
Salt
About ¼ teaspoon white pepper
6 ounces lump crabmeat (6 tablespoons), carefully picked over
Cilantro sprigs

1. Heat the butter in a saucepan. Add the squash, carrots, and *apio;* stir occasionally over moderate heat for about 5 minutes.

2. Add the bay leaf and 5 cups of stock; bring to a boil. Cover and simmer until tender, about 20 minutes. Uncover and boil for 5 minutes. Let cool for about 30 minutes. Remove the bay leaf.

3. Puree in batches in a blender or processor until smooth. Add the ½ cup cream, or to taste. Heat through over low heat. Add the ginger, Worcestershire, and salt and white pepper to taste. Adjust the thickness by adding more cream or stock, if necessary.

4. Divide into 6 soup cups. Top with crab and cilantro sprigs.

Note: *Called pumpkin soup on the hotel's menu, the vegetable of choice is the orange-fleshed, fairly large* calabaza, *also known by a variety of local names, including West Indian pumpkin. The fine-grained, medium-sweet, fairly large squash (often sold by the slice) is similar in taste and texture to butternut squash, which substitutes perfectly if there is no Puerto Rican, Cuban, or West Indian market in your neighborhood.*

6 SERVINGS AS A FIRST COURSE

Wine Soup with Peppered Cheese, Onions, and Croutons
UNITED STATES

Assembling the ingredients that remained after preparing a microfiche on the subject of French cheeses, Dieter Hannig, director of the Food Research Center, came up with this intense, peppery-winy cold country brew. There is an Alpine feeling to this rich, strong soup—which is best served in small portions. It is delightful as a restorative après-ski, with no other accoutrements, or as a first course.

---

5 tablespoons butter
4 medium onions, thin-sliced (about 3 cups)
1 cup chicken broth
8 fairly thin slices from a narrow loaf of French bread (*baguette*)

1¼ cups dry white wine (see Note)
4 ounces *crottin poivre* cheese (see Note), grated (about 1¼ cups)
Salt and pepper
Minced parsley

---

1. Preheat the oven to 400°. Melt 4 tablespoons butter in a heavy 2–3-quart saucepan; stir in the onions. Cook over moderately low heat, stirring often, until soft and translucent but not browned, about 10 minutes. Add the broth. Scrape into a processor and puree thoroughly.

2. Meanwhile, place the bread slices in a single layer on a baking sheet; bake until golden, about 10 minutes.

3. Return the onion mixture to the saucepan. Add the wine and bring to a simmer. Remove from the heat; gradually stir in the cheese. Season with salt and pepper to taste.

4. To serve, ladle soup into 4 small bowls; top with the warm toast. Cut the remaining tablespoon butter into 8 pieces and set a dab on each crouton. Sprinkle with parsley and serve at once.

Note: *Wine is the flavor here. Use a dry, big-bodied white, preferably French. Avoid fruity, semi-dry wines.*
   Crottin poivre is a firm, cylindrical cheese made of cow's or sheep's milk and coated with a distinctively grooved black wax. It originates in the Auvergne, home of a number of zesty, rustic cheeses. Shot through with whole peppercorns, its pungent bite is considerable, although the cheese is nutty and not aggressively strong. Its high salt content pleasantly balances the brisk pepper.
Advance preparation: *Most soups to which cheese is added cannot be made ahead—but this one can. The slightly granular texture and appearance of the finished soup do not change when reheated.*

4 SERVINGS AS A FIRST COURSE

COLD BEET SOUP WITH SCALLOPS

UNITED STATES

Brunch, that leisurely late-morning meal for weekends and holidays, is a well-established American pastime, yet virtually unknown in the rest of the world. After receiving many requests from abroad, Dieter Hannig developed a microfiche on the subject for use among chefs—particularly those outside the United States.

This updated version of a Slavic classic is substantial, but light-tasting, an unusual offering for a spring-to-summer brunch. Shocking-pink soup thick with maroon beet shreds, scallops, ribbons of ham, and cucumbers is seasoned with snippets of scallion and dill and served refreshingly chilled.

10–12 small beets, (about 2 pounds, weighed with 2-inch tops)
7½ cups chicken broth, skimmed of all fat
1 pound sea scallops
2 medium cucumbers
8–9 ounces sliced ham, trimmed of fat, then cut into thin julienne (about 2 cups)

¾ cup thin-sliced scallion greens
2–3 tablespoons red wine vinegar
3–4 tablespoons lemon juice
1¼ cups (10 ounces) sour cream
About 2 tablespoons minced dill plus 6 small sprigs for garnish
Salt and pepper

1. Scrub the beets and drop them, unpeeled, into boiling salted water. Boil, uncovered, until very tender when pierced with a skewer; timing varies, but 20 minutes is average. Drain, cool slightly, then slip off the skins and stems. Cut in thin slices, then thin strips.

2. Bring 1½ cups broth to a simmer in a small saucepan. Add the scallops and keep under a simmer until barely cooked, about 2 minutes. Cool in the stock, then refrigerate.

3. Peel, halve, and seed the cucumbers. Cut each half lengthwise in half again, then cut across into thin slices. Combine in a bowl with the beets, ham, scallions, 2 tablespoons vinegar, and 3 tablespoons lemon juice. Whisk together the sour cream and 2 tablespoons minced dill. Gradually whisk in the remaining 6 cups stock. Strain the poaching liquid from the scallops and add it to the bowl. Cut the scallops in thin slices and add to the soup.

4. Chill thoroughly. Season to taste with additional salt, pepper, vinegar, lemon juice, and dill. Divide the soup among the serving bowls, then garnish with dill sprigs.

Serving: *Buckwheat waffles make an interesting accompaniment, as do rye muffins.*
Advance preparation: *Although the soup should be made long enough in advance to chill and blend the flavors, a few hours will suffice. More than that and the cucumbers exude too much liquid and the solids will turn a rather livid pink.*

6 SERVINGS AS A MAIN COURSE; 10 AS A FIRST COURSE

WISCONSIN DICED VEGETABLE AND SORREL SOUP

UNITED STATES

A fresh first course for any time of the year, this soup is served at the American Harvest Restaurant. Based on a recipe from the Wisconsin County Cookbook and Journal *by Edward Harris Heth (1956), this subtle combination of soft-cooked diced vegetables in broth tastes sweetish at first, then tart and grassy from the acid sorrel.*

2 medium leeks (about 1 pound), dark green tops and roots removed
3 tablespoons butter
1 medium-large onion, chopped (about 1 cup)
2 medium turnips, peeled and cut into ¼-inch dice (about 2 cups)
2 medium carrots, peeled and cut into ¼-inch dice (about 1½ cups)

1 small wedge of cabbage, cut into ¼-inch squares (about 1 cup)
2 quarts chicken stock
7 ounces fresh sorrel
1 tablespoon finely slivered basil
½ teaspoon minced fresh marjoram
Salt and pepper

1. Quarter the leeks lengthwise. Wash meticulously, then cut into ¼-inch squares (you should have about 2½ cups). Heat the butter in a large, heavy pot. Stir in the leeks and onion; cook over moderate heat until translucent, but not browned, about 5 minutes.

2. Add the turnips, carrots, and cabbage; cook for 4–5 minutes, stirring now and then. Add the chicken stock. Simmer, partly covered, for 20 minutes.

3. Meanwhile, strip off and discard the sorrel stems. Cut the leaves into thin strips, using a stainless-steel knife. (You should have about 4 cups lightly packed leaves.)

4. Add the sorrel, basil, marjoram, and salt and pepper to taste to the soup. Simmer, uncovered, for 3 minutes and serve hot.

8 SERVINGS AS A FIRST COURSE

CARROT AND WALNUT SOUP

UNITED STATES

Lightly sweet and thick, with a natural vegetable taste (not spiced as this type of soup often is), this puree is the kind usually associated with family celebrations (particularly Thanksgiving), for it seems to please all ages. The walnuts lend depth, meatiness, and a curry-yellow color. Another from the American Harvest Restaurant, where the seasons are marked by a menu that features such autumnal pleasures as this.

2 tablespoons butter
1 very small onion, chopped
1 pound carrots (weighed without
    tops), sliced (about 3 cups)
⅔ cup (2 ounces) walnuts, chopped
About 3½ cups chicken stock

1 cup heavy (or whipping) cream
Salt and pepper
Garnish
⅓ cup walnuts
About 1½ tablespoons thin-sliced
    chives

1. Melt the butter in a saucepan over moderate heat. Add the onion and stir for a few minutes until translucent, but not browned. Add the carrots and cook for 2–3 minutes, stirring often. Add the chopped walnuts and 2½ cups stock. Bring to a boil, stirring from time to time. Simmer the soup gently, covered, for 30 minutes.

2. Puree in a food processor until smooth. Return to the saucepan with the remaining 1 cup stock and the cream. Bring to a simmer. Add salt and pepper to taste. Add more stock, if needed, to obtain the desired consistency.

3. Divide the soup among heated bowls or cups. Place the walnuts for garnish in a rotary cheese grater; grind over the soup. Garnish with chives.

6 SERVINGS AS A FIRST COURSE

SEVEN GREENS AND MUSSEL GUMBO

UNITED STATES

Served at Vista's Greenhouse Restaurant, an airy glass enclosure set amid the soaring skyscrapers of the World Trade Center in New York City, this rough-textured soup is hot and herbal, smoky and briny, rich in the flavor of good bitter greens—and as backcountry as the setting is urban.

Although the tremendous quantity of greens requires considerable cleaning and chopping time, the soup is straightforward to cook, and improves if made in advance.

(continued)

Seven Greens and Mussel Gumbo

8 tablespoons butter
2 cups chopped onions
1 tablespoon minced garlic
1 cup dry white wine
36 cultivated mussels (about 2 pounds), rinsed and cleaned (see page 324)
½ pound precooked garlic sausage, such as *andouille* or kielbasa, coarsely chopped
1 cup chopped celery
2 cups chopped green bell peppers
About 2½ teaspoons salt
¼–1 teaspoon ground red pepper (see Note)
1½ teaspoons paprika
¼ teaspoon crushed red pepper (pepper flakes)

1 teaspoon dried thyme
½ teaspoon dried oregano
1 teaspoon dried basil
2 bay leaves, crumbled
1 cup coarsely chopped parsley
1 bunch watercress, stems removed, chopped
4 very green large romaine lettuce leaves, cut into wide slices
1 pound spinach, stems removed, leaves rinsed and cut into wide slices
6 outer leaves chicory or escarole, cut into wide slices
1 bunch scallions, chopped
4 outside leaves iceberg lettuce, cut into wide slices
1 tablespoon filé powder (see Note)

1. Melt 7 tablespoons butter in a large pot over moderate heat. Add 1 cup onions and the garlic; stir until softened. Add the wine and 1 cup water. Add the mussels. Cover and bring to a boil; the mussels should open up. Lift out the mussels. Shell and reserve them, along with the cooking liquid.

2. Heat the remaining 1 tablespoon butter in a soup pot. Add the sausage and fry for a few minutes to render some fat. Add the remaining 1 cup onions and the celery and bell peppers. Cook over moderate heat until soft. Add 2 teaspoons salt, ground red pepper, paprika, pepper flakes, thyme, oregano, basil, and bay leaves; stir. Add the parsley, watercress, romaine, spinach, chicory, scallions, and iceberg lettuce (you may want to add them gradually, pushing in each green as the others reduce in volume).

3. Add the reserved cooking liquid and 7 cups water. Simmer, uncovered, for 30 minutes.

4. In a food processor, puree the gumbo in batches to a rather coarse texture. Return to the pot; heat through. Remove 1 cup of the mixture and stir in the filé powder. Return mixture to pot and heat again until hot, but not boiling.

Note: *Lovers of fiery food may want to go for the full teaspoon of ground red pepper, but delicate palates should begin with ¼ teaspoon. You can always add more later.*

Filé powder, made of dried, ground sassafras leaves, contributes a unique herbal flavor to soups; at the same time it adds thickness and a slightly slippery texture. It should not be boiled, as it may become sticky and ropy. Rather, simply heat through to bind and flavor the gumbo. Purchase the powder in many specialty stores and in supermarkets throughout much of the southern United States.

If you're in no mood to tackle 7 varieties of greens, a lesser quantity will be as delicious, if different.

6–7 SERVINGS AS A MAIN COURSE

CAPE COD'S BOOKBINDER RED SNAPPER SOUP

UNITED STATES

During cold weather, Chicagoans come to The Drake hotel to down this by the boatload, along with overflowing baskets of rolls and crackers. It is a buttery, thick American-style soup that brings out the goodness of seafood: no Mediterranean seasoning, no cream or egg finishing—just mild vegetables and fish. The soup is served in the hotel's extremely popular Cape Cod Room, in fact a cozy clutch of rooms, decorated with nautical Americana—ancient cauldrons, a gargantuan crab, a stuffed swordfish, brass sconces that may have traveled the seven seas, copper and pewter ware from New England.

The recipe on which the sturdy pottage is based comes from Bookbinder's Seafood House in Philadelphia. The original version, a soup special to that area and to southern New Jersey, has quite a different snapper as its featured ingredient—snapping turtle.

Stock
**Head and bones from filleted red
  snapper (below)**
**About 1½ pounds additional fish
  bones and head(s)**
2 onions, quartered
2 celery ribs with leaves, sliced
1 large carrot, sliced
1 bay leaf
Soup Assembly
14 tablespoons (7 ounces) butter
1 small carrot, chopped
3 small celery ribs, chopped
2 medium onions, chopped

1 medium garlic clove, minced
1 bay leaf
15 white peppercorns, crushed
½ teaspoon dried thyme
1 cup all-purpose flour
¼ cup tomato paste
**3–3½-pound red snapper, filleted
  and skinned (head and bones
  used in stock)**
About ½ cup dry sherry
Salt and pepper
**Optional: medium-dry sherry for
  finishing the soup (see Note)**

---

1. Make the stock: Rinse the fish bones and heads and combine in a stockpot with all of the other stock ingredients and 4 quarts water. Bring to a simmer, skimming. Simmer gently for 20 minutes. Ladle through a strainer and set aside (you should have about 14 cups).

2. Assemble the soup: Melt 12 tablespoons (1½ sticks) of the butter in a large heavy pot; add the chopped carrot, half the celery, half the onions, and the garlic; stir over moderate heat for 2 minutes. Add the bay leaf, peppercorns, thyme, and flour: stir for another few minutes.

3. Blend together the tomato paste with 1 cup of the stock. Add this, then the remaining stock to the pot. Whisk over high heat until the soup boils. Lower the heat and simmer, uncovered, for 20 minutes, skimming occasionally.

4. Meanwhile, cut the snapper fillets into ½-inch squares. Heat the remaining 2 tablespoons butter in a wide skillet. Add the remaining onion and celery; stir over moderate heat for a few minutes, to just soften. Add the fish and stir for about 1 minute; add the dry sherry and toss for another minute.

5. Add the mixture to the soup. Simmer for about 15 minutes, until thickened and savory. Season with salt and pepper; taste for additional sherry.

Note: *At The Drake, caramel color is added to the soup to change it from a shrimpy peach to a distinctly mahogany hue. This can be done at home as well, if preferred.*

Also, miniature carafes of medium-dry sherry are offered to the diners so that they can adjust the sherry to taste.

Advance preparation: *Although at The Drake this soup is never kept beyond the day it is made, we found it to be mellow and delicious after 24–48 hours in the refrigerator.*

6–7 SERVINGS AS A MAIN COURSE; 12 SERVINGS AS A FIRST COURSE

A shellfish extravaganza in the Cape Cod Room of The Drake

The American Harvest Restaurant: Regional Bounty, Traditional Food in a Fine Dining Room

The timing was on target. By the end of the '70s it was no longer necessary for diners in-the-know to prefer minestrone to mixed vegetable soup, or *tarte Tatin* to apple pie à la mode. American food was coming out of the shadows into the California (Florida, New Mexico, etc.) sunshine. At Hilton International, what began as research for an American Bicentennial celebration to be held in its hotels became the basis for the American Harvest Restaurant at the Vista hotel in New York City—the company's first entry into the U.S. market after 32 successful years managing 89 hotels elsewhere on the globe. Thus began the formidable task of creating a menu which could represent all regions of a country with more ethnic groups than any other, and present a panorama of dishes to highlight the abundance of its fields, forests, ponds, streams, and oceans at its seasonal best.

The result is a menu unique to each month: Buttered fiddlehead ferns and sesame-fried soft-shell crabs appear in May; June's tart of wild American morels or creamed, minted green peas might follow; Wisconsin vegetable and sorrel soup, blueberry cream puffs, and raspberry summer pudding denote July; sunny Martha's Vineyard green corn pudding means August; tomatoes and sweet onions with basil dressing belong to

September; while a pumpkin cheesecake, Ozark Apple Pudding, and apple pies, cobblers, and compotes leave no doubt that October is upon us.

The small group that developed the restaurant concept arrived at these and more than 300 other exemplary American recipes after five years of plowing through cookbooks, periodicals, and historical documents. In typical American fashion, the backgrounds of the principal players were diverse—the food consultant, chefs, and key Hilton International executives hailing from the Midwest, Austria, France, Germany, Britain, Holland, Pennsylvania, and New York. Journeying back and forth between Montreal (where the Food Research Center was located at the time) and New York, members of the team cooked, sampled, and rated some 1,500 home recipes. Seventy potato dishes from almond-studded to walnut-crusted were candidates; 110 chicken recipes from batter-fried to stewed with dumplings were in the running at the start of the competition; 75 cookies from apricot bars to wagon wheels were tasted—as were comparable quantities in some 50-odd categories ranging from soup to nuts. Given the possible scenarios, it seems amazing that the internecine skirmishes were so few and that the "learning process" prevailed. For a trial clambake, for example, executive chef Walter Plendner (born in Austria) served the largest steamer clams he could find, not realizing that they were to be broth-dunked and eaten whole, as clambake etiquette dictates. French pastry chef Alain Roby, who trained at the celebrated Pâtisserie Lenôtre, kept turning out perfect tiny *tartelettes* and petits fours, balking at the American preference for voluminous desserts. After a crash course in American taste, the steamers were appropriately petite, the Shaker lemon pies and walnut chiffon cakes full-blown, and many such peculiarities set in their proper perspectives. But with comments, scores, and ultimate agreement required for each recipe, the final 350 choices were hard-won.

All this attention is focused on a restaurant that is a quiet, 90-seat oasis in the center of New York's hectic financial district, where the Vista was the first major hotel to be built in 145 years. Prior to its opening, there were few (or no, depending on your definition) truly American upscale restaurants in the city. The American Harvest embraces a quintet of intimate-feeling dining areas that suggest a modern melding of townhouse, Shaker barn, and Southern colonial home (a curious environment for the "power breakfasts," and corporate lunches that are frequently held there). Tiny geometric shapes dot the pastel silk upholstery, a dark oak table holds baskets of the season's harvest, and spongeware pottery and stenciled cups grace a pale, antique wooden breakfront. Conservative, tasteful, the decor is in keeping with the fresh, simple food, which is presented attractively, with relatively little embellishment. Salt, pepper, and butter are the main seasonings for the wide palette of honest American vegetables and generous helpings of fresh fish and meat. Handsome glassware and soft-hued napery, a sprinkle of parsley on the thick squash puree, a crumble of nuts on the pumpkin cheesecake are sufficient decoration.

As much of the United States leaps to create a glamorous new hybrid cuisine, the American Harvest seems a safe place to savor the past—modified ever so slightly to fit the tastes of a broad spectrum of contemporary diners who are happy with tradition, updated. This is accomplished not only with monthly menus that salute its culinary heritage, but with annual celebrations that single out the cooking of groups of Americans who have had abiding influences—the Shakers, Pennsylvania Dutch, and American Indians, for example. It is a place for some to feel nostalgic, for some to feel at home, for others to learn about their heritage, and to dignify simple American fare.

MARTHA'S VINEYARD GREEN CORN PUDDING

UNITED STATES

Sweet corn is a fairly recent agricultural development. Before it became common, "green corn," well sugared, was the vegetable that appeared in preparations such as this one. "Green corn" is the term for fresh (not dried) field corn or "critter corn," the starchy grain that is used for animal feed or ground into meal.

A favorite old-fashioned summer dish at the American Harvest Restaurant, this pudding has a memorably intense flavor that depends entirely on the quality of corn itself—so choose only the very freshest. A bit messy and time-consuming to prepare, you must be a real corn-lover to appreciate the goodness of this delicacy.

The recipe on which the pudding is based is attributed to Mrs. Charles L. Foote of West Tisbury, Massachusetts, on the island of Martha's Vineyard. The original, which appears in The Yankee Cookbook *by Imogene Wolcott, was "dry enough to be cut into squares" after 2–3 hours baking. The American Harvest adaptation is tender and baked in individual dishes for less than half an hour.*

---

12 medium ears of fresh sweet corn, preferably white, husks and silk removed (see Note)
2 eggs

½ teaspoon salt
2 tablespoons melted butter
1 cup milk

---

1. Preheat the oven to 350°. With a sharp knife cut lengthwise through the center of each row of kernels. With the dull side of a butter knife, press and rub the kernels to extract their pulp. Do not scrape the kernels from the cob. You should have 3 cups of corn pulp.

2. Blend together the eggs, salt, and butter in a mixing bowl. Add the corn. Add the milk.

3. Divide the mixture evenly among eight 6-ounce (¾ cup) buttered ramekins, cocottes, or custard cups, stirring the mixture so that the corn is equally distributed as you spoon it. Set the cups on a baking sheet in the center of the oven.

4. Bake for 20–25 minutes, until the centers are barely set. Serve hot, warm, or lukewarm.

Note: *The yield will vary considerably with the size and freshness of the kernels, from 8 to 16 ears being required. Buy a few extra ears of corn and measure as you scrape the pulp from the cobs.*

The custard can also be baked in a shallow 5–6 cup dish for 25 minutes or so.

Serving: *Enjoy this delightful dish for breakfast or brunch along with ham or smoked chicken or turkey. Or offer it as an appetizer, with a pat of butter, as is done at the American Harvest Restaurant.*

8 SERVINGS AS A SIDE DISH OR FIRST COURSE

Manitoba Wild Rice Croquettes

CANADA

Manitoba, a central Canadian province, is home to deep-brown wild rice, the seed of a native American grass. The crunchy crumb-coating of these croquettes breaks open to reveal chewy grains bound with creamy béchamel.

1¼ cups wild rice
6 tablespoons (3 ounces) butter
¼ cup all-purpose flour
2½ cups milk
¼ cup minced shallots
¾ cup (¼ pound) minced ham
¼ teaspoon mace
½ teaspoon salt

¼ teaspoon pepper
2 tablespoons minced parsley
For coating and frying
½ cup all-purpose flour
3 eggs, beaten
2½ cups fine dry white bread crumbs
Light vegetable oil for deep frying

1. Combine the rice and 3½ cups water in a small heavy saucepan and bring to a rolling boil over high heat, stirring. Turn heat to its lowest point and cover the pot. Cook until no longer hard within, but still rather firm-textured; this can vary from 25 minutes to 1 hour, depending upon the rice. Check now and then, adding water if necessary. Drain any liquid that remains. Cool the rice, then chill.

2. In a small saucepan, heat 4 tablespoons butter; stir in the flour. Cook for 30 seconds over low heat; add the milk all at once. Bring to a boil, stirring. Lower heat; simmer for 5 minutes, stirring often.

3. Melt the remaining 2 tablespoons butter in a medium skillet. Add the shallots and ham; stir over low heat for 2 minutes. Add the rice; stir for 3–4 minutes. Add the white sauce, mace, salt, and pepper. Add the parsley. Let the mixture cool.

4. Line a baking sheet with waxed paper. Using a pastry bag with a ¾-inch plain tube, pipe mixture in long strips onto the sheet. Freeze until firm. Wrap strips tightly; freeze.

5. When ready to coat and fry the croquettes, preheat oven to 150–200°. Cut frozen strips into 2-inch lengths (you can fry as few as suits the meal: reduce the coating ingredients to suit). Dust the still-firm croquettes with flour, then coat with beaten eggs. Roll in the crumbs, being sure there are no bare spots. Set on waxed paper.

6. Heat 2 inches of oil to 325° in a wide electric skillet or fryer (or a large saucepan into which you've placed a deep-fat thermometer, if you have no thermostatically controlled equipment). Leaving plenty of "swimming" room, fry the croquettes in batches until golden brown, but not dark—about 3 minutes. Place them on a towel-covered dish in the warm oven until all are ready. Serve hot.

Advance preparation: *Uncoated croquettes can be frozen for months, then crumbed and fried as you like. Or they can be prepared through Step 5, then refrigerated for up to a day (uncovered) before frying.*

56 SMALL CROQUETTES

Woodsy Buckwheat

UNITED STATES

An updated variation of an old-world favorite, kasha (roasted buckwheat groats) and mushrooms, from Dieter Hannig—a lively new-world chef with training in the classical school. Earthy and wild-flavored, the fluffy grains of buckwheat are generously laced with chewy black Chinese mushrooms and morels and punctuated with the fruitiness of sun-dried tomatoes. Serve as a light main course or roast accompaniment.

---

16 medium-size dried morels (about ½ ounce)
16 dried Chinese black mushrooms (shiitake, Forest mushrooms)
1 tablespoon olive oil
2 tablespoons butter
¼ cup chopped shallots
1 teaspoon minced garlic

2 ounces sun-dried tomatoes, chopped (about ⅓ cup)
1½ cups chicken stock
1 egg, beaten
1 cup roasted buckwheat kernels (medium granulation)
2 small scallions, trimmed and sliced thin

---

1. Combine 2 cups water, the morels, Chinese mushrooms, and olive oil in a saucepan. Bring to a boil, then remove from the heat and let cool. Lift out the mushrooms; strain the remaining liquid slowly through several layers of dampened cheesecloth to remove any soil or sand. (You should have about ½ cup.)

2. Quarter the morels, rinsing if necessary. Trim off the black mushroom stems and reserve for stock-making. Quarter the caps.

3. Heat the butter in a skillet over moderately high heat. Add the shallots, garlic, and mushrooms; toss for 3 minutes. Lower the heat; add the tomatoes, stir for 2 minutes longer. Add the chicken stock and mushroom liquid and bring to a boil.

4. Meanwhile, heat a skillet over moderate heat. Mix together the egg and buckwheat to coat well. Add the mixture and flatten and stir the kernels in the hot pan for 3–4 minutes, until they are dried and separated.

5. Being careful to avoid splatters, add the grains to the hot stock. Cover and cook over lowest heat for 10 minutes. Remove from the heat and let stand 5–20 minutes before serving, sprinkled with the scallions.

Advance preparation: *If the mushrooms are soaked in advance, the dish can be quickly assembled.*

4 MAIN COURSE SERVINGS; OR 6 AS A SIDE DISH

A Vegetarian Thanksgiving Feast

UNITED STATES

Although this recipe looks formidable, it yields a full meal, will take less time to prepare than a "regular" Thanksgiving dinner, can be done in substantial part a day in advance— and provides a colorful, bountiful feast for vegetable lovers (vegetarians or not).

Adapted from a prize-winning creation of Franz Kranzfelder, senior sous-chef at The Drake hotel in Chicago, it is a merry medley: bread dumpling slices marbled with chestnuts and figs are served with a cranberry red-wine sauce; maple-glazed sweet potatoes are embellished with golden raisins and pecan halves; porcelain-pretty striped sweet dumpling squash are heaped with a nutmeg-perfumed carrot puree, arranged with crescents of acorn squash topped with coins of zucchini, and set around a tumble of baby ears of corn.

Cranberry-Wine Sauce
12-ounce package (3 cups) fresh
  cranberries, sorted and rinsed
1¼ cups dry red wine
½ cup sugar
¼ teaspoon ground cinnamon

Chestnut-Fig Bread Dumplings
½ pound fresh chestnuts
1 pound day-old bakery hard rolls
  (6–8 high-quality medium size)
2 tablespoons vegetable oil
½ cup diced onion
1 cup diced celery
1 egg, beaten to blend (see Note)
8–9 dried figs, cut in ½-inch dice (or
  enough to equal 1 cup)
1½ teaspoons minced fresh sage
About ¼ teaspoon salt
¼ teaspoon pepper
¼ teaspoon nutmeg

Carrot Puree with Nutmeg
2 pounds large carrots (weighed
without tops), peeled and sliced
  ¼ inch thick
½ teaspoon nutmeg
½ teaspoon salt
3 tablespoons margarine or butter

Vegetables
3 medium-large sweet potatoes
  (about 10 ounces each), peeled
  and halved lengthwise
6 sweet dumpling squash (about 6
  ounces each) *or* 3 squash (about
  13 ounces each)
Salt and pepper
1 acorn squash (about 1½ pounds)
½ cup pure maple syrup
3 tablespoons margarine or butter
½ cup golden raisins
½ cup pecan halves
2 medium zucchini (10–12 ounces),
  sliced thin
Two 15-ounce cans baby corn-on-
  the-cob, drained

1. Preheat the oven to 425°. Combine the cranberries, red wine, sugar, and cinnamon in a medium nonaluminum saucepan. Bring to a boil, stirring occasionally. Boil about 2 minutes, until most of the skins pop. Press through the medium disk of a food mill. Cool the sauce, cover, and refrigerate.

2. Make the dumplings: Cut a cross through the tip of each chestnut. Bake in a pan in the center of the oven for 10 minutes. While still hot, remove the shells and husks. Cut into ½-inch dice (you should have about 1 cup).

3. Halve and slice the rolls; soak in 4 cups cold water for 15 minutes or more, tossing occasionally. Meanwhile, heat the oil over moderate heat in a medium skillet. Add the onion; stir for 3 minutes. Add the celery; stir until it is somewhat tender, but has not lost its crunch—about 4 minutes.

4. Squeeze the water from the rolls. Combine in a mixing bowl with the chestnuts, onions and celery, beaten egg, figs, sage, and salt, pepper, and nutmeg to taste. Squeeze and knead to blend thoroughly. Divide the mixture into 4 parts. Roll each to form a cylinder about 2½ inches in diameter. Roll each in a length of plastic wrap. Twist the ends tightly, then fold underneath each roll. Refrigerate for about 24 hours.

5. Make the carrot puree: Combine the carrots, nutmeg, salt and margarine with 1½ cups water in a saucepan over high heat. Simmer, covered, for about 15 minutes, until soft. Uncover and boil briefly, if necessary, until almost no liquid remains. Transfer to a food processor; whirl to a smooth puree. Cool, cover; refrigerate.

6. Drop sweet potatoes into a pot of boiling, salted water. Boil until tender, 15–20 minutes. Lift out carefully with a slotted spoon; cool. Cut crosswise into ½-inch slices. Arrange in a single layer in an 8 × 11-inch baking dish. Cool, cover; refrigerate.

7. *About 40 minutes before you plan to serve dinner:* Preheat the oven to 375°. Cut out the stem ends of the sweet dumpling squash (or halve larger ones); scoop out the seeds; salt and pepper. Set in a baking pan; add in water to just cover the bottom of the pan. Cover tightly with foil. Halve the acorn squash; scoop out seeds; then cut each half lengthwise in thirds. Place in a baking dish, sprinkle with salt and pepper, add water to barely cover the bottom of the dish. Cover tightly with foil. Bake both types of squash until just tender, 25–40 minutes (check frequently). Remove from the oven but leave the oven on; let the squash stand, covered, while you complete the meal.

8. While the squash bake, finish the sweet potatoes: Combine the maple syrup, 1 tablespoon of the margarine, the raisins, and pecans in a small pot; bring to a boil. Pour over the potatoes. As soon as the squash is removed from the oven, set the potatoes in the center; bake for 15 minutes, until browned and bubbling.

9. At the same time, set the dumpling logs on a steamer rack over boiling water. Cover tightly; steam for 10 minutes. Remove; let stand for 5 minutes.

10. Meanwhile, attend to these simultaneously: Heat 2 very large skillets over high heat; add 1 tablespoon of margarine to each. Toss the zucchini in one until just tender, about 2 minutes. In the other, toss the corn until slightly colored, about the same amount of time. Warm both the carrot puree and the cranberry sauce (which should be thick, but pourable; add red wine if it is too dense).

11. Tip juices out of the sweet dumpling squash; arrange around the edge of a very large, heated platter. Divide carrot puree into them. Place acorn squash between the dumpling squash. Heap corn in the center of the platter. Spoon the zucchini onto the acorn squash. (The platter can wait for 10 minutes in the turned-off oven.)

12. Unwrap the dumpling logs; cut each into 6 diagonal slices. Arrange in a warm dish; serve with the cranberry sauce alongside.

Advance preparation: *Steps 1–6 can be accomplished a day in advance.*

6 SERVINGS

The Drake: Great Expectations
Fulfilled—and the Role of the Roll

In the Chef's Office of The Drake hotel, a place for brainstorming and conferring

The 67-year-old brick oven of The Drake hotel in Chicago, Illinois, United States of America, is delivered of at least 8,000 golden, light-textured rolls (cheese, caraway-rye, sesame, onion, and on) each day. Once a year the oven must be cooled, cleaned, and refired. During this three-day period the management is invariably alerted to the complaints of regular diners who object to the "imports," and there may even be an empty table (an unheard-of occurrence at this popular meeting place) from a *regular* regular who may not wish to dine in such dire conditions.

A staff of life for Chicagoans, a monument (recognized officially as an historical landmark), a place of substance: The Drake is an elegant *grande dame* who will have no truck with "glitz" or shortcuts. It offers deep comfort, a gracious pace; walnut-paneled, mirrored elevator cars with salmon and pale-green seats are operated by polite, efficient "elevator ladies." Though discreetly (beautifully and expensively) refurbished, the massive building has retained its special personality. It would be wise to do so, or the clientele—many of whom request the same spacious rooms and suites year after year—would mutiny. The American Association of Railway Surgeons has held its annual dinner at The Drake for 51 years; the Arden Shore Home for Boys for 50. Staff members go back 35, 40, and 50 years. (And the fancy powder room—still so-called in this liberated age—is rated the finest in Chicago.)

If radical changes were made in its menus, there would probably be a revolt by the diners, who daily overflow the 54-year-old Cape Cod Room, the bright Oak Terrace, and the Club International, a private association of 3,500. Executive chef Leo Waldmeier, without tampering with the revered dishes, has honed the style of the food and techniques of the cooks. In fact, in his brief tenure he has so sharpened the edge that the team has pulled in 27 medals and six trophies in national culinary competitions during the last four years. From a raised, glass-windowed office in a kitchen built before the days of real estate sold by the foot, Waldmeier surveys an area the size of three basketball courts—including a pastry area that would engulf many modern main kitchens, soup tanks that would hide an ox, and vats of sauces.

Excellence on a grand scale is expected—and expectations are met, in full Midwestern style. Portions are hearty, food is piping hot, impeccably fresh, and cooked exactly as ordered. Fish is flown in daily from both coasts, coffee is strong and just-brewed, orange juice is always the real thing, and leftover soups are discarded every evening (Bookbinder's Red Snapper Soup, a dense, mahogany, pottage brimming with fish chunks is consumed at the rate of 35 gallons a day). For the most part (though Waldmeier and staff have introduced some eloquent exceptions), the menu is American at its finest—simple and straightforward: What you see is what you get. When a family looks forward to the sparkling fresh local whitefish or sweet crabmeat cakes, all members will depart the cozy Cape Cod Room beaming, satisfied. Blond and blue-eyed debutantes relaxing in the sunny Oak Terrace after a morning of shopping at Neiman-Marcus and Marshall Field tuck into the utterly simple chicken salad (chunks of tender meat in a light mayonnaise with a touch of celery) and are never disappointed. An elegant couple finishing their pre-theater dinner with the custardy rice pudding with golden raisins (25 years on the menu) will be as pleased with it as was the late Mrs. Maurice L. Rothschild, who lived at The Drake for 58 years, until her death at age 102 in 1980. A businessman entertaining European clients in the Club International can be justly proud of the Dover Sole Meunière, the well-aged sirloin, or the day's specials—oyster stew with linguine and yellow pepper sauce or lamb fillet with Burgundy and onion ragout.

People are comfortable at The Drake. There, one feels special, but easy. It seems to instill devotion for generations. An example among many is the tap dancer who met her husband-to-be in the Camellia House (now The Drake Room), where he was a drummer in the 1930s. They married and honeymooned at The Drake, conceived their first child there—and named him Drake. Camille was their second. They recently celebrated their 40th anniversary—in The Drake Room.

"We like a hotel that has poise and yet is not stilted; that offers luxury without ostentation, convenience without conscious effort, and calm with its activity. We like a hotel that will charm and make you feel that you belong to its family," wrote a couple in 1925. In 1986 one letter of praise was from a widow with seven grandchildren: "I have stayed at The Drake since 1943 during World War II when I was on my honeymoon. I . . . have the pleasure of bringing [my grandchildren] (one at a time!) to Chicago for special little trips for fun and sightseeing. . . . I feel as safe there as in a friend's home." The same month a young woman extolled the present management and explains that "I have been coming to The Drake for 30 years—first with my parents and now as an adult." Another: "this weekend is the gift of our five daughters. They were wise in selecting The Drake for our 25th wedding anniversary." Chances are good that the couple's grandchildren will celebrate life's passages in the same place—with a toast in the Cape Cod Room.

CRAB CAKES WITH LIGHT MUSTARD SAUCE

UNITED STATES

Large pieces of sweet crab are melded with mashed potato and egg yolk, seasoned with a generous quantity of pepper and Tabasco, dredged in soft crumbs, pan-fried, then served with a creamy mustard sauce. At The Drake hotel's bustling Cape Cod Room (a series of dim, cozy rooms that feel like an old inn and overflow with nautical antiques and good cheer) these are a best-selling item.

---

1 medium all-purpose potato (about 6 ounces)
About ¼ teaspoon Tabasco sauce
3 egg yolks
1 pound lump crabmeat, carefully picked over and slightly flaked
1½ cups soft white bread crumbs (from about 3 slices bread)
3 tablespoons minced red bell pepper (see Note)
½ teaspoon salt
¼ teaspoon pepper

Mustard Sauce
1 cup dry white wine
1–1½ teaspoons dry mustard
1 tablespoon butter
3 tablespoons minced shallots
1 cup fish stock, *or* ⅔ cup clam juice mixed with ⅓ cup water
½ cup dry vermouth
1 cup heavy (or whipping) cream

4 tablespoons clarified butter for frying

---

1. Boil the potato until soft, about 25 minutes. Mash with a fork and let cool completely.

2. Blend the Tabasco and egg yolks. Combine with the crab, ½ cup crumbs, the bell pepper, salt, and ground pepper. Mix well. Form into 8 cakes about 1 inch thick and 3 inches in diameter.

3. Prepare the sauce: Blend together 2 tablespoons of the wine with 1 teaspoon dry mustard and set aside. Melt the butter in a small pan over moderately low heat. Add the shallots and stir for about 2 minutes, until softened. Add the remaining white wine, the fish stock, and dry vermouth. Boil to reduce to 1 cup—about 15 minutes.

4. Add the cream; boil again to reduce to about 1 cup, or the desired consistency. Add the mustard mixture. Taste and stir in additional dry mustard, as desired (first dissolving in water), and salt. Strain.

5. Dredge the cakes in the remaining bread crumbs. Heat the clarified butter in a wide skillet over low heat. Fry the cakes for 6 minutes on each side. Raise the heat to moderate; fry for 1 minute longer on each side, until golden. Heat the sauce; pour into a warm sauceboat. Serve alongside.

Note: *Both red and green peppers are used at the Cape Cod Room, 1½ tablespoons of each.*
Advance preparation: *The crab cakes can be fried until light golden, cooled, then covered and refrigerated. Heat through in a 400° oven to serve. The sauce can be cooled, covered, then refrigerated until serving time. Reheat over low heat, adding a little white wine or fish stock to restore the consistency.*

4 SERVINGS AS A MAIN COURSE; 8 AS A FIRST COURSE

SCALLOPS IN LIME AND GREEN PEPPERCORN SAUCE

UNITED STATES

White rounds of scallops sprinkled with fine strands of pungent lime zest blend in a thin buttery sauce sharpened by green peppercorns. To prepare this special served in the Cape Cod Room at The Drake, cook the scallops over highest heat in the widest pan available—or they will exude too much juice and wind up stewed instead of sautéed.

1½ pounds sea scallops
1½ teaspoons drained, rinsed, water-
  packed green peppercorns
Salt and white pepper

1½ teaspoons very fine julienne-cut
  lime zest
4½ tablespoons butter
2 tablespoons lime juice
1 teaspoon coarsely grated lime zest

---

1. Slice the larger scallops horizontally in half; leave smaller ones whole. Mince (or crush) 1 teaspoon of the peppercorns. Sprinkle the scallops with the salt and white pepper. Drop the lime julienne into boiling water, return to a boil, then drain.

2. Heat a wide skillet (12 inches or so) over moderate heat. Add 3 tablespoons butter; as the butter stops foaming spread the scallops in the pan in a single layer. Turn the heat to high and cook for 1 minute. Flip over the scallops and cook 1 minute longer.

3. Add the lime juice, grated zest, and minced peppercorns. Toss for a moment. Cut the remaining 1½ tablespoons butter into bits and add all at once. Off the heat stir to melt. Season to taste.

4. Scoop into a warm serving dish, sprinkle with the lime julienne and the ½ teaspoon whole peppercorns. Serve at once.

Serving: *The Drake offers a cornucopia of bright vegetables: asparagus tips, shiitake, green beans, snow peas, baby carrots, and tiny potatoes boiled with saffron. For a simple meal, steamed pink potatoes do well.*

4 SERVINGS AS A MAIN COURSE

LEFT: **Scallops in Lime and
Green Peppercorn Sauce**
RIGHT: **Crab Cakes with Light
Mustard Sauce**

SALMON STRUDEL

UNITED STATES

This is chef Leo Waldmeier's adaptation of the Russian kulebiaka *(or* coulibiac*), simplified by the use of phyllo instead of brioche. He offers it at The Drake's Cape Cod Room as a menu special, or for banquets, where it is often accompanied with a beurre blanc or basil cream sauce. Rich salmon is centered in a coating of chopped, dill-seasoned millet, eggs, and mushrooms, then rolled in a buttery phyllo pastry. Extremely moist and rich, the strudel is tender and juicy enough not to require a sauce, should you prefer.*

¼ cup hulled millet (available in health food stores)

1¼ ounces (1 "skein") rice noodles (see Note)

13–14-ounce skinned salmon fillet

¼ cup dry white wine

2 hard-cooked eggs, chopped fine

¼ pound mushrooms, trimmed, cleaned, and chopped fine

2 tablespoons minced dill

1–2 tablespoons lemon juice

½ teaspoon salt

¼ teaspoon pepper

1 small package (1 pound) phyllo or strudel dough (see Note)

6 tablespoons butter, melted

1 egg yolk blended with 1 tablespoon water

Optional sauce: About 1 cup sour cream, mixed with lemon juice, dill, and salt and pepper to taste

1. Preheat the oven to 400°. Drop the millet into a pot of boiling salted water; boil for 20 minutes, or until tender, but not soft. Rinse, drain, and spread on a plate to dry. Boil the rice noodles for 3 minutes in salted water. Drain, rinse, dry, then chop fine (you should have about ¾ cup).

2. Remove any stray bones from the salmon with narrow pliers or tweezers. Halve the fish lengthwise. Pour the wine into a baking dish or pan to hold the fillets closely, then set them in the pan. Set in the center of the oven and bake until half-cooked, 6–8 minutes, depending on the thickness. With a spatula, transfer to a plate to cool. Reduce the oven temperature to 375°.

3. Combine the millet, rice noodles, chopped eggs, mushrooms, dill, 1 tablespoon lemon juice, and the salt and pepper. Add additional seasoning to taste, overflavoring slightly.

4. Spread one leaf of phyllo or strudel on a clean, dry dish towel, a long side toward you. Brush with the melted butter to coat completely. Continue layering and buttering until five of the leaves are used. Spread ½ cup filling on the fifth layer to cover evenly.

5. Place two more buttered sheets on the stack. Form a rectangle with the remaining filling, leaving a 2–3-inch margin all around. Match up one salmon fillet with the lower left corner of the stuffing rectangle, placing the narrow tip of the fillet inward. Place the other fillet along the right hand corner so that its narrow end overlaps the other fillet. Fold over the short edges of phyllo where they meet the filling, then the long sides. Butter these folded leaves. Begin rolling from the long side close to you (do not roll very tightly) using the towel to shape a neat cylinder.

6. Place seam side down on a buttered baking sheet. Brush with the egg wash. Bake in the center of the oven for 20–25 minutes, until nicely browned.

7. Let stand for about 15 minutes before slicing with a serrated knife. Serve with or without sour cream sauce alongside.

Note: *Rice noodles, also called rice flour noodles,* mi fun, *long rice, and Chinese vermicelli are widely available in Oriental markets; if you prefer, use the clear cellophane noodles (also called glass noodles, silver noodles, or bean threads). Both noodles serve as a textural substitute for the sturgeon spinal marrow (viziga) that is used at The Drake. Obviously, if you have access to this delicacy, it is to be preferred. Prepare by boiling for 6–8 hours until it can be easily crushed or broken with your fingers. Wash with cold water, then clean off the white particles, keeping only the shiny, clear mass. Chop fine with a heavy knife.*

You'll need seven sheets of 7 × 12-inch phyllo, or a size close to that (the dough is available in many supermarkets). Have a few extra sheets in case of breakage.

4 SERVINGS AS A MAIN COURSE; 8 AS A FIRST COURSE

SALMON WITH MUSSELS IN WATERCRESS SAUCE

CANADA

Albert Schnell of the Hilton International Toronto makes use of salmon from British Columbia and local shellfish in this updated version of an haute cuisine classic. Tender fillets of pale salmon garnished with plump mussels bathe in pools of buttery watercress sauce (the blanching and pureeing remove all bite, but retain the brilliant green color). Halved, the recipe makes an elegant first course.

2 bunches watercress (about 10
   ounces total weight), all stems
   removed (except 12 small sprigs
   reserved for garnish)
½ cup plus 1 tablespoon dry
   white wine
3 tablespoons dry vermouth
2 tablespoons minced shallots
24 mussels (about 1 pound),
   scrubbed and beards removed
   (see page 324)

¾ cup heavy (or whipping) cream
⅛ teaspoon dried tarragon
10 tablespoons (5 ounces) cold
   butter, cut into ½-inch bits
About 1 teaspoon lemon juice
Salt and pepper
1 tablespoon melted butter
12 skinned salmon fillets (about 2
   ounces each)

1. Drop the watercress into a pot of boiling, salted water; return to a full boil. Drain, chill in ice water. Drain again. Puree thoroughly in a processor or blender.

2. Combine ½ cup of the wine, the vermouth, and shallots in a wide nonaluminum pot; bring to a boil. Add the mussels; cover tightly and bring to a boil over high heat. Remove from the heat as soon as the mussels open, about 2 minutes.

3. Strain the liquid through a dampened cheesecloth-lined sieve. You should have about ½ cup; if more, boil to reduce to this amount. Remove the mussels from their shells; set aside in a small nonaluminum pan with 2 tablespoons of the stock.

4. Preheat the broiler. Add the cream and tarragon to the stock; boil to reduce to ½ cup. Off heat, whisk a piece of butter into the sauce. Continue to add bits of butter, whisking just until the last is nearly incorporated. Set the pan over very low heat now and then to keep the butter melting, but not long enough to turn it oily. The sauce should be a creamy suspension. Add lemon juice, salt, and pepper to taste. Blend in the watercress. Set the saucepan in a skillet of barely simmering water to keep warm.

5. Blend the remaining 1 tablespoon wine with the melted butter. Paint a wide flame-proof serving dish with half this mixture. Arrange the fillets in a single layer in the dish; brush with the remaining stock-butter mixture. Sprinkle with salt and pepper.

6. Set as close to the broiling element as possible. Broil until barely cooked through, 2–2½ minutes. Reheat the mussels at the same time.

7. Divide the sauce (see Option) among 6 *barely* warmed serving plates, tilting to distribute neatly. Arrange the salmon on top of the sauce, garnish with the reserved cress sprigs and mussels. Serve at once.

Option: *If you have one of the handy electric rods with a tiny high-speed blade at the tip that is variously called a hand- or immersion- or stick-blender, place it directly in the sauce pot and whiz to create a lovely froth, as the chef does.*

6 SERVINGS AS A MAIN COURSE

Baked Sea Bass with Caraway

UNITED STATES

When Kazuhito Endo was sous-chef of the Vista International in New York, he created this simple and attractive dish, and a number of other low-calorie, low-sodium main courses for the changing menus, which regularly feature light, health-wise specials.

Slivers of Belgian endive and tomato, dressed with a light curry vinaigrette touched with tarragon, form an unusual backdrop for the caraway-topped sea bass fillets, decorated with their natural motif of black netting. Surprisingly big flavor and satisfying texture make this dish a success with dieters—as well as other customers. If you prefer salt, add to taste—but the natural bitter-sweetness of the endive and the punch of curry and caraway will be sufficient seasoning for most.

½ teaspoon curry powder
¼ cup tarragon vinegar
½ cup light vegetable oil
Lemon juice
Four 5-ounce sea bass fillets with
  skin (for this you'll need two bass,
  each weighing 1¼–1½ pounds)
2 teaspoons caraway seeds

1 pound small Belgian endives,
  halved, cored, and cut crosswise
  into thin slices
1 medium tomato, peeled, seeded,
  and cut into thin strips
Fresh tarragon leaves or chervil
  sprigs

---

1. Preheat the broiler. Blend together the curry powder and vinegar in a small bowl. Beat in the oil gradually, then add lemon juice to taste.

2. Place the fillets, flesh side down, on an oiled broiler pan. Score the skin diagonally every 1½ inches or so. Sprinkle with the caraway. Set the pan under the broiler at the middle level. Cook for about 5 minutes, until just opaque throughout.

3. Meanwhile, toss together the endive, tomato, and tarragon leaves with the dressing. Arrange on 4 serving plates.

4. Arrange a fillet on each salad; serve at once.

Serving: *This dish should be served as soon as the fish emerges from the broiler to enjoy the contrast of the juicy-firm hot sea bass and the cool, crisp salad.*

4 SERVINGS AS A MAIN COURSE

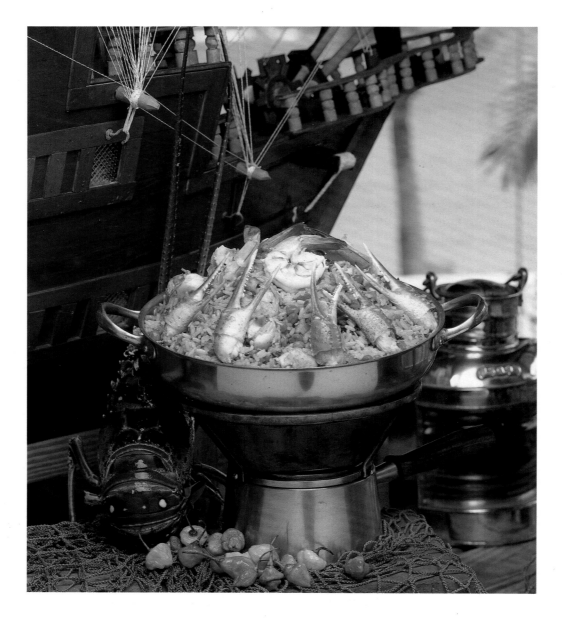

SHELLFISH WITH RICE, HAM, MUSHROOMS, AND BRANDY
"El Pescador"

PUERTO RICO, UNITED STATES

El Pescador *is a mild seafood and rice dish that has been featured in the main dining room of the Caribe Hilton International since 1956. Prepared at tableside, the simple flavors (reminiscent of paella) and generous amount of luxury shellfish please guests of all ages and backgrounds.*

4 rock lobster tails (fresh, or frozen, defrosted; 8–10 ounces each)
12 medium-large shrimp in the shell
1 cup long-grain or converted long-grain white rice
1/4–1/2 teaspoon saffron threads
1/2 cup blanched (or frozen, defrosted) peas
1 whole large canned pimiento, cut into fine dice (about 1/3 cup)
2 tablespoons margarine or butter
2 ounces salt pork, cut into 1/2-inch dice (about 1/3 cup)
2 ounces cooked ham, cut into

1/2-inch dice (about 1/2 cup)
2 teaspoons minced garlic
1 medium green bell pepper, cut into 1/4-inch dice (see Note)
3 ounces small mushrooms, thin-sliced (about 1 cup)
1 medium tomato, peeled, seeded, and cut into 1/2-inch dice
1/4 cup minced cilantro leaves
1/3 cup brandy, preferably Spanish
1 cup chicken stock (see Note)
Salt and pepper
8 cooked king crab claws for garnish (optional)

1. Place the lobster tails in a skillet of boiling salted water to cover. Simmer for 3 minutes. Add the shrimp and simmer for another minute. Drain and cool until you can remove the shells. Devein the shrimp; cut the lobster into 1/2-inch slices.

2. Meanwhile, combine the rice and saffron with 1 3/4 cups water in a small saucepan. Bring to a boil, stirring. Turn heat to lowest point, cover, and cook for 20 minutes. Remove from the heat; let stand, covered, 15–30 minutes, as convenient. Stir in the peas and pimiento.

3. Heat the margarine in a very wide skillet. Add the salt pork; cook over moderately high heat until lightly colored, about 1 minute. Add the ham and toss. Add the garlic and toss for 30 seconds. Add the bell pepper, mushrooms, tomato, and cilantro. Toss for 2 minutes.

4. Add the brandy and ignite, shaking the pan. Add the broth; boil for 1 minute. Add the seafood; return to a boil, tossing.

5. Add the rice mixture; toss for about 2 minutes, to heat through. Add salt and pepper to taste. Heap onto a serving plate and garnish with the crab claws, if desired.

Note: *The tiny, distinctively aromatic sweet chili-peppers known as* ajies dulces *add an inimitable flavor to the dish when it is prepared in Puerto Rico. If they are available, substitute for one-third of the green bell pepper.*

   Brown sauce or mushroom sauce is commonly used at La Rotisserie in place of chicken stock; substitute either, if on hand.

Advance preparation: *The components for the dish can be prepared through Step 2 a day ahead, then cooled, covered, and refrigerated.*

Options: El Pescador *has been prepared at the Mayaguez Hilton International with cooked* gandules *(pigeon peas) instead of green peas for a more Puerto Rican flavor. For those who like a stronger ocean taste, substitute fish stock for the chicken, and add the seafood raw, increasing the cooking time slightly to almost cook through, rather than simply heat.*

4 SERVINGS AS A MAIN COURSE

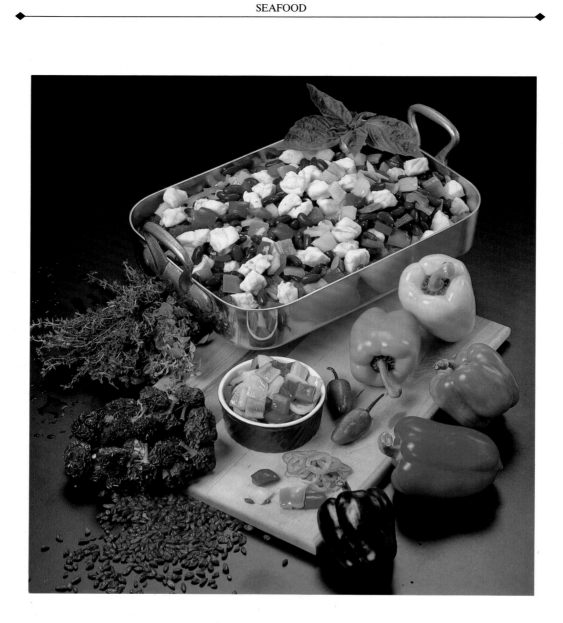

MONKFISH CHILI

UNITED STATES

This culinary hybrid from executive chef Walter Plendner of the Vista International Hotel in New York City is a product of both the Deep South and the Southwest. It was created as a result of the Cajun foodfest at the hotel's Greenhouse restaurant, undertaken in collaboration with the popular Louisiana restaurateur-chef-celebrity Paul Prudhomme.

Completely inauthentic, this unusual mixture may astound chile (and chili) purists but pleases a large number of diners who order it regularly at the Vista's elegant American Harvest Restaurant. The firm-fleshed fish holds its shape, the red and green pepper dice add color and texture, the beans soften, thickening the sauce—which is richly hot-sweet.

2 tablespoons vegetable oil
2 medium onions, cut into ½-inch dice
2 medium green bell peppers, ribbed, seeded, and cut into ½-inch dice
2 medium red bell peppers, ribbed, seeded, and cut into ½-inch dice
1 teaspoon salt
½ teaspoon ground cumin
¼ teaspoon ground red pepper
¼ teaspoon crushed red pepper (pepper flakes)
½ teaspoon dried thyme
½ teaspoon dried oregano

½ teaspoon dried basil
3 bay leaves, crumbled
½ teaspoon dried marjoram
2 pounds monkfish (*lotte,* goosefish, angler), cut into 1½-inch dice
¼ cup pure mild chile powder (see Note)
6 tablespoons tomato paste
3 large tomatoes, peeled and diced
3 cups fish stock (see page 326), *or* 1 cup bottled clam juice mixed with 2 cups water
4 cups cooked drained red kidney beans

1. Heat the oil in a wide casserole or deep skillet about 11 inches in diameter. Cook the onions over moderately low heat until soft and translucent, about 10 minutes. Add the bell peppers and toss for 1 minute.

2. Blend together the salt, cumin, ground red pepper, crushed red pepper, thyme, oregano, basil, bay leaves, and marjoram. Add to the pan; cook for 5 minutes, stirring occasionally.

3. Add the fish and chile powder; stir over moderate heat until the fish whitens on the outside. Add the tomato paste and stir gently for 2 minutes. Add the tomatoes and fish stock; bring to a boil. Add the kidney beans and bring to a boil again. Simmer for 5 minutes. Cool, then cover and refrigerate.

4. To serve, reheat over low heat, stirring gently so as not to break up the beans or fish.

Note: *A powder of ground whole chili-peppers (usually New Mexican)—and nothing else—is vastly superior to any of the commercial spice mixtures. It is available in many supermarkets and in stores that carry Mexican and New Mexican ingredients. If you must use the combination of spices called "chili powder," buy the one with the shortest list of ingredients on the label.*
Serving: *This is a casual, easy party dish that keeps well on a hot tray. Accompany with unsweetened cornbread, a salad of bitterish greens and citrus, and plenty of icy beer.*
Advance preparation: *Like most stewy dishes, this one improves with reheating, the flavors becoming more mellowed and balanced.*

8 SERVINGS AS A MAIN COURSE

STUFFED HALIBUT STEAMED IN ROMAINE WITH CAVIAR BEURRE BLANC

UNITED STATES

Franz Kranzfelder, senior sous-chef at The Drake hotel (but a very young man, indeed), invented this dish for the 1985 National Restaurant Association competition—and won a gold medal for the "Most Original Piece of the Show." The delicate flavor and texture of snowy halibut are maintained by brief steaming in a stylish cloak of romaine. The sea-sweet fish in a pool of butter sauce is sparked by lustrous salmon eggs.

2 halibut steaks (each about ¾ pound), cut about 1½ inches thick
1 medium-large head of romaine lettuce (about 1 pound)
Salt and pepper
1 medium-large tomato, peeled, seeded, and diced (about ½ cup)
3–4 ounces mushrooms, cut into fine dice (about 1 cup)

1 tablespoon minced parsley
1 tablespoon minced shallot
½ cup dry white wine
12 tablespoons (6 ounces) cold butter, cut into 24 pieces
4 tablespoons salted salmon eggs (about 3 ounces)

1. Divide each halibut steak into 2 natural sections by cutting out the bone. Remove the skin from each section. Cut a pocket into the long flat side of each piece.

2. Remove 10 large leaves from the romaine. Drop them into a wide skillet of boiling salted water; return to a boil. Drain, refresh in ice water, then spread flat between towels to dry.

3. Sprinkle the fish with salt and pepper. Combine the tomato, mushrooms, and parsley in a bowl. Add salt and pepper to taste. Place each halibut slice on 2 overlapping romaine leaves. Divide the filling evenly in the pockets, stuffing generously. Enclose each piece of fish in the lettuce, wrapping neatly and firmly.

4. Boil the shallot, white wine, and a sprinkling of salt and pepper in a small nonaluminum skillet until reduced to a scant 2 tablespoons; set aside momentarily.

5. Arrange the fish packets on a buttered steamer rack. Set the rack inside the steamer over boiling water; cover. Steam for 11–12 minutes, until the fillets are just opaque throughout.

6. Meanwhile, heat the wine reduction. Off the heat, whisk in 1 piece of butter. When it has nearly melted, whisk in another. Over lowest heat, continue adding butter, one piece at a time, incorporating another just as the last almost melts. Remove the pan from the heat occasionally so that the butter does not become oily. Maintain a pale, creamy suspension. Remove from the heat and stir in the salmon roe. Season to taste.

7. As soon as the fish is cooked, set the packets on a cutting board. Cut in half or into ¾-inch crosswise slices. Arrange at once on individual serving plates; spoon 3 tablespoons of the sauce alongside each. Serve immediately.

Presentation and serving: *The colorful halved packets or slices and rich sauce need no more than rice as an accompaniment.*
Advance preparation: *The stuffed, wrapped fish packets can be prepared hours ahead of cooking time and refrigerated.*
Options: *The steamed fish makes a lovely first course or salad when chilled and served with a light mustard vinaigrette.*

4 SERVINGS AS A MAIN COURSE

RED SNAPPER FILLETS WITH CILANTRO SAUCE

VENEZUELA

Silvery red snapper patterned with its distinctive rosy netting is imbued with the vivid aroma of cilantro (fresh coriander), the parsley of South America, in this simple presentation from Frank Muller, executive chef of the Caracas Hilton International. The fish is steamed on a thick bed of the herb, then the fragrant cooking liquid is strained, slightly reduced, and finished with butter and feathery cilantro leaves.

The success of the deliciously pure ensemble depends entirely upon the beauty and freshness of the fish—and a sense of timing: The fish must not be overcooked. The simple savor is best underscored by no more than steamed baby potatoes and a cool Chablis or Meursault.

---

2 medium-large bunches (5 ounces) cilantro, preferably with roots
4 red snapper fillets with skin (each about 6 ounces)

Salt and pepper
⅔ cup chicken stock
1 cup dry white wine
4 tablespoons butter

---

1. Turn the oven to its lowest heat, about 150°. Strip enough cilantro leaves from their stems to make ¾ cup, very lightly packed. Rinse and dry the leaves and reserve for the sauce. Dunk the remaining cilantro leaves and stems in several changes of water to remove all traces of sand and soil.

2. Halve the fish crosswise, on the diagonal, to make 8 more-or-less equal pieces. Sprinkle with salt and pepper. Set 4 serving plates in the warm oven.

3. Combine the cilantro stems and leaves, chicken stock, and white wine in a wide nonaluminum pan large enough to hold the fish in a single layer. Bring to a boil, covered.

4. Place the snapper fillets skin side up on the cilantro; return to a boil. Cover the pan and cook over low heat until not quite cooked through—about 2 minutes. With a spatula carefully transfer the fillets to the plates in the oven.

5. Strain the cooking liquid into a nonaluminum saucepan; boil to reduce to about ¾ cup. Turn off the heat and stir in the butter, a little at a time. Add the reserved cilantro leaves and salt and pepper to taste. Spoon the sauce over the fillets and serve at once.

4 SERVINGS

FRICASSEE OF BABY HENS WITH WINE VINEGAR SAUCE
(Fricassée de Poussins au Vinaigre de Vin)
CANADA

A fine, traditional French family dish as refined by Albert Schnell, area executive chef for Hilton Canada, Inc.—no small realm. The tan cream sauce, tomato-flecked, is poured over the hens in old-fashioned fricassee style. Because the generous quantity of savory sauce is natural and liquid, not thickened, noodles suit perfectly.

4 *poussins* (baby chickens) *or*
   Rock Cornish hens (about 1½
   pounds each)
1 teaspoon salt
¼ teaspoon pepper
5 tablespoons butter
2 tablespoons vegetable oil
8 unpeeled garlic cloves
⅓ cup white wine vinegar

2 teaspoons Dijon mustard
1 teaspoon tomato paste
1 cup dry white wine
¼ cup Armagnac or brandy
⅔ cup heavy (or whipping) cream
2 tomatoes, peeled, seeded, and
   diced (about 1 cup)
About 2 teaspoons minced chervil
   or parsley

1. Preheat oven to 375°. Remove loose fat deposits from hens. Cut off the wing tips; cut out the backbones; wrap and freeze for stock-making. Cut each hen in quarters (see Note). Sprinkle with the salt and pepper.

2. Heat 1½ tablespoons butter and 1 tablespoon oil in a wide skillet over moderate heat. Brown half the pieces lightly on both sides, then transfer to a roasting pan. Add 1½ tablespoons more butter and the remaining 1 tablespoon oil to the skillet; add the remaining hen and the garlic cloves to the pan. Brown these, then add to the roasting pan. Discard the fat from the skillet, but do not wash it.

3. Set the hens, uncovered, in the oven. Roast until the juices just run clear, about 20 minutes. Remove the garlic from the pan; slip off the skins, mash the garlic with the side of a knife blade and reserve. Pour the vinegar into the skillet in which the hens were browned. Scrape and stir over moderate heat to loosen all the brown bits. Pour over the birds, then set over moderate heat; boil for a few minutes, until the vinegar and juices have thickened. Transfer the hens to a platter in the turned-off oven.

(continued)

4. Set the roasting pan over moderate heat; add the mustard and tomato paste and stir to blend. Add the wine and Armagnac and mix well (see Note). Boil for about 5 minutes; stirring, to reduce to ¾ cup. Strain; return to the pan along with the mashed garlic and cream. Season with salt and pepper. Bring to a boil, whisking. Off the heat, stir in the remaining 2 tablespoons butter.

5. Sprinkle the birds with the tomato dice. Pour the sauce over all. Sprinkle with chervil or parsley and serve.

Note: *For a more refined presentation, remove the breast bones and hip (pelvic) bones from the quartered hens. Do not take out the bones from drumstick, second joint, and wing, which give the birds their shape.*

   If you prefer a completely smooth sauce, add the mashed garlic at the same time as the wine, rather than at the end.

6 SERVINGS AS A MAIN COURSE

SAUERKRAUT-STUFFED DUCK BREASTS WITH SWEET RED PEPPER SAUCE
UNITED STATES

A fine example of traditional cuisine, updated and refined by Dieter Hannig, who remembers a heavy, fatty (albeit delicious) version of this dish from his childhood and years of apprenticeship in Germany. In this elegant transformation, duck breasts (their skin and fat removed, cubed, and crisped) are stuffed with a small quantity of sauerkraut, onion, grated potato and the browned fat cubes, then briefly roasted and served with a bright, fresh red bell pepper sauce.

4 boneless duck breast halves with skin attached
2 small onions, sliced
2 cups (about 1 pound) sauerkraut, drained and rinsed
1 cup dry white wine
1 teaspoon sugar
½ small bay leaf

1 small potato (about 3 ounces)
Salt and pepper
2 large, thick-skinned, smooth-sided red bell peppers
4 tablespoons butter
⅓ cup minced shallots
1 cup chicken stock

1. Carefully remove the fat and skin layer from the duck breasts without cutting into the flesh. Wrap and refrigerate the meat.

2. Cut the fat into small cubes (you should have about 2 cups). Spread these in an 8–9-inch skillet and cook over moderately low heat, stirring often, until the fat is rendered and the cubes are brown and crisp. With a slotted spoon, transfer the pieces to a dish.

3. Pour out all but 3 tablespoons fat from the skillet. Add the onions and cook over moderately low heat for about 5 minutes, until tender but not browned. Add the sauerkraut, wine, sugar, and bay leaf. Bring to a boil, stirring. Reduce the heat and simmer, covered, for 20 minutes. Shred the potato on the fine blade of a food processor or hand grater. Stir into the sauerkraut. Simmer for 2 minutes. Add salt and pepper to taste. Blend in the duck fat cubes. Let cool.

4. Meanwhile, grill the peppers directly in a gas flame until blistered and blackened almost all over. (Alternatively, you can cook the peppers as close as possible to the heating element of a broiler.) Wrap in damp toweling and let stand for 5–10 minutes. Slip off the skin, scraping off stubborn bits with a knife. Halve the peppers; remove the ribs and seeds; cut the flesh into small pieces.

5. Melt 1 tablespoon butter over moderately low heat in a small saucepan. Add the shallots and stir for 2 minutes. Add the peppers and stir for another 2 minutes. Add the chicken stock and bring to a boil, stirring. Reduce heat to low, cover, and simmer for 10 minutes.

6. Preheat the oven to 400°. Pour the contents of the saucepan into a food processor. Puree to a fine consistency (you should have about 1½ cups). Scoop back into the saucepan and simmer to reduce to about 1 cup. Season.

7. Cut a horizontal lengthwise pocket in each breast, being careful not to pierce through the sides. Divide the stuffing evenly among the 4 breast pieces, packing tightly. Secure with a toothpick or string, if necessary. Heat 2 tablespoons butter in an ovenproof skillet over moderate heat. Brown the duck lightly on both sides. Set in the oven for 5 minutes (medium-rare) or 7 minutes (medium). Let stand for 5–10 minutes.

8. Heat the pepper sauce over low heat. Stir in the remaining 1 tablespoon butter. Divide onto 4 warmed plates. Cut each breast in 6 long slices and arrange around the sauce.

Advance preparation: *The final cooking of the lean, meaty breasts requires less than 10 minutes, making for easy—and smokeless—entertaining. The sauce and stuffing can be made ahead, cooled, and refrigerated. Or if you prefer, the duck breasts can be filled with the chilled stuffing, then wrapped and refrigerated for up to 2 days.*

4 SERVINGS AS A MAIN COURSE

Beef Tenderloin with Fresh Goat Cheese Sauce
CANADA

When chef Albert Schnell of the Hilton International Toronto first served these plump rounds of fillet napped with a cocoa-colored sauce (accompanied by Manitoba Wild Rice Croquettes, page 68), it was for a chefs' convention at the time when interest in regional specialties was just burgeoning. The beef was from the province of Alberta and the tart, fresh cheese from Quebec. Although there were just a handful at the time, now there are 160 goat farmers in that province.

The sauce is not a creamy one, as might be expected, but rather a winy-meaty gloss lightened and sharpened by the acid goat cheese.

---

4 beef tenderloin (fillet) steaks (5–6 ounces each), trimmed and tied
Salt and pepper
1 tablespoon light vegetable oil
2 tablespoons Armagnac or brandy
2 tablespoons butter
2 teaspoons minced shallot
⅔ cup dry red wine

1 cup brown veal stock or beef stock (see Step 1 of Beef Steaks with Mustard Cream, page 292)
2 ounces fresh (not aged) white goat cheese, crumbled
Lemon juice
1 teaspoon thin-sliced chives

---

1. Preheat the oven to 150°. Season the beef with salt and pepper. Heat the oil in a medium skillet over moderate heat; brown the meat on both sides, cooking to the desired degree of doneness (about 4 minutes for medium-rare). Pour out the fat. Add the Armagnac; light it, shaking the pan until the flames die out. Transfer the beef to a platter and set in the warm oven. (Set 4 plates in the oven to warm as well.)

2. Add the butter to the pan; stir in the shallot. Cook over moderately low heat until softened, but not browned, about 2 minutes. Add the red wine and boil over high heat until almost syrupy—about 5 minutes. Add the stock and boil to reduce to about ½ cup.

3. Off the heat, stir in 1½ ounces of the cheese, and salt, pepper, and lemon juice to taste.

4. Spoon about 2 tablespoons sauce on each round of beef. Arrange the remaining cheese in small dabs on these. Garnish with the chives. Serve at once, on heated plates.

4 SERVINGS AS A MAIN COURSE

Executive chef Albert Schnell selects fresh goat cheese from a local supplier

STUFFED, POT-ROASTED BEEF, PUERTO RICAN STYLE
(Carne Mechada)
PUERTO RICO, UNITED STATES

There are probably three or four versions of this dish for each of the Spanish-influenced Caribbean countries, and a few more in Central America. Garlicky, but mellow, this fancified pot roast in russet gravy has a salty-smoky Puerto Rican flavor, but is lighter than the version prepared at the Caribe Hilton International. You might serve the beef with potatoes, plain rice, yellow rice—or try cornmeal mush for a delicious side dish.

Seasoning mixture
1 medium onion, chopped
1 medium green bell pepper (see
  Note), chopped
1 cup cilantro leaves
3 large garlic cloves, minced
1 teaspoon salt
Pot Roast and sauce
3½-pound beef round eye (or eye
  round) roast, tied
4 ounces end-cut cooked ham, cut
  into ¾-inch-wide strips (see Note)
3 ounces salt pork, rind removed,
  cut into ¾-inch-wide strips

3–4 ounces slab bacon, cut into
  ¾-inch-wide strips
4 tablespoons vegetable oil
1 large carrot, cut into ½-inch pieces
2 medium onions, cut into 1-inch
  chunks
1 large celery rib, cut ½ inch wide
¼ cup tomato paste
2 large tomatoes, coarsely chunked
1½ cups dry red wine
2 bay leaves
1 whole large canned pimiento,
  cut into ¼-inch dice
2 tablespoons minced parsley

1. Preheat the oven to 350°. Combine the ingredients for the seasoning mixture on a chopping surface. Mince with a large knife until they become almost a paste.

2. Insert a long knife into one end of the beef and saw gently to make a 2-inch-wide slit that extends to the center of the meat; do the same from the other side to meet in the middle. Rub 1 tablespoon of the seasoning mixture into each end of the opening. Stuff in the strips of ham, salt pork, and bacon to form a tight, neat core. Rub a few tablespoons more seasoning on the meat.

3. Heat 2 tablespoons of the oil in a 4–5-quart Dutch oven or heavy casserole. Brown the meat well on all sides; transfer to a dish. Scrape out the solids and pour out the fat. Add the remaining 2 tablespoons oil and place over moderately high heat. Add the remaining seasoning paste and stir for a few seconds. Add the carrot, onion, and celery slices; stir for a few minutes to color lightly. Add the tomato paste; stir for 2 minutes on moderate heat. Add the tomatoes and wine and stir.

4. Add the meat. Add enough water (about 4 cups) to almost cover the meat. Add the bay leaves. Bring to a boil. Cover and set in the oven. Simmer until tender, about 2½ hours. Uncover and simmer for ½ hour longer. Turn the heat to 150°–200°.

5. Transfer the meat to a platter, cover with foil, and place in the oven. Strain the sauce. Skim off the fat. Boil in a saucepan to reduce to a medium consistency, about 2 cups. Add the minced pimiento and parsley and bring to a boil.

6. Cut the meat in about 12 slices. Arrange on a platter, spoon over a generous quantity of sauce, and serve the remainder in a heated sauceboat.

Note: *In Puerto Rico the tiny, distinctively aromatic sweet chilis called* ajies dulces *are part of the seasoning mixture. If available, add enough to make about 3 tablespoons, finely minced.*
  An end-cut is called for simply so that you get a small quantity if purchasing ham just for the recipe.
Advance preparation: *The meat can be cooled, covered, and refrigerated and the sauce refrigerated separately. To heat, slice the meat, cover with sauce, and place in a moderate oven until heated through.*
Options: *You also can serve it chunky: simply skim the unstrained mixture, then boil to reduce to the desired consistency. For a more Caribbean flavor, substitute cilantro for the parsley used in the sauce.*

6–8 SERVINGS

CORNCAKE TOPPED WITH LAMB, GOAT CHEESE, AND MUSHROOMS

UNITED STATES

A golden custardy corncake is topped with slices of pink lamb, pale goat cheese, and tomato and mushroom dice. An unusual dish of equally weighted, solid flavors, this rather labor-intensive presentation will be a delight for lovers of lamb and rich food—from Dieter Hannig, director of the Food Research Center.

Although the intense lamb jus *(essence), a must in fine dining rooms, will add complexity and distinction to the dish, you might skip it if short of time or inclination.*

Lamb jus

Lamb bones and trimmings from rib
  roast of lamb (see below), bones
  and trimmings chopped or sawed
  into small pieces, and fat
  discarded (see Note)
1 medium carrot, sliced
1 celery rib, sliced
1 small garlic clove, crushed
  or minced
1 medium onion, chopped
2 tablespoons tomato paste
¼ teaspoon dried thyme
¼ teaspoon dried rosemary
1 bay leaf
8 peppercorns, bruised
½ cup dry white wine

Cornmeal cake, lamb, and garnish

8½ ounces (1½ cups) yellow cornmeal
2¼ cups milk

6 tablespoons (3 ounces) butter
½ teaspoon salt
⅛ teaspoon nutmeg
½ cup (about 2 ounces) grated
  Parmesan cheese
1 egg yolk
2 tablespoons chopped onion
½ teaspoon minced garlic
¼ pound mushrooms, thin-sliced
1 medium tomato, peeled, seeded,
  and diced
Bone-in rib roast (rack) of lamb
  (8 ribs), meat removed in one
  long cylinder (see Note)
Pepper
1 tablespoon olive oil
5½-ounce cylinder (1½-inch
  diameter) fresh (not aged), soft
  goat cheese, cut into 8 slices
Basil sprigs for garnish

---

1. Prepare the lamb *jus:* Preheat the oven to 425°. Place the lamb bones and trimmings in a deep skillet or wide saucepan with an ovenproof handle. Roast in the preheated oven for 30 minutes; drain the fat. Roast for another 30 minutes until well browned; drain again. Add the carrot, celery, garlic, onion, and tomato paste; roast for 15 minutes longer.

2. On stovetop, add the thyme, rosemary, bay leaf, and peppercorns. Add the wine and bring slowly to a boil, stirring. Add 4 cups water. Barely simmer, partly covered, for 1½ hours. Strain. Boil to reduce to ½ cup.

3. Blend together the cornmeal and 2 cups water. In a heavy saucepan, combine the milk, 4 tablespoons of the butter, the salt, and nutmeg; bring to a boil, stirring. Add the cornmeal mixture, stirring constantly. Reduce the heat and simmer, stirring, for about 3 minutes.

4. Remove from the heat and stir a moment to cool; stir in the Parmesan cheese, then the egg yolk. Pour into a buttered round 11-inch pan (or set an 11-inch flan ring on a sheet of buttered foil and fold in the edges to improvise a pan; set on a baking sheet). Smooth with a spatula before the cornmeal begins to cool.

5. Melt the remaining 2 tablespoons butter in a skillet; add the 2 tablespoons chopped onion and stir over low heat for 2 minutes; add the garlic and stir over moderate heat for 1 minute. Add the mushrooms; toss for a few minutes to cook through. Add the tomato; toss over high heat for 30 seconds. Set aside.

6. Thirty minutes before serving, set the corncake in a preheated 375° oven. Sprinkle the lamb with salt and pepper. Heat the olive oil in a skillet with a heatproof handle. Sear on all sides; pour off the fat. Set in the oven with the corncake (which will have baked for about 10 minutes). Roast the lamb for 8 minutes, or until the internal temperature reaches 125° for rare meat. Set aside, covered, while you finish the corncake.

7. When the cake has baked 30 minutes and is lightly golden, remove it from the oven; slide onto a heatproof serving dish. With a sharp knife, lightly score the surface into 8 wedges. Divide an equal quantity of the mushroom mixture onto each wedge, placing it toward the wide end. Set a round of cheese on this. Return the cake to the oven until the cheese begins to melt, about 5 minutes.

8. Meanwhile, reheat the lamb *jus*. Slice the rack into 16 pieces. Place 2 pieces on each wedge of the cornmeal cake. Set a sprig of basil in the center and serve at once, with a spoonful of the lamb essence alongside each serving.

Note: *Have the butcher remove the rack and saw the bones for you, unless you're equipped with heavy-duty tools to hack the bones into small pieces.*
Serving and presentation: *Although the corncake slices are not large, the components are very rich and filling. You might serve a salad beforehand, as a first course, and fresh fruit afterward.*
Advance preparation: *The unbaked corncake and lamb* jus *can be made up to 2 days ahead.*

8 SERVINGS AS A MAIN COURSE

Albert Schnell of the Hilton International Toronto: Discipline and Details, or Mignardises for Multitudes

Albert Schnell, executive chef of the Hilton International Toronto and area chef of Hilton Canada, Inc.

I magine the task of running a hotel where 4,500 can lunch together in a convention center, where any one of a possible thousand hotel guests can order a dainty repast or hearty meal from the room service menu—at any moment, day and night—and where a sunny restaurant accommodates 250 at dinner and lunch— with a good 35 dishes making up the buffet service. Meanwhile, an airy coffee shop adjacent to the svelte, spacious lobby seats about 300 from early breakfast to midnight snack-time, a bar offers drinks and nibbles to as many as 200 suave sippers, and one hundred elegant lounge lizards may decorate the tailored sofas of the lobby, ordering an espresso or sandwich, Cognac or orange juice. Imagine that in an evening, the tall-backed club-style chairs of the fine dining room embrace up to 140 diners, while a private room adjoining the restaurant sets the scene for thematic gastronomic tours de force that private club members gather to enjoy.

And imagine that beneath the polished floors and ornate Chinese carpets, beneath a lobby bubbling gently with French, English, German, Italian, and Japanese is a vast labyrinth of chilly storerooms into which pour quantities of the highest quality ingredients, from woodsy-wild chanterelles to loquats, pheasants to fresh foie gras, tins of saffron and other sweet spices. Figure that during one week 115 cooks of the combined restaurants typically make use of 4,100 eggs—and the same number of pounds of chicken—1,300 pounds of butter, 275 pounds of chocolate, 350 quarts of cream, 700 pounds of onions, 500 of carrots, at least 300 pounds of lobster, and about 175 prime ribs of beef (each weighing about 15 pounds). And, finally, imagine that the 2,020 various food items required are specified by one man, the same man responsible for the quality of every dish that leaves the kitchens, whether a cheeseburger or an elixir of ringneck pheasant with morels under a puff pastry crust.

Albert Schnell—imposing, quietly authoritative, with a smile that is as ingenuous as it is mischievous—orchestrates (with help from his all-seeing sous-chefs, Tadashi Katoh and Daniel Lamy) such extravaganzas every day. A firm, disciplined man, his many years at the mammoth Queen Elizabeth in Montreal and the Harbour Castle in Toronto and a concurrent 20 years as the Area Chef for Hilton Canada, Inc., make him one of the very few executive chefs who could possibly be equal to the task of coordinating not merely the workings of a giant hotel, but all of Hilton International's kitchen operations in Canada.

Despite these overwhelming responsibilities, Schnell's attention to detail is such that he might well be garnishing each portion himself (the Swiss-born chef began as a pastry apprentice and has earned awards in this exacting culinary realm). Before each menu is drawn up, he will specify which plates must be used for each course, where the food should be placed, how the napkins must be decoratively folded under the bowl of pheasant consomme, how many doilies should grace the dessert saucer, the color of the rose petals to be frozen in ice bowls to hold sorbet, and just how far the pool of raspberry puree should extend into the outer rim of creme anglaise on the plate. He is deeply engaged in each undertaking; it is a personal affair to him each time a meal is set out, whether for four or 4,000. He thinks that if the finest food is served at a huge event, many more diners will leave better educated, aware of the refinements. Teaching is of the utmost importance to him, and he has trained, honed, and contributed to the success of students who take his message worldwide, wherever fine dining flourishes.

Schnell's gala dinners, whether for the prime minister of Japan, Queen Elizabeth, or the Opera Ball, are tailored to fit the occasion: The concept of an entire meal, from the typeface of the menu to the shape of the tray for the after-dinner sweets, is his medium. For the prime minister, for example, he included a number of local ingredients to introduce the best of Canada: Brome Lake duck, Manitoba wild rice, the fine beef of Alberta, spring vegetables from the Okanogan Valley. At the same time he welcomed the Japanese guests with *La terrine de saumon des Maritimes escortée de sushi aux crevettes,* sesame seeds on the cheese straws, and a ragout of shiitake. The dinner for the queen finished appropriately with *La couronne glacée aux pêches de Niagara accompagnée de mignardises* (a selection of tiny pastries and bonbons)—for 2,100. The whimsical took over at the Opera Ball when Schnell served such creations as Noisettes of Lamb under a Veil of Seven Herbs with Love-Apples (Salome-inspired), followed by Carmelite Salad on Oakleaf Lettuce and Rose Petals Sprinkled with Virgin Olive Oil (The Dialogue of the Carmelites).

It was not surprising that shortly after we returned home from visiting this chef who has an eye for the whole picture and the finest detail, he sent a gracious, personal note and enclosed a meticulous recipe for a dessert that had been a favorite during our sampling, the fresh, sweet-scented Pear Souffle which follows.

PEAR SOUFFLÉ WITH VANILLA PEAR SAUCE

CANADA

A meal in the Hilton International Toronto proceeded as follows: crêpes with golden caviar filling; pigeon breast sautéed with herbs and garnished with asparagus, endive, and mâche in rose petal vinaigrette; duckling consommé with quail egg yolk; ragoût of minute morsels of crayfish tail, salmon, and frogs' legs in a beurre blanc with leeks; and spinach with golden raisins. This was followed by a pear soufflé of sheer perfection. Only years of honing and experimenting from chef Albert Schnell (whose career began as a pâtissier) *could have produced such a refined, satiny, and beautiful soufflé. The result is worth every moment of the undeniably lengthy preparation.*

Soufflé Base
1 cup milk
½ vanilla bean pod, halved
   lengthwise
⅓ cup granulated sugar
¼ cup all-purpose flour
Pinch of salt
4 egg yolks

Vanilla Sauce
½ vanilla bean pod, halved
   lengthwise
¾ cup heavy (or whipping) cream
2 tablespoons granulated sugar
2 egg yolks

Assembly
About 2 pounds canned pears in
   heavy syrup (11–12 halves),
   drained
4–5 tablespoons *eau-de-vie de poire*
   (clear pear brandy)
Melted butter
Granulated sugar for coating
   the molds
4 egg yolks, at room temperature
5 tablespoons granulated sugar
5 egg whites, at room temperature
Confectioners' sugar

1. Prepare the soufflé base: Combine the milk and vanilla pod in a heavy medium saucepan and bring to a simmer, stirring. Combine the sugar, flour, and salt in a mixing bowl. Blend in the yolks with an electric mixer. Slowly pour half the hot milk into the mixture, beating on low speed. Scrape into the remaining milk, stirring to blend. Stir over moderate heat until thick and pasty. Remove the vanilla pod and scrape the beans into the pot. Scoop into a small bowl; set a film of plastic on the surface and cool.

2. Prepare the vanilla sauce: Bring the vanilla pod and cream to a boil over low heat in a small pan; cover and reserve. Combine the sugar and egg yolks in a small bowl and whip with an electric mixer until thick and pale, the texture of soft meringue. Pour the cream into this mixture, beating on low speed. In a clean saucepan, stir the sauce over lowest heat until it just barely thickens and tiny wisps of steam begin to puff out. Immediately strain into a bowl set in a pan of ice water to stop the cooking. Once lukewarm, remove from the ice. *(continued)*

3. Preheat the oven to 400°. Puree 6 pear halves to a smooth consistency in a processor or blender. (You should have about 1 cup.) Stir 3 tablespoons of the puree into the vanilla sauce. Add 1–2 tablespoons pear *eau-de-vie*, to taste.

4. Paint ten individual soufflé dishes or ramekins, each about 3⅝ inches in diameter × 1¾ inches high, with melted butter. Coat with granulated sugar, tapping off the excess.

5. Combine the remaining pear puree with 2½ tablespoons pear *eau-de-vie*. Divide evenly among the dishes, tapping to coat smoothly. Thinly slice 5 more pear halves; divide evenly to cover the puree in all the dishes.

6. Blend the 4 egg yolks into the cooled soufflé base. Beat the egg whites and 5 tablespoons granulated sugar to form firm but not stiff peaks. Blend one-quarter of the whites into the base to mix thoroughly, then fold in the remainder delicately. Spoon evenly over the pears.

7. Set the dishes on a folded dish towel in a large baking pan; pour in boiling water to reach halfway up the molds. Set in the center of the hot oven and bake for 20 minutes.

8. Lift the soufflés from the water bath with a wide spatula. Immediately sieve confectioners' sugar over the tops and serve, accompanied with the vanilla pear sauce.

Advance preparation: *The soufflé can be prepared ahead through Step 5.*
Options: *For a dramatically high-rising petite soufflé, use dishes 3⅜ inches in diameter and 1½ inches high. Although the mixture will reach to the top before baking, the soufflés will not topple if carefully handled.*

10 SERVINGS

BANANA PUDDINGS WITH COFFEE-RUM SAUCE
VENEZUELA

Warm, smooth banana desserts unmold easily to be cloaked with a tawny caramel sauce in this recipe from Frank Muller, executive chef of the Caracas Hilton International. Surprisingly fresh and fruity, the firm, cream-beige pudding contains no additional sugar, drawing its sweetness from the fruit alone (which should be over-ripe). It is briskly complemented by the bittersweet sauce, which coats sleekly, not stickily.

Sauce
⅓ cup sugar
½ tablespoon butter
¼ cup coffee liqueur
¼ cup dark rum
1 cup heavy (or whipping) cream
½ teaspoon instant coffee
Banana pudding
1 pound 10 ounces very ripe bananas
    (5 medium bananas)

1 egg
3 tablespoons banana liqueur
1 cup heavy (or whipping) cream
1 teaspoon lemon juice
Softened butter for the molds
Garnish
½ cup heavy (or whipping) cream,
    whipped

1. Preheat the oven to 300°. *Prepare the sauce:* Combine the sugar and 2 tablespoons water in a small, heavy pan. Let stand for 3–4 minutes, to dissolve somewhat. Set the pan over moderately low heat; let bubble, without stirring, until the syrup begins to brown. Meanwhile, combine the butter, coffee liqueur, rum, cream, and instant coffee. As the syrup browns, swirl the pan to prevent burning. When the caramel is a rich brown, slowly add the cream mixture, stirring (don't worry when the caramel lumps; it will melt). Stir over moderate heat until the sauce is reduced to about 1⅓ cups, when it should be thickish and shiny. Set aside.

2. *Prepare the pudding:* Cut off, wrap, and reserve ½ banana. Slice the remaining fruit into the container of a food processor. Add the egg, banana liqueur, cream, and lemon juice. Blend until smooth.

3. Coat six ½–¾-cup custard cups, timbale molds, or ramekins with the softened butter. Divide the custard mixture into these. Set the molds on folded paper towels in a roasting pan. Pour in boiling water to come halfway up their sides. Bake for about 35 minutes, until just firm in the center. Let stand for about 15 minutes.

4. To serve, slip a knife around each pudding and unmold onto a dessert plate. Divide the sauce over each, then slice the reserved banana into 18 thin rounds and place 3 slices on top of or alongside each pudding. Serve the whipped cream separately.

Advance preparation: *The sauce can be made ahead, chilled, then returned to room temperature or warmed slightly. The mixture for the puddings (which should be served warm, but cannot be reheated) can be made and refrigerated, tightly covered, for up to 8 hours before baking, although the color will darken slightly— but it is so quickly assembled that it hardly seems worth it.*

6 SERVINGS

FOOLPROOF COCOA SOUFFLÉ

PUERTO RICO, UNITED STATES

It is no wonder that in high season as many as 160 portions of this dessert are served each night at the Caribe Hilton International. You have to try this to believe it: an utterly unflappable soufflé that is easy, impressive, and can be made almost completely in advance. Smooth-crowned, its sugar-crisped sides rise high, and its bittersweet center, reminiscent of a light steamed pudding, remains tender. Do not forgo the ice cream which perfectly complements the barely sweet, rather firm soufflé with its cool softness and sweetness.

2 tablespoons melted butter
Sugar for coating the molds
4 tablespoons (2 ounces) cold butter
⅔ cup plus 3 tablespoons sugar
⅔ cup (3 ounces) bread flour (high-gluten flour)

½ cup (1½ ounces) unsweetened cocoa powder
2 cups milk
7 eggs, separated and at room temperature
Vanilla ice cream

1. Paint 10 ramekins (individual soufflé dishes) about 3¾ inches in diameter and 1¾ inches high with the melted butter; coat generously with sugar. Preheat the oven to 400° with the rack set in the center.

2. Combine the cold butter, ⅔ cup sugar, the flour, and cocoa in a processor or blender; whirl to form a crumbly mixture.

3. Bring the milk to a boil in a medium saucepan, stirring. Whisk in the cocoa mixture. Return to a boil, stirring. Scoop into a mixing bowl, then whisk in the egg yolks, one at a time.

4. Combine the egg whites and the remaining 3 tablespoons sugar in a mixing bowl. With an electric beater, whip until soft, not stiff, peaks form. Stir one-third of the whites into the warm cocoa mixture to blend completely. Gently fold in the remainder.

5. Set the molds on a folded dishtowel in a roasting pan. Pour in boiling water to reach halfway up the sides of the molds. Set in the center of the oven and bake for 17–20 minutes, until the center no longer seems liquid—but not until baked firm.

6. Serve at once, with the ice cream.

Note: *Although the service is simpler and more attractive and the soufflés hold their shape better if made individually, you can prepare the dessert in a 2-quart soufflé dish by making the following adjustments: Use ¾ cup plus 2 tablespoons sugar in the soufflé mixture combined in the processor. Set the dessert on the lower rack of the oven, rather than in the center. Bake for about 40 minutes. Presented this way, you'll have about 6 servings.*

Advance preparation: *The soufflé mixture can be prepared and portioned 3–4 hours ahead, then left at room temperature (preferably cool) to pop into the oven as the dishes are cleared away.*

10 SERVINGS

APPLE TIMBALES ROUGEMONT WITH MAPLE SYRUP AND VANILLA SAUCE

CANADA

Rougemont is the center of apple production in Canada, and Quebec of maple syrup. Executive chef Albert Schnell chose these native ingredients to reinterpret the classic upside-down tarte Tatin *in individual presentation. Neatly petaled apple slices, sweetened with caramel-y maple syrup, are inverted on a pastry crust and surrounded with thick vanilla sauce.*

Pastry
¾ cup (3¼ ounces) all-purpose flour
⅛ teaspoon salt
5 tablespoons (2½ ounces) chilled
 butter, cut into bits
About 3 tablespoons ice water
Vanilla Sauce
¼ large vanilla bean pod, halved
 lengthwise
¾ cup heavy (or whipping) cream

2 tablespoons sugar
2 egg yolks
Filling
¼ cup pecans
4 medium-small Golden Delicious
 apples
2 tablespoons lemon juice
2 tablespoons butter
¼ teaspoon ground cinnamon
¾ cup pure maple syrup

1. Make the pastry: Blend the flour and salt in a bowl. Cut in the butter with a pastry blender until it resembles oatmeal flakes. Gradually sprinkle on the ice water, tossing with a fork until the dough can be massed together easily into a ball. Form a flat disk, wrap; refrigerate for 1 hour or longer.

2. Preheat the oven to 300°. Prepare the vanilla sauce: Bring the vanilla pod and cream to a simmer over low heat in a small pan; cover and reserve. Combine the sugar and egg yolks in a small bowl and beat until pale and thick, similar to the texture of soft meringue. Pour half the cream into this mixture, whisking briskly. Pour the egg mixture into the remaining cream.

3. Set over low heat and stir constantly until the cream just barely begins to thicken as tiny wisps of steam begin to puff out. Immediately strain into a bowl set in a pan of ice water to stop the cooking. Stir now and then as the sauce cools. Refrigerate.

4. Make the filling: Spread the pecans in a cake pan and roast for 10 minutes in the oven. Remove and cool. Increase the oven temperature to 400°. Peel, quarter, and core the apples; toss with the lemon juice. Cut each quarter into 3 lengthwise wedges. Heat ½ tablespoon butter in a 9-inch nonstick skillet. Sauté half the wedges over moderate heat until pale gold on both sides. Sprinkle with half the cinnamon; transfer to a plate. Repeat with another ½ tablespoon butter and the remaining apples and cinnamon.

5. Chop the roasted nuts; reserve ½ tablespoon. Chop 12 of the apple wedges and mix with the remaining nuts.

6. Boil the maple syrup in a small saucepan until it is reduced to ½ cup. Add the remaining 1 tablespoon butter and remove from the heat. Place 1 tablespoon of the syrup in each of 4 individual straight-sided ramekins or soufflé molds about 3¾ inches in diameter and 1¾ inches high (or slightly larger).

7. Place 3 of the sautéed apple wedges overlapping against the dish to leave a hole in the center. Arrange 3 more over these, then another 3 on top of them. Fill the other 3 molds the same way. Stuff the chopped mixture into the center holes, tamping tightly. Spoon maple syrup into this section.

8. On a lightly floured work surface, roll out the pastry to form a circle large enough to cut 4 circles that will just fit within the rim of each dish. Place a round of pastry in each dish on top of the apples, but do not press down the edge.

9. Bake in the upper level of the hot oven for 20 minutes, until the dough is golden brown. Place on a rack; cool to lukewarm (see Serving).

10. To serve: divide the vanilla sauce onto 4 large serving plates, then tilt to distribute. Unmold each timbale onto a slotted spatula, then set carefully in the center of each pool. Sprinkle with the reserved nuts.

Serving: *The amount of juice that accumulates as the timbales bake can vary enormously. If there seems to be a large quantity after the desserts have cooled, pour some off before unmolding so that the sauce is not diluted or the pastry softened by the liquid.*
Advance preparation: *The sauce can be prepared completely in advance. The timbales can be completed through Step 8. Add 5 minutes to the baking time if refrigerated.*

4 SERVINGS

SHAKER LEMON PIE

UNITED STATES

During the late eighteenth and early nineteenth centuries, communities of the religious society that came to be known as Shakers were established throughout the United States. These self-sufficient groups were renowned for their beautiful handicrafts and simple, good cooking—particularly baking. The American Harvest Restaurant in New York's Vista Hotel has featured the food of the Shakers, drawing inspiration from many of the settlements. The following easy and unusual lemon pie—one of 35 pie recipes in The Best of Shaker Cooking *by Amy Bess Miller and Persis Fuller (Collier Books, 1976)— is based on a recipe from North Union Shaker Village in Ohio.*

A powerful lemon-rind aroma leaps through the cross-cut center of the sugar-glazed crust. The flavor is surprisingly complex and vivid for a filling that has but three ingredients. Bittersweet, pungent, brimming with sunny slices of fruit with its peel, this is for devoted lemon-lovers only. Plan a day ahead for this dessert, as the fruit must be macerated for 24 hours.

---

3 lemons, preferably thin-skinned
1 cup plus 1 teaspoon sugar
1¾ cups (9 ounces) all-purpose flour
½ teaspoon salt
12 tablespoons (6 ounces) chilled, unsalted butter, cut into small bits

5–6 tablespoons cold milk
3 eggs
1 egg beaten with 1 tablespoon water and a pinch of salt for egg wash

---

1. Cut the lemons into paper-thin slices, removing seeds as you go (you should have 2 cups). Combine in a mixing bowl with 1 cup of the sugar. Cover and let stand at room temperature for about 24 hours.

2. Whisk together the flour and salt in a mixing bowl. With a pastry blender, work in the butter until the mixture forms small flakes. Sprinkle in the milk 1 tablespoon at a time, tossing the flour mixture to incorporate evenly. Press the dough together gently to form a ball; if the pieces separate, add a few more drops of milk. Form the dough into 2 disks. Wrap each in plastic and refrigerate for at least 1 hour.

(continued)

3. Preheat the oven to 450°. Roll out one piece of pastry on a lightly floured board to form an 11-inch circle; trim with scissors to form an even round. Fold the dough in quarters, place the center point in the middle of a 9-inch pie pan, then unfold gently, easing into the pan.

4. Roll the remaining dough to form a circle ½ inch larger than the pan rim; trim neatly. Cut an X in the center.

5. Beat the eggs to blend; stir into the lemon and sugar mixture, stirring to dissolve any remaining sugar. Pour into the shell; distribute the slices with a fork. Paint the exposed rim of pastry with the egg wash; lay the top crust on this, pressing lightly. Fold the overhanging pastry over this. Press, then seal with the tines of a fork. Paint the crust lightly with the egg wash. Fold open the corners of the X to make a square. Sprinkle the crust evenly with the remaining 1 teaspoon sugar.

6. Set on the lowest rack of the hot oven. Bake for 15 minutes. Reduce the heat to 350° and bake for about 20 minutes longer, until well browned. Cool on a rack.

Option: *For a milder, slightly more tender and sweet variation, substitute 2 cups halved, thin-sliced oranges for the lemons.*

6–8 SERVINGS

CALVADOS SHERBET

UNITED STATES

Fruity and flowery, this golden ice is clean and fresh, but has plenty of character—and alcohol. It is particularly suited to rich autumnal meals, those based on game or pork, for example. Although it is possible to prepare this in other ways, the ice cream makers that contain their own freezing elements are the surest routes to a fine-textured, light dessert. This comes from a series of microfiches devoted to frozen desserts that was developed by the Food Research Center.

¾–1 cup sugar (see Option)
3½ cups apple cider, chilled
¾ cup Calvados or other apple
    brandy, such as applejack

2–3 tablespoons lemon juice
1 egg white

1. Combine the sugar and 2 cups water in a small pot; swirl over high heat until the syrup boils, then lower the heat, cover, and simmer for 2 minutes. Cool and chill.

2. Combine the cooled syrup, cider, and Calvados. Add the lemon juice to taste. Stir 1 cup of the mixture into the egg white. Blend well, but do not beat until foamy; pour this into the cider mixture.

3. Pour into the container of an ice cream maker. Freeze according to the manufacturer's directions. Scrape into a freezer container, cover tightly, and freeze for at least 6 hours or up to a week.

4. To serve, soften slightly in the refrigerator.

Option: *If you like a strong Calvados flavor and tart edge to the sherbet, use the smaller amount of sugar. If you prefer a more traditional sweetness, use the larger quantity.*

ABOUT 2 QUARTS

CRANBERRY-APPLE SHERBET

UNITED STATES

If you enjoy serving a palate refresher during a rich meal, this tart fruity sherbet, made with the minimum quantity of sugar, does a brisk job. For a ruby-pink, fine-textured dessert, use the maximum amount of sugar and offer the sherbet in tulipe *cookie cups or decorated with fancy-cut apple slivers.*

12 ounces cranberries, rinsed and picked over

2 cups apple juice
¾–1 cup sugar (see Note)

1. Combine the cranberries, juice, sugar, and 2½ cups water in a nonaluminum saucepan. Bring to a simmer; cook for a few minutes until all of the berry skins pop. Set the pan in ice water to cool.

2. Puree the berries and liquid in a food processor until not quite smooth, then press through a fine sieve. (Or simply press through the fine disk of a nonaluminum food mill.)

3. Pour the mixture into the container of an ice cream maker. Freeze according to the manufacturer's directions. Scoop into a container and freeze for 6 hours up to a week.

4. Let the sherbet soften slightly in the refrigerator before serving.

Note: *Since berries may vary in ripeness and acidity, taste and add more sugar if necessary after you've pureed the fruit.*

ABOUT 1½ QUARTS

AMERICAN HARVEST PUMPKIN CHEESECAKE

UNITED STATES

A best-seller at the Vista New York's fine dining room, this oozingly rich cake is for devoted cream-cheese lovers. The spice blend tints the cake a pale beige (rather than the orangy color you might expect) and adds subdued undertones to the pumpkin, which lightens the texture of the dense cheese.

Amusingly, the recipe, which evolved from one published in the December, 1979 issue of Gourmet *magazine ("Cheesecake Creations" by Margaret H. Koehler), was later requested from the restaurant by editors of the same magazine.*

8 gingersnaps (or ½ cup dried gingerbread or spice cookie crumbs)
1 tablespoon melted butter
2 pounds plus 3 ounces cream cheese, at room temperature
1½ cups sugar
5 eggs
1½ teaspoons grated orange zest
1½ teaspoons grated lemon zest
1-pound can pumpkin puree

¼ teaspoon ground cinnamon
½ teaspoon nutmeg
2 teaspoons ground anise
1 teaspoon ground cloves
2 teaspoons ground coriander
¼ cup heavy (or whipping) cream
¼ cup sour cream
3 tablespoons Bourbon whisky
⅔ cup walnuts, chopped medium-fine

1. Preheat the oven to 350°. Buzz the gingersnaps in a processor or blender to form fine crumbs. (There should be ½ cup.) Paint a cake mold about 10 inches in diameter and 3¼ inches deep with the melted butter. Coat evenly with the crumbs.

2. Cut the cheese into small chunks. In the large bowl of a standing mixer, beat until creamy; gradually beat in the sugar and work until very soft, with no lumps remaining. On low speed, add the eggs, one at a time. Beat in the grated zests, pumpkin, cinnamon, nutmeg, anise, cloves, and coriander. Add the cream, sour cream, and Bourbon. Beat to blend.

3. Pour the cheese mixture into the pan; sprinkle evenly with the nuts. Place in a roasting pan; pour in boiling water to reach halfway up the sides. Set in the center of the hot oven and bake for 1½ hours.

4. Set on a rack to cool completely. Refrigerate for at least 8 hours, or up to 2 days.

5. To unmold, dip the pan into very hot water for about 30 seconds. Run a knife carefully around the edge. Invert the cake onto a board, then invert onto a serving plate, so the nuts are on top. To serve, dip a wide cake knife in hot water to cut each slice (which may not be perfectly neat, as the cake is quite soft).

12–14 SERVINGS

Hazelnut Rice Pudding

UNITED STATES

The Vista Hotel won first prize in a competition in search of the best rice pudding in New York City with a dessert of creamy white rice flecked with wild rice and bound with richly perfumed ground hazelnuts (adapted below). The prize tied in neatly with an American Indian food festival that was held shortly thereafter at Vista's American Harvest Restaurant and which featured the distinctive native grain.

½ **cup hazelnuts**
½ **cup wild rice**
½ **cup long-grain white rice**
2¼ **cups milk**
Pinch of salt

½ **cup raisins**
½ **cup lightly packed dark brown sugar**
Whipped cream
¼ **cup grated semisweet chocolate**

1. Preheat the oven to 375°. Toast the hazelnuts in a pan in the hot oven for 10 minutes, until the husks split and the nuts are lightly browned. While still warm, rub together vigorously in a dish towel to remove as many husks as possible.

2. Combine the wild rice and 2 cups water in a small heavy saucepan; bring to a boil, stirring. Cover and cook over low heat until tender, but not mushy, testing occasionally. Timing can vary considerably, from 25 minutes to 1 hour. Drain and cool.

3. Meanwhile, combine the white rice in a small heavy pot with the milk and salt. Bring to a boil, stirring. Cook over very lowest heat, uncovered, until the rice is almost tender and the milk is thickened and creamy, about 20 minutes; stir often. Add the raisins and cook 5 minutes longer, stirring frequently. Remove from the heat.

4. Combine the nuts and brown sugar in a processor; whirl to a fine texture. Add ¼ cup water and whiz to a puree. Add another ¼ cup water and continue processing until smooth. Stir this mixture into the white rice, blending well. Add the wild rice and mix thoroughly.

5. Cool to room temperature, stirring now and then. Spoon into 8 parfait or champagne glasses. Refrigerate until serving time (or ½ hour prior, for the most flavor and texture).

6. To serve, decorate with whipped cream rosettes and sprinkle the grated chocolate over all.

8 SERVINGS

RECIPES

APPETIZERS

Cornmeal Squares with Blue Cheese, Tomatoes, and Basil *(Switzerland)* 120
Shrimp on Leaf Salad with Fluffy Mustard
Mayonnaise *(United Kingdom)* 122
Mussels with Fennel in Saffron Butter *(Italy)* 123
Fish Fillets with Asparagus in Herb Sauce *(Austria)* 124
Poached Salmon with Sherry Cream and Tomato Parfait *(Germany)* 126

SALADS

Fennel Salad with Apples and Walnuts *(Switzerland)* 132
Farmer's Kale Salad *(Switzerland)* 133
Spinach, Bacon, and Egg Salad *(Belgium)* 135
Fillets of Sole with Sautéed Apples and Salad Greens *(France)* 137
Salad of Endive with Poached Egg and Bacon *(France)* 138

SOUPS

Alsatian Beer Soup *(France)* 139
Forest Mushroom Broth *(United Kingdom)* 140

VEGETABLES, GRAINS, AND PASTA

"Ratatouille" with Mint *(Switzerland)* 144
Potato Dumplings, Alsatian-Style *(France)* 145
Potato Pancakes with Cheese and Caraway *(Switzerland)* 147
Risotto with Mint *(Italy)* 148
Spinach Noodles with Mandarin Cream Sauce *(Italy)* 149
Spinach and Carrot Tofu Cakes in Tomato Sauce *(Switzerland)* 150
Vegetable Strudel with Herbal Cream *(Austria)* 152

PREVIOUS PAGE: **Chef Eduard Mitsche, of the Hilton International Wien, displaying a selection of pastry in front of a monument to Johann Strauss in the beautiful Wiener Stadtpark adjacent to the hotel**

SEAFOOD

Lobster, Red Snapper, Scallops, and Flounder with
Vegetable Strands in Light Stock *(Austria)* 156
Fish Terrine with Basil *(Belgium)* 158
Fish Fillets in Red Wine Butter Sauce *(Germany)* 160
Brochettes of Monkfish and Salmon with Lime *(Switzerland)* 161
Sea Bass Fillets with Artichokes and Cilantro *(Switzerland)* 165
Monkfish Fillet with Fennel and Red Onion *(United Kingdom)* 166

MEAT AND POULTRY

Lamb with Minted Red Wine Sauce and
Mustard Seeds *(United Kingdom)* 171
Sweetbreads with Honey Sauce and Melon *(Belgium)* 172
Veal Medallions with Apples and Walnuts *(Switzerland)* 174
Squab and Endive with Salad Greens *(France)* 176
Duck in Two Acts: Crackling Salad and Sliced Duck with
Spring Vegetables in Broth *(United Kingdom)* 178
Breast of Hen with Green Beans in Hazelnut Dressing *(Austria)* 183
Chicken Breasts with Red Pepper Sauce *(Switzerland)* 184
Chicken Breasts Stuffed with Liver in
Light Basil Cream Sauce *(United Kingdom)* 186
Rabbit and Endive in Cream with Walnut Dressing *(France)* 187

DESSERTS

Layered Orange and Chocolate Parfait with Pear Sauce *(Belgium)* 192
Frozen Poppy Seed and Cinnamon Parfait with Rum Dates *(Austria)* 194
Honey-Ginger Ice Cream with Papaya and Mango *(Austria)* 196
Ice Cream with Melon and Jasmine Tea Sabayon *(Germany)* 197
Champagne Sorbet with Campari *(Switzerland)* 198
Engadine Nut Cake *(Switzerland)* 199
Flamed Blackberries with Pernod and Ice Cream *(Switzerland)* 200
Gâteau Devidal (Chocolate Mousse Cake) *(Switzerland)* 203
Thurgau Apple Cake *(Switzerland)* 204
Baked Apple Custard with Caramel Pepper Sauce *(Germany)* 206
Dialogue of Fruit Purees *(Austria)* 207
Prune Terrine with Sabayon Cream *(Switzerland)* 208
Berries Perfumed with Kümmel *(France)* 212

CORNMEAL SQUARES WITH BLUE CHEESE, TOMATOES, AND BASIL
SWITZERLAND

Ticino is the Italian canton of Switzerland, and the source of this savory appetizer that is served by chef Franz Kuhne at the casual Café de la Marine Suisse in the Hilton International Basel.

The butter-bright yellow squares of cornmeal porridge (polenta in Italian cuisine) are topped with tomato wedges and tangy blue-veined cheese in abundance (Gorgonzola being the Italian choice). The snippets of fragrant green basil are no longer strictly Italian, but part of a storehouse that is common to most fine restaurants in much of the world.

---

1 cup milk
4 tablespoons butter
¼ teaspoon salt
¼ teaspoon nutmeg
¾ cup (4 ounces) fine-to-medium ground yellow cornmeal
1 egg yolk

1 generous cup (4 ounces) crumbled blue-veined cheese (see Options)
½ teaspoon minced garlic
4 smallish tomatoes (about 1 pound), peeled, seeded, and each cut into 12 wedges
2 tablespoons slivered basil leaves
Pepper

---

1. In a small heavy saucepan, combine the milk, half the butter, the salt, and nutmeg; bring to a boil. Combine the cornmeal with 1 cup water. Add to the milk mixture, stirring constantly.

2. Bring to a boil; lower the heat and stir for 5 minutes. Off the heat, stir in the egg yolk. Spread on a baking sheet to form a 7-inch square. Let cool for 30 minutes or so, until rather firm. Meanwhile, preheat the oven to 425°.

3. Cut the cooled cornmeal into 16 squares. Scatter the blue cheese on top, then tamp it down. Set in the hot oven and bake for 7–8 minutes, until bubbly. Meanwhile, heat the remaining 2 tablespoons butter in a medium skillet. Stir in the garlic; add the tomatoes, basil, and salt and pepper to taste. Sauté over moderate heat just to warm through.

4. Place 4 corn cakes on each of 4 serving plates; arrange the tomatoes in the center.

Serving and presentation: *For a pretty effect you can also arrange the tomatoes directly on the cornmeal squares. An icy white wine from Northern Italy, such as a Riesling or Pinot Bianco from the Alto Adige, would do beautifully with this—as would a Fendant from Switzerland, if it is available.*

Advance preparation: *All but the tomato mixture can be prepared up to a day in advance. Simply slip the corn-cheese squares into the oven to heat while you assemble this savory topping.*

Options: *Any number of blue-veined cheeses will suit this dish: Danish blue, French bleu d'Auvergne, Italian Gorgonzola. Or try one of a number of Swiss toppings: snails, sausage, wild mushrooms, or tomato-herb sauce.*

4 SERVINGS AS A FIRST COURSE

Shrimp on Leaf Salad with Fluffy Mustard Mayonnaise

UNITED KINGDOM

Chef Graham Cadman, who confesses he is not by preference "a banquet person," was relieved and delighted when he came up with this appealing appetizer for a party of 400 at the Gatwick Hilton International. A new twist on a shrimp cocktail: shrimp are bathed in an ivory cream in which blanched mustard seeds pop like caviar as you bite them.

1 tablespoon plus ¼ teaspoon salt
16 very large shrimp in the shell
  (about 1¾ pounds; see Serving)
1 egg yolk
1½ teaspoons Dijon mustard
1 teaspoon white wine vinegar
¼ cup light vegetable oil
¼ cup light olive oil
2 teaspoons lemon juice

White pepper
1 tablespoon mustard seeds
¼ cup heavy cream
1 medium head of Bibb lettuce
  (about 4 ounces), cored, rinsed,
  and dried
1 bunch mâche (corn salad; about 2
  ounces), trimmed, rinsed, and
  dried

1. Bring 3 cups water and 1 tablespoon of the salt to a boil; add the shrimp. Cover and bring to a simmer over highest heat. Remove from the stove, uncover, and let cool in the liquid for 30 minutes.

2. Meanwhile, in a small mixing bowl, whisk together the egg yolk, mustard, the remaining ¼ teaspoon salt, and vinegar. Very gradually whisk in the vegetable oil, a tiny bit at a time, until completely incorporated. Add the olive oil in larger quantities, beating continually. Add the lemon juice. Season with white pepper.

3. Drop the mustard seeds into boiling water to cover generously. Boil for 20 seconds. Drain and rinse in cold water. Add to the mayonnaise. Whip the cream in a small bowl until thickened and fluffy, but not firm enough to mound; it should be liquidy. Fold into the mayonnaise. Chill until serving time.

4. Peel off the shrimp shells, leaving the tail section intact. Remove the veins; rinse the shrimp in the cooled cooking liquid. Serve, or cover and refrigerate until serving time (see Note).

5. Spoon about 2 tablespoons of the sauce onto each of 4 large plates. Cut a slit halfway down the body on the back of each shrimp. Open each one and place cut side down so that it stands in the dressing. Distribute the salad greens.

Serving: *For less than hearty eaters, serve 3 shrimp as an appetizer. For a lunch main course, serve 5–6 shrimp per person and arrange on a platter, family-style.*

  For optimum tenderness and flavor, the shrimp are at their best if served warm or at room temperature, if your schedule permits.

Options: *Offer cruets of oil and vinegar for those who prefer their salad greens dressed.*

4 SERVINGS AS A FIRST COURSE

MUSSELS WITH FENNEL IN SAFFRON BUTTER

ITALY

Fennel is the dominant note in this first course served at La Pergola restaurant in the Cavalieri Hilton International in Rome. The pale green strips of this quintessentially Italian vegetable are accompanied by a small quantity of mussels which, in their buttery sauce, lend softness and succulence.

2 medium-small fennel bulbs (with 2-inch tops; about 1½ pounds total weight)
6½ tablespoons butter
2 tablespoons minced onion
24 small-medium (or 16 large) cultivated mussels, cleaned (see page 324)

¼ teaspoon saffron threads
¾ cup dry white wine
Salt and pepper
1 medium tomato, peeled, seeded, and diced
Basil sprigs

1. Cut off and reserve the stalks of fennel for another use. Cut the core out of the base. Slice the fennel bulb into thin layers about 2 inches long.

2. Heat 2 tablespoons of the butter over moderately high heat in a 10-inch saucepan; stir in the onion and cook until softened. Add the fennel strips and toss over moderate heat for 2 minutes, until shiny and brightly translucent.

3. Add the mussels, saffron, and wine. Cover and boil for a few minutes, just until the mussels open. Remove them with a slotted spoon; set aside and cover four of them for garnish. Shell the remaining mussels.

4. Continue cooking the fennel in the sauce over moderate heat until tender; 3–4 tablespoons of liquid should remain. Place the mussels on the fennel; cover the pan and remove from the heat.

5. In a small skillet, sauté the tomato in ½ tablespoon butter for 2 minutes, or until just softened; set aside. Cut the remaining 4 tablespoons butter into small pieces. Set the mussels and fennel over lowest heat and stir in the butter. Season with salt and pepper.

6. Divide into 4 small, shallow dishes, placing a mussel in the shell in each. Top with the tomato and basil.

4 SERVINGS AS A FIRST COURSE

FISH FILLETS WITH ASPARAGUS IN HERB SAUCE

AUSTRIA

The dishes offered by Eduard Mitsche at the opulent Rôtisserie Prinz Eugen in the Hilton International Wien are deceptively simple. Arranged in a gay, almost random fashion, the ingredients sparkle with freshness: colorful fish fillets with their iridescent skin are pearly moist; the vivid asparagus are cooked just à point; dressings are room temperature, when appropriate—as here. The success of this dish, less tricky than most of the demanding split-second creations that emerge from the vast kitchen, depends entirely on the quality of fish and asparagus—nothing less than perfect will do. Although the ingredient list looks ominously long, the cause is no more than easy-to-prepare dressings.

2 red mullets or red snappers (each
    ¾–1 pound; see Options), filleted
    with skin intact and bones and
    heads reserved
¼ cup dry white wine
½ bay leaf
½ teaspoon lightly crushed
    peppercorns
1 very small shallot, chopped
12 medium asparagus (about 1
    pound), peeled and trimmed

Balsamic Vinaigrette
4 teaspoons balsamic vinegar
3 tablespoons olive oil
½ teaspoon minced shallot
Salt and pepper

Creamy Herb Vinaigrette
1 egg yolk

1 tablespoon Dijon mustard
2 teaspoons white wine vinegar
4 teaspoons sherry vinegar
2½ tablespoons dry white wine
⅔ cup olive oil
1 teaspoon minced parsley
1 teaspoon minced chervil (or
    substitute parsley)
1 teaspoon minced chives
½ teaspoon minced fresh tarragon
    leaves
Salt and pepper

Assembly
Butter for the skillet
1 small head of soft lettuce, such
    as oakleaf
8 cherry tomatoes, halved
Chervil or parsley sprigs for garnish

1. Remove the gills and innards. Wash the fish bones and heads well; chop into fairly small pieces. Combine in a saucepan with 2 cups water, the wine, bay leaf, peppercorns, and shallot. Bring to a simmer and skim. Barely simmer for 20 minutes. Strain the fish stock and reserve (you should have about 2 cups).

2. Meanwhile, place the asparagus in skillet; cover with boiling water. Simmer until tender, but not soft—5–8 minutes; they should be on the firm side. Refresh in ice water. Drain, dry, and set in a close-fitting dish.

3. Prepare the balsamic vinaigrette: Combine the balsamic vinegar, olive oil, minced shallot, and salt and pepper to taste. Spoon half over the asparagus. Do not refrigerate.

4. Prepare the creamy vinaigrette: Combine the egg yolk, mustard, vinegars, and wine in a processor or blender; whiz to mix well. With the motor running, gradually pour in the olive oil. Add the minced herbs and blend. Add salt and pepper to taste.

5. Salt the fish fillets. Butter a skillet and spread the fillets in it, skin side up. Pour the fish stock over these. Poach just until the fish is no longer translucent in the center, about 4 minutes. Set on a plate to cool for a moment.

6. Meanwhile, toss the lettuce with the remaining balsamic vinaigrette; arrange on 4 large serving plates. Place a fillet on the lettuce. Halve the asparagus and arrange over and around this, with the tomatoes. Spoon 2 tablespoons of the creamy vinaigrette alongside each fillet, garnish with chervil or parsley, and serve.

Advance preparation: *You can prepare the fish stock, both sauces, and asparagus many hours in advance, leaving only the few minutes of fish poaching for the last moment.*

Options: *To prepare as a main course dish for lunch or brunch, substitute fish of about 1¾ pounds or so. The extra dressing can be refrigerated and used during the week.*

4 SERVINGS AS A FIRST COURSE; SEE *OPTIONS* AS A MAIN COURSE

Poached Salmon with Sherry Cream and Tomato Parfait

GERMANY

Breathtakingly productive, chef Pierre Pfister, of the Hilton International Mainz, is well known in Germany through his gala banquets, television and radio appearances, and books. Experience has given him a sense of just which dishes can be reproduced by the home cook. The following recipe, for example, is easily accomplished in stages, without the last-minute flourishes that distinguish his restaurant food.

Like most of Pfister's dishes, this one contains an element of surprise—in this case, the temperatures: The sherry-touched mayonnaise-like sauce that coats the plate is room-temperature; the slice of salmon is warm, just poached, while the tart and peppery tomato "parfait" (a slightly fluffy gelatine-bound mixture) is cold. Try this fashionable first course on connoisseurs of contemporary cuisine.

1 packet unflavored gelatine
2/3 cup tomato juice
2 large tomatoes (about 1 pound)
1/2 teaspoon celery salt
Generous amount of white pepper
1 egg yolk
1/3 cup plus 1 tablespoon dry white wine, preferably Riesling (see Note)
1 teaspoon sherry vinegar

1 teaspoon dry sherry
Salt
1/2 cup light olive oil
3 tablespoons walnut oil
1/3 cup heavy (or whipping) cream
About 1 tablespoon butter
18–20 ounces skinned salmon fillet, cut on the bias into 6 slices
Small celery leaves for garnish

1. Sprinkle the gelatine over the tomato juice in a tiny nonaluminum pot. Peel and halve the tomatoes; squeeze out and discard the seeds. Combine the pulp in a processor or blender with the celery salt and white pepper to taste. Whiz just to liquefy (there should be 1–1¼ cups). Heat the tomato juice mixture until almost simmering, swirling the pot to blend. Add to the puree and whirl only until smooth; do not continue to fluff mixture. Pour into six ⅓–½-cup timbale (dariole, baba) molds (see Option). Chill for 2 hours or longer.

2. Combine the egg yolk, 1 tablespoon white wine, sherry vinegar, sherry, and salt and pepper in a blender or processor; whirl to mix. Combine the olive and walnut oils and cream in a cup. With the machine running, pour in the liquid and whiz until light. Scoop into a bowl, cover, and refrigerate (or use within 1 hour).

3. Preheat the oven to 400°. Near serving time, remove the sauce from the refrigerator. Poach the fish: Butter a wide casserole (about 12 × 8-inches) and place the fish in this in a single layer, not touching. Pour over the remaining ⅓ cup wine. Set in the center of the hot oven until barely cooked through, 6–10 minutes depending upon the thickness.

4. Meanwhile, spoon the sherry cream onto 6 plates and tip to distribute evenly. Loosen the tomato parfait by running a knife around the molds, then dipping the base into warm water for 15 seconds. Unmold onto a spatula and slip one timbale on each plate.

5. With a spatula transfer the fish fillets to a towel to dry for a minute. Set on the sherry cream; decorate with the celery leaves.

Note: *It is important to use particularly light, high-quality dry wine for the poaching, as the balance of flavors depends upon the fresh taste of the fish and light seasoning of the sauce.*

Option: *Small timbale molds (⅓–½ cup) or any straight-sided small dishes or molds do a nice job. However, you may also pour the tomato mixture into a pan or dish to come to a depth of about 1 inch. This can be scooped into "quenelles" with teaspoons, rather than unmolded.*

6 SERVINGS AS A FIRST COURSE

Hilton International Mainz: Expect the Unexpected When You're Entertained by Pierre Pfister

A palate refresher, Pfister-style

D iners seated in the thickly carpeted, richly upholstered Rheingrill can gaze directly into the romantic river through vast windows accented by a brass railing. The ambience is of a sleek cruiser lounge or nautical club. This is Mainz, on the Rhine, and the presumed menu might be fresh trout from the river garnished with baby new potatoes, or a selection of local smoked meats and a profusion of hearty beers.

What arrives at the table, however, is a nouvelle cuisine key signature (introduced by Michel Guérard): A white china eggcup bears what at first glance might be a soft-cooked egg, but is, in fact, custard-soft "scrambled" eggs nestled in a shell, topped generously with caviar. Surprised, but pleased at the execution of the lush appetizer, you smile as the hovering waiter adds more heavy Christofle silver to the already impressive array. As he removes the wide-based eggcup, he uncovers a curious morsel that had been hiding on the underplate: a petite round of toast, spread with a tartare of beef fillet on which shines the tiniest of yolks—quail, an ovoid exclamation point!

Apparently enjoying extremes, the chef then sends in a "serious" plate: A severe arrangement of diamonds of blanched leek and carrot graces the center of a small, flat soup bowl. Over this the waiter trickles a classically pure consommé of cèpes, deep and woodsy. Creamy layered lasagne follows—but lasagne with a difference: Moist salmon strips are tucked between the filmiest of noodle strata—which are black, tinted with cuttlefish ink—and set in a pool of saffron cream. Although almost austere to behold, it is voluptuous to savor.

A frivolously ornate arrangement arrives (is it dessert?): Fine-drawn wings of chocolate piping, filled in with a mirror of chartreuse and rose confiture, adorn the plate. In the center is a swirled butterfly of pale orange passion-fruit and wine-dark cassis sorbet. Sweet as it is, it must surely be a palate cleanser, as this meal looks as though it will be banquet-length.

Tradition, miniaturized, ensues in the form of fanned slices of baby lamb fillet, two infant carrots with stems, a tiny potato pancake and peeled cherry tomato.

Solemnly, the waiter announces that two desserts are on their way, as he sets a shining white plate on the crocheted doily on the silver presentation plate beneath. In comes an ice cream cone: a real, street-vendor's wafer cone filled with light, smooth nougat ice cream. This is followed by an unmolded hazelnut soufflé surrounded by vanilla sauce and a toss of raspberries.

If one, two, or three thousand guests are invited, Pierre Pfister revels in the challenge and meets it with similar style. *"Je fais tout,"* exclaims the Alsatian-born chef, *"banquets, cuisine esthétique—hamburgers!"* The annual *Ball des Sports,* a giant Olympic fund-raiser, catches his imagination. Not content with the feat of a *dégustation* meal for 2,500, he may add dancing girls (or elephants), Siberian tigers, or gymnasts between courses of Symphony of Luxury Fish in Turtle Aspic with Two Sauces and Veal Medallions with Creamed Mushrooms and Melted Mozzarella, and has been known to finish off with handmade pulled-sugar roses for all. Or in another mode entirely, a city block-size bash at the Frankfurt airport featured tables covered in miles of fresh, tender salad greens over which guests sprinkled vinaigrette from watering cans.

But make no mistake. The wild take-offs are somersaults based on firm ground rules. Escoffier is Pfister's hero, he vows, and his cuisine is based on stringent traditional techniques. "To create as I do, to play, you must have a firm grasp of the reality of food, a serious base to lean on," he says proudly.

Stashed in the maze of rooms beneath the vast convention hall of the Hilton International Mainz where Pfister reigns over all events (and indeed, some of his dinners could be called happenings), a cache of props attest to the playful side: clown trappings; frying pans large enough to hold a pig or a hundred eggs; Beethoven busts in sugar; balloons, favors, and sprinkling cans for the salad dressing. Numerous plaques, medals, diplomas—tacked to every available scrap of wall—are testament to the mastery of his craft.

One of Pfister's favorite mad creations, an "homardburger," offers an irresistible and inimitable example of his culinary philosophy: While McDonald's launched a particularly visible advertising campaign in the picture-perfect town of Mainz, Pfister featured an haute cuisine facsimile of the notorious layered burger. Presented on a domed silver platter, the top was removed to reveal the infamous styrofoam container in which rested a sesame-sprinkled "bun" of the finest puff pastry cradling a "burger" of the tenderest lobster meat, scrupulously dressed and seasoned.

Fennel Salad with Apples and Walnuts

SWITZERLAND

Franz Kuhne, executive chef at the Hilton International Basel, describes this as a typical Swiss farmer's salad. The fine strips of crisp red and yellow apple and satiny fennel make a particularly toothsome accompaniment to smoked meats, game, and terrines.

2 medium fennel bulbs with 1½-inch
   tops (about 1½ pounds), chilled
2 medium apples, preferably one red
   and one yellow
About 3 tablespoons lemon juice
About 5 tablespoons dry white wine

Salt
White pepper
¼ cup walnut oil (see Note)
¾ cup walnuts (2 ounces), coarsely
   chopped

1. Cut tops from fennel and reserve for another use; save a few sprigs of leaves for garnish. Cut out the core from the base. Remove strings, if necessary, from outer layers (or discard the layers, if less than perky). Cut the bulbs into thin julienne about 2½ inches long (there should be about 5 cups).

2. Core the apples and cut into thin julienne the same length as the fennel. Combine both in a mixing bowl and toss with 3 tablespoons lemon juice.

3. Add 5 tablespoons wine and salt and pepper to taste, tossing. Add the walnut oil. Toss thoroughly. Taste and season with additional lemon juice, wine, salt, and pepper as desired.

4. Arrange the salad on 4 plates; sprinkle with the nuts; garnish with fennel sprigs.

Note: *Walnut oil, available in most specialty stores, is an extremely assertive and delicious flavor—for those who know and love it. Those unfamiliar with its charms may wish to blend it with an equal amount of light vegetable oil. Those who are familiar may wish to use even more. It spoils rapidly and should be stored in the refrigerator.*

Presentation: *For a more formal presentation, as is done in restaurants, blanch the largest outer layers of fennel bulbs to make individual cases for the salad, then garnish with decoratively cut apple slices.*

4 SERVINGS AS A SIDE DISH

PREVIOUS PAGE: Pierre Pfister selecting wines to match his menu

FARMER'S KALE SALAD

SWITZERLAND

The title tells the tale: a sturdy affair, strong and simple. The rough flavors and textures are independent and contrasting: salty, bitter, oniony, winy, smoky—and good. Served at the coffee shop of the Hilton International Basel, the Café de la Marine Suisse, this warm toss of wilted kale is not a salad in the traditional sense, but more a cooked dish that takes the place of a first-course salad.

1½ pounds small-stemmed kale
5 ounces thick-cut bacon, cut crosswise into ¼–½-inch strips
1 large onion, cut in half, then
   sliced thin
1 teaspoon minced garlic

2 tablespoons white wine vinegar
½ cup dry white wine
Salt and pepper
1 teaspoon caraway seeds, chopped
   (see Option)
1 tablespoon thin-sliced chives

1. Dunk the kale into a sink filled with cool water. Swish around, then lift out gently so that any debris sinks to the bottom. Repeat, as needed. Pull the stems from the leaves and discard them. Cut the leaves into strips.

2. Heat the bacon over low heat in a wide nonaluminum skillet until it begins to render some fat, then raise the heat to moderate and toss until lightly browned. With a slotted spoon, transfer the bacon to a plate. Lightly color the onion in the fat remaining in the skillet.

3. Add the garlic and kale; toss for a moment. Add the vinegar and wine. Toss briefly on high heat until most of the liquid has evaporated and the kale has softened sufficiently. Do not cook until tender, but until pleasantly chewy. Season with salt and pepper.

4. Transfer to a serving plate (or 4 individual dishes). Sprinkle with cumin or caraway, bacon, and chives.

Serving/Presentation: *This dish can be served at room temperature or warm. Accompany with a robust wine— the same that you've used for the preparation of the dish. Follow with veal shanks, or another plain, savory roasted meat.*

Option: *The word "cumin," which appeared in the original of this recipe, is used in parts of France, Germany, and Austria to describe what we call caraway. We tested the dish with both (substituting ½ teaspoon ground cumin for the teaspoon of caraway) and found each to be intriguing: the cumin tastes flowery, musky and blooms slowly, while the caraway has a more forthright perfume.*

4 SERVINGS AS A FIRST COURSE OR SIDE DISH

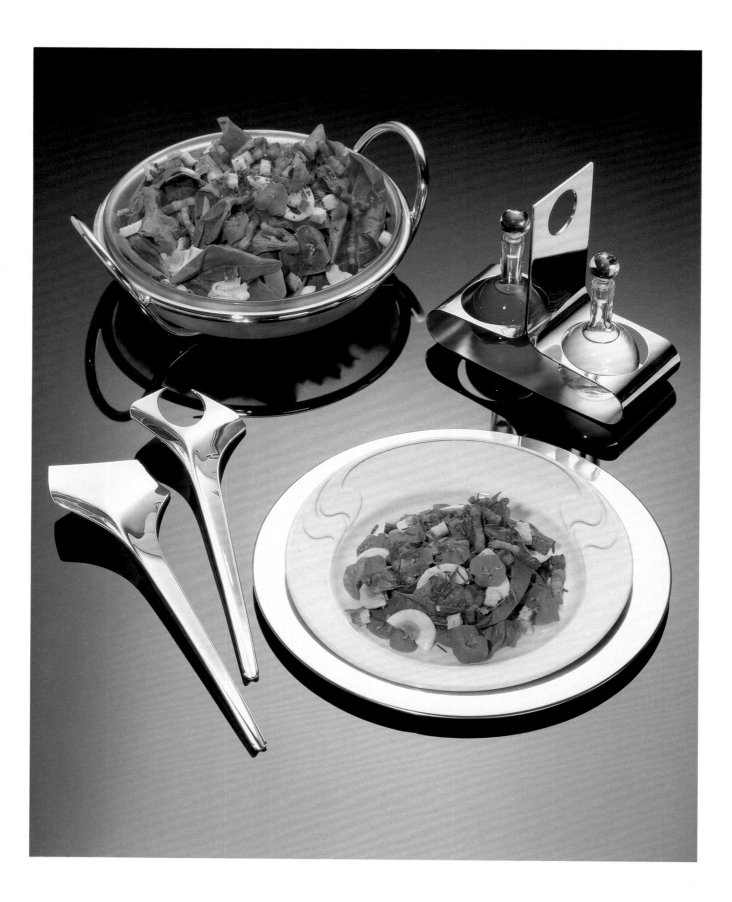

Spinach, Bacon, and Egg Salad

BELGIUM

Chunks of bacon, sturdy slices of egg, a heap of baby spinach leaves, and a creamy mustard-garlic dressing make this traditional country-style dish worth reviving. Although similar salads would be equally at home in much of Europe, this version comes from Michel Theurel at the Hilton International Brussels.

---

1 pound small-leafed, thin-stemmed spinach

3 slices sandwich bread, crusts trimmed, cut into ½-inch squares

4 hard-cooked eggs, peeled and halved

1 small garlic clove, crushed or minced

2 tablespoons Dijon mustard

1 tablespoon lemon juice

2 tablespoons sherry vinegar

¼ cup olive oil

¼ cup peanut oil

4 ounces thick-cut bacon, cut crosswise into ½-inch strips

---

1. Preheat the oven to 375°. Dunk the spinach into a sink filled with cool water. Swish around, then lift out carefully so debris falls to bottom. Repeat as needed. Strip the stems from the leaves and discard them. Spin-dry the leaves (or wrap in soft, absorbent towels); wrap and chill.

2. Toast the bread dice in a pan in the oven until golden, about 15 minutes.

3. Separate the egg whites and yolks; slice the whites and set aside. Mash the yolks in a salad bowl. Add the garlic, mustard, lemon juice, and 1 tablespoon vinegar; blend well. Gradually whisk in the olive oil, then the peanut oil.

4. Sauté the bacon over moderate heat in a medium skillet until browned lightly on all sides. Drain off the fat from the pan. Add the remaining 1 tablespoon vinegar; remove from the heat and stir to deglaze the pan.

5. Add the spinach to the bowl with the dressing; toss lightly, using your hands. Divide the mixture onto 4 serving plates. Top with the bacon, croutons, and sliced egg whites.

Serving: *The salad is sufficient as a main course for a light lunch, or serve it as a side dish to grilled meats, or a preamble to a hearty soup meal.*

4 SERVINGS AS A MAIN COURSE

Fillets of Sole with Sautéed Apples and Salad Greens

FRANCE

Warm strips of sole, yellowy-green tart apple slivers, and feathery leaves of salad are as elegant and beautiful as Oriental porcelain. This surprisingly suited bouquet of tastes and textures comes from executive chef Dominique Michou in Strasbourg, who excels in elegant, understated salads.

1½ pounds fillet of sole or other firm white fish fillets
Salt and pepper
4½ tablespoons light olive oil
1 tablespoon sherry vinegar
4 medium Granny Smith apples (about 1½ pounds)

3 tablespoons butter
¼ pound (about 1 medium head) imported curly chicory (*chicorée frisée*) or 2 medium Belgian endives, trimmed, rinsed, and dried
1 large bunch (1½ ounces) mâche (corn salad), rinsed and dried

1. Cut the sole fillets crosswise on the diagonal into slices 2½–3 inches wide with a very sharp knife (you should have about 24 pieces). Set on a sheet of waxed paper. Sprinkle with salt and pepper, then paint each slice with olive oil. Turn over the slices, salt and pepper them, then paint with oil (you'll use about 2 tablespoons of the oil). Place the slices on a baking sheet. Preheat the oven to 525°.

2. Combine the sherry vinegar and the remaining 2½ tablespoons olive oil with salt and pepper to taste.

3. Core and peel the apples; cut them lengthwise into very fine julienne. Heat the butter in a wide skillet and sauté the apple strips over high heat until just lightly softened and hot, but not cooked through, about 2 minutes. Arrange 3 small heaps around the edge of each of 4 serving plates.

4. Set the fish in the oven for about 3 minutes, to barely cook through. Meanwhile, toss the greens and dressing; set in the center of the plates. Arrange the fish between the apple heaps.

Serving: *This delicate dish works well for a light summer lunch or supper. Accompany with a chilled Riesling or Sauvignon Blanc. Begin the meal with a consommé madrilène or light pureed vegetable soup, such as asparagus. Although the salad cannot be prepared in advance, it is very easy to assemble and extremely effective.*

4 SERVINGS AS A MAIN COURSE

SALAD OF ENDIVE WITH POACHED EGG AND BACON
FRANCE

Lunch at the flowery, wicker-decorated Le Jardin in the Hilton International Strasbourg can be as simple as a hamburger; as sturdily Alsatian as Sauerkraut with Strasbourg sausages, salt pork, black pudding and pork hocks; a spontaneous and luxurious invention of the creative chef, Dominique Michou; or somewhere in between—such as the following. Fresher and lighter than traditional French bacon-garnished salads, this bistro-style brunch or lunch dish of herb-stippled endive and poached egg is given a contemporary twist with the nutty dressing, which complements the smoky bacon.

14 ounces thick-cut bacon, sliced
   across into ¾-inch strips
Salt and white pepper
2 tablespoons red wine vinegar
2 tablespoons hazelnut oil

1¼ pounds medium Belgian endives
1½ tablespoons minced parsley
1½ tablespoons thin-sliced chives
2 tablespoons distilled white vinegar
4 eggs (see Note)

1. Drop the bacon into boiling water; return to a boil. Drain and rinse. Mix together ⅛ teaspoon each salt and white pepper, 1 tablespoon red wine vinegar, and the oil.

2. Halve the endives and cut out the cores. Soak briefly in water to clean. Drain and spin dry or blot well with towels. Cut the spears across into ¼–½-inch slices. Toss with the dressing.

3. Gently cook the bacon in a wide skillet until slightly crisp, tossing often. With a slotted spoon, transfer to a plate. Discard all but ¼ cup fat. Add the remaining 1 tablespoon red wine vinegar; stir to deglaze the pan. Pour over the endive and toss. Add the bacon, parsley, 1 tablespoon chives, and salt and pepper. Divide onto 4 plates.

4. Poach the eggs in the following manner: In a 10-inch skillet or saucepan, bring 2 inches of salted water to a boil with the white vinegar. Break each egg into a cup. Slip one at a time into the water and gently scoop up the whites and turn to form neatly covered eggs.

5. When all the eggs have been added, poach below a simmer for 1½ minutes, or until the yolks are not quite set. Lift out with a slotted spoon and drain well.

6. Set an egg on each plate. Sprinkle with the remaining ½ tablespoon chives.

Note: *Poached eggs often have a way of misbehaving, so it makes sense to cook an extra one unless you're very practiced.*

4 SERVINGS AS A LIGHT MAIN COURSE

ALSATIAN BEER SOUP

FRANCE

While this version of beer soup hails from Alsace, others warm up wintry evenings in Germany and Switzerland. They can be bound with a pale roux *(such as the following) or a deeply browned one, or with eggs, cream, or bread. Some are spicy and sugary, some savory and sharp—and this recipe lies in between: bittersweet, with a fruity-yeasty tang, the soup is barely thickened—as if enriched by eggs, although there are none. The zesty, palest beige cream makes a wonderful conversation piece, for few guess the ingredients.*

Be careful about the beer that you choose, for the flavor is intensified—as will be the bitterness. A light, but complex taste will produce the most interesting result.

---

8 tablespoons (4 ounces) butter
⅓ cup all-purpose flour
Four 12-ounce bottles light beer, preferably French (Alsatian is best)
About ¾ teaspoon coarse kosher salt

About ¼ teaspoon white pepper
About 3 tablespoons confectioners' sugar
½ teaspoon ground cinnamon
1 cup heavy (or whipping) cream
6 slices French bread

---

1. Melt 4 tablespoons butter in a saucepan over moderate heat; stir in the flour. Whisk until golden. Gradually stir in the beer. Add ¾ teaspoon salt, ¼ teaspoon pepper, 3 tablespoons confectioners' sugar, and the cinnamon.

2. Bring to a boil, stirring. Simmer gently for 20 minutes, uncovered. Add the cream and stir until hot through. Remove from the heat. Add salt, pepper, confectioners' sugar, and cinnamon to taste.

3. Heat the remaining 4 tablespoons butter in a wide skillet. Fry the bread over moderate heat until browned on both sides.

4. Place a slice of bread in each serving dish; ladle in the soup.

6 SERVINGS AS A FIRST COURSE

Forest Mushroom Broth

UNITED KINGDOM

At the Gatwick Hilton International, Graham Cadman put together this deep-brown soup, thick with woodsy-wild mushrooms, then topped it with a froth of whipped cream for contrasts of color, flavor, and texture—à la Irish coffee. Easy and unusual.

5 cups full-flavored chicken stock
About ½ ounce dried morels (¾
   cup, or 20 smallish mushrooms)
6 ounces small wild or "exotic" fresh
   mushrooms, preferably a combination—such as *chanterelles* and
   oyster mushrooms
2 tablespoons butter
2 tablespoons minced shallots

About ¼ cup brandy
About ½ teaspoon fresh thyme
   leaves, plus sprigs for garnish
About 3 tablespoons fine-sliced
   chives
Salt and pepper
½ cup heavy (or whipping) cream,
   whipped to form firm peaks

1. Heat 1 cup of the stock; combine with the morels. Soak for 2–3 minutes, until tender enough to slice. Trim off the tough tip of the base, then quarter each mushroom lengthwise. Rinse lightly in the broth. Strain the soaking liquid through dampened, fine-meshed cheesecloth, pouring slowly to keep out any sand.

2. Trim the fresh mushrooms, removing any heavy or tough stems. Cut into thin slices. Melt the butter in a wide saucepan. Add the dried and fresh mushrooms. Soften slightly over moderately high heat, about 1½ minutes. Add the shallots; stir for 1 minute. Add ¼ cup brandy and ½ teaspoon thyme and stir for 1 minute.

3. Add the remaining 4 cups chicken stock (and the strained stock used to soften the morels). Simmer for 10 minutes. Add 2 tablespoons chives. Season with salt and pepper and additional brandy, thyme, and chives, to taste.

4. Ladle into 4 cups or small bowls, preferably glass, distributing the mushrooms equally. Spoon the cream into the bowls, sprinkle with the remaining chives and garnish with thyme sprigs. Serve at once.

Note: *At Gatwick the soup is ladled into flameproof glass goblets, topped with the cream, then glazed under intense heat.*
Advance preparation: *The soup mellows and develops more body if made a day or two before serving.*

4 SERVINGS AS A FIRST COURSE

Basel: A Melting Pot for
Eclectic Contemporary Cuisine

Trains that run from Geneva in the south to this city in northwest Switzerland, trains that slip punctually alongside groves of espaliered fruit trees, plowed earth the color of pumpernickel, diminutive terraced vineyards, and café au lait cows, have their signs printed in German, Italian, French, and English (for tourists). Although Basel is only ten minutes from France and two minutes from Germany, its inhabitants speak Swiss-German *(Schwyzerdeutsch),* while those in Geneva are as likely to speak French. In broadest terms there are three regions in the Swiss Confederation: the Deutsch-Schweiz, the French-speaking Suisse-Romande, and the Italian Ticino. Composed of 25 self-governing cantons, this tiny country has a wealth (or confusion, depending upon your point of view) of cooking styles to draw from.

Franz Kuhne, executive chef of the Hilton International Basel, was trained at the hotel school in his native town Lucerne, and has cooked his way around the country—and several others. While steeped in the multicultural cuisine of Switzerland, he acknowledges that his culinary thinking has been equally affected by a summer spent with chef Jacques le Divellec at La Rochelle, France, where he became enamored of the "creative cuisine" that has changed the thinking of so many cooks today. Both influences are clearly visible in the techniques and ingredients of the dishes served in the Wettstein Grill (named after the 17th-century mayor of Basel who, after the Thirty Years War, negotiated the treaty that recognized Switzerland as independent from the German Empire), such as the following graceful dinner assortment:

—A petite slice of rich, deep-flavored goose liver pâté with *cèpes* affirms that Alsace is just across the border

—A light vinegar-touched broth with a scattering of brown lentils and bright vegetable dice has roots in local peasant fare

—An innovative presentation of braided sole fillet in a chive-flecked sauce, accompanied with surprisingly hot-peppery strands of sweet leek and carrot and tender pasta, is a strictly personal expression, inspired by the training with le Divellec

—Fat, soft white asparagus from a nearby farm are blanketed with thin, moist slices of salmon (one of the favorite fish of Switzerland) and napped with orange-scented butter

—A quick-cooked crisp and fresh version of ratatouille reminds us of the Mediterranean's proximity, while the generous mint seasoning is Kuhne's own touch

—The yielding, spicy-winy terrine of prunes with fragile sabayon cream is based on a traditional Swiss dessert (which Kuhne has adapted and lightened)—astonishingly complex in flavor, considering its few ingredients and ease of preparation.

The progression is enhanced by wines and spirits of the country, from a refreshing Fendant to a full-bodied Dézaley, through a berryish, light Pinot Noir, to the unforgettable kirsch and raspberry *eau-de-vie* renowned throughout the world.

OVERLEAF: **Executive chef Franz Kuhne (left) with head cheesemaster Alex Stadelmann of the Basel Dairy Cooperative selecting a prime Emmentaler**

"RATATOUILLE" WITH MINT

SWITZERLAND

Swiss-born chef Franz Kuhne calls this vegetable mélange ratatouille, *although it is not prepared in the same manner as the traditional provençal dish. (Perhaps this is to remind diners who think Swiss food means cheese and chocolate of the country's connection to Mediterranean cuisines.) The final fillip of mint is Kuhne's own, and delightfully refreshing. Although the dicing takes some time, the quick-cooking method more than compensates.*

5–6 tablespoons full-flavored olive oil

¾ pound firm eggplant, cut into ½-inch dice

¾ pound small zucchini, cut into ½-inch dice

¾ pound red bell peppers, cut into ½-inch dice

1 pound (about 4 medium) tomatoes, peeled, seeded, and diced

1 large garlic clove, minced or crushed

2–4 tablespoons minced fresh mint leaves

Salt and pepper

---

1. Heat 3 tablespoons of the oil in a wide skillet over moderate heat. Add the eggplant; toss over high heat until tender, 5–6 minutes.

2. At the same time, heat 2 tablespoons oil in another wide pan; toss the zucchini and peppers over high heat until almost tender, about 4 minutes. Add the tomatoes and toss another minute to heat through. Add the garlic; toss another minute.

3. Add the eggplant to the zucchini-pepper mixture. Add the mint and salt and pepper to taste.

4 SERVINGS AS A SIDE DISH

POTATO DUMPLINGS, ALSATIAN-STYLE

FRANCE

While creative contemporary cuisine is the principal focus at the Hilton International Strasbourg, Alsace has a vast repertoire of rich and memorable dishes that have sustained the well-fed inhabitants for centuries. One standard, potato gnocchi or knepfles *(this Alsatian word varies in spelling, ingredients, and garnish from one part of the region to another) seems to please diners from the simplest and most sophisticated backgrounds. Soft, chive-dotted, irregular-shaped oval dumplings are strewn with crunchy, butter-drenched croutons.*

Serve as a hearty side dish with beef or venison stew—with or without the bread garnish. Or set the dumplings and croutons on tomato sauce and scatter sage leaves over all for a simple main course. Substitute crumbled, butter-fried pumpernickel crumbs for the white bread cubes, in a more German mode. Or omit the chives and serve as a light supper or brunch, accompanied by apples, pears, or plums poached in a light syrup.

1½ **pounds medium all-purpose potatoes, scrubbed**
3 **slices white sandwich bread, crusts removed, cut into ½-inch squares (about 1¼ cups)**
8 **tablespoons (4 ounces) butter**
½ **teaspoon salt**
¼ **teaspoon white pepper**

¼ **teaspoon nutmeg**
1 **whole egg**
1 **egg yolk**
3 **tablespoons fine-sliced chives**
1 **cup (4½ ounces) all-purpose flour**
¼ **cup grated imported** *Gruyère* **cheese**

---

1. Bake the potatoes in a 400° oven until very tender when pressed, 40–60 minutes. During the last 10 minutes of baking, place the bread cubes in a pan in the oven to toast to golden.

2. Holding the hot potatoes with a cloth, halve them and scoop out the pulp. Press through a sieve or the fine disk of a food mill. Stir in 3 tablespoons butter; add the salt, pepper, and nutmeg. Stir in the whole egg, then the yolk, then 2 tablespoons chives. Gradually stir in the flour; add the cheese.

3. Using two soup spoons, form oval dumplings (figure on about 20) from the mixture, placing them on strips of lightly oiled waxed paper.

4. Drop the dumplings into a wide pot of boiling, salted water. Keep at a bare simmer for about 12 minutes, or until done to taste. Meanwhile, melt the remaining 5 tablespoons butter in a medium skillet until golden-brown; add the croutons and toss until tawny.

5. With a slotted spoon, transfer the dumplings to a heated dish. Add the croutons; sprinkle with the reserved 1 tablespoon chives. Serve at once on warmed plates.

4–5 SERVINGS AS A SIDE DISH; 2–3 SERVINGS AS A LIGHT MAIN COURSE

POTATO PANCAKES WITH CHEESE AND CARAWAY

SWITZERLAND

Flat, brown cakes of shredded potato, soft within, are crisped outside, then topped with one of the incomparable cheeses of Switzerland, warmed to barely melting. Caraway seeds, freshly ground over the cheese, lend their pungent scent. (If you don't have an extra mill, simply remove the peppercorns from your grinder and replace with caraway.) At Le Cygne, *in the Hilton International Genève, Chef Dupont serves the rich concoction alone, as a cheese course, with* vieux vacherin de Fribourg *the cheese of choice; but imported* Gruyère *is an excellent alternative.*

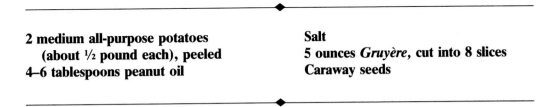

2 medium all-purpose potatoes (about ½ pound each), peeled	**Salt**
4–6 tablespoons peanut oil	**5 ounces *Gruyère*, cut into 8 slices**
	Caraway seeds

1. Preheat the oven to 375°. Grate the potatoes on the wide holes of a standing grater (you should have about 1½ cups).

2. Heat 2 tablespoons of the oil over moderate heat in a wide skillet, preferably nonstick. Measuring scant ¼ cupfuls of the potato (and stirring each time you measure), spread to form 2 or 3 thin cakes, as will fit easily. Flatten to form neat, rounded cakes. Sprinkle with salt.

3. Cook over moderately low heat until golden, about 2 minutes per side. Set on paper towels to drain. Continue making pancakes (you should have 8), adding oil generously, as often as needed, to keep the cakes from sticking.

4. Transfer the cakes to a baking sheet; top with the cheese slices. Set in the upper level of the hot oven. Bake until the cheese just melts, 3–4 minutes.

5. Grind a bit of caraway over each and serve hot.

Serving: *Paired with the pleasantly rustic Kale Salad (page 133), also a Swiss specialty, the pancakes make a hearty lunch. In a German version, tart apple compote is the accompaniment.*
Advance preparation: *Surprisingly, the pancakes reheat very well. They can remain in a single layer on a baking sheet for hours at room temperature, or longer, refrigerated. At serving time, top with cheese and bake.*

4 SERVINGS AS A SIDE DISH

RISOTTO WITH MINT

ITALY

Although the following dish from the Cavalieri Hilton International in Rome adheres to the techniques of traditional risotto-making, the brisk seasoning of fresh mint is in line with the gastronomia creativa *of contemporary Italian chefs. Because mint's intensity varies considerably depending upon the season and variety, you may need more or less. Buy more than you think you'll need, and add gradually, to taste.*

When the dish is served for a first course (which is most common), more broth should be added to the green-flecked grains to achieve a creamy-soupy consistency. As an unconventional side dish to accompany grilled or roasted pork or lamb, less is needed.

About 8 tablespoons (4 ounces) butter
½ cup finely minced onion
About 8 cups chicken stock (see Note)
2 cups (1 pound) arborio rice (see Note)

About 4 cups mint leaves stripped from their stems, measured without packing, rinsed
Salt and pepper
Mint sprigs for garnish

---

1. Heat 4 tablespoons butter in a heavy, wide (10-inch) saucepan or sauté pan. Stir in the onion and soften over low heat for a minute or two. Meanwhile, heat the stock to simmering in another pan.

2. Add the rice to the onions and stir for 2 minutes. Ladle in about ¾ cup hot stock. Adjust the heat so that the rice simmers, but does not boil and stick; stir often until the liquid is almost absorbed. Continue adding hot stock in ¾ cup increments and stirring as needed until it is almost absorbed. Meanwhile, mince enough mint leaves to equal about 1 cup, lightly packed (do not use a food processor).

3. After about 25 minutes the rice should be properly firm-tender in texture; that is, it should be softish on the outside, but remain firm (but not hard) in the center of the kernel. Remove from the heat; stir in three-quarters of the mint, then additional hot stock, as needed (the mixture will thicken as soon as you remove it from the heat, so add a little more than you gauge necessary).

4. Season with salt and pepper, then add more mint, to taste. Stir in the remaining 4 tablespoons butter, or more or less to taste. Spoon into heated bowls. Serve at once, garnished with mint sprigs.

Note: *Because a considerable quantity of stock is cooked down to produce the risotto, it should not be salted, or the finished dish will be much too salty.*

Arborio rice, a short-grain Italian rice, is required in order to achieve the special sticky-creamy texture of this dish. It is available in many markets and all Italian specialty shops.

6 SERVINGS

SPINACH NOODLES WITH MANDARIN CREAM SAUCE

ITALY

At La Pergola in the Cavalieri Hilton International in Rome, lemon, lime, and various mandarin seasonings are particularly fashionable, as they are in trendy dining rooms throughout France, Switzerland, Austria, and Germany. The unusual Clementine perfume and color add a mysterious undertone to the incredibly rich, cream-glossed soft green noodles. Although cheese may seem incongruous, it seems to add saltiness and texture, rather than a defined flavor of its own.

3 small Clementines, *or* 2 larger
   mandarins (tangerines)
3 tablespoons butter
¼ cup dry white wine
1⅔ cups heavy (or whipping) cream
Big pinch of ground red pepper

¾ pound fresh (not dried), thin-cut
   spinach egg pasta (homemade or
   store-bought)
¾ cup grated Parmesan cheese (1½
   ounces)
Salt, if desired
4 basil or mint sprigs

1. Grate fine enough Clementine zest to equal 1 teaspoon. With a very sharp knife cut off and discard the rind and pith from 2 fruits; cut neatly between the membranes to free each section. Squeeze and reserve the juice from another ½ fruit—to equal about 2 tablespoons.

2. Heat the butter in a wide, rather deep skillet—about 10 inches in diameter. Add the grated zest and stir over low heat for 30 seconds. Add the wine and stir over moderately high heat until just a small quantity of liquid remains. Add the cream and a pinch of ground red pepper. Bring to a boil; cook gently for another minute or so to thicken very slightly. Remove from the heat.

3. Drop the noodles into boiling salted water; cook until not quite tender, only a minute or so (they will continue to cook in the sauce). Drain, rinse lightly. Immediately add to the pan of sauce.

4. Simmer, stirring gently, until the noodles and sauce have reached the desired consistency—only a minute or so (leave extra liquid, as the noodles continue to absorb cream when removed from the heat).

5. Take the pan from the stove. Gradually add the reserved Clementine juice to taste; add the Parmesan, tossing gently. Season to taste with ground red pepper and salt. Spoon onto 4 heated plates; garnish with the fruit sections and basil sprigs and serve immediately.

Serving: *A crisp Alsatian Riesling or Italian Grave del Friuli might accompany the pasta. Plan on a light follow-up to the ultra-creamy opener: a salad of seafood with radicchio and arugula, for example.*

4 SERVINGS AS AN APPETIZER

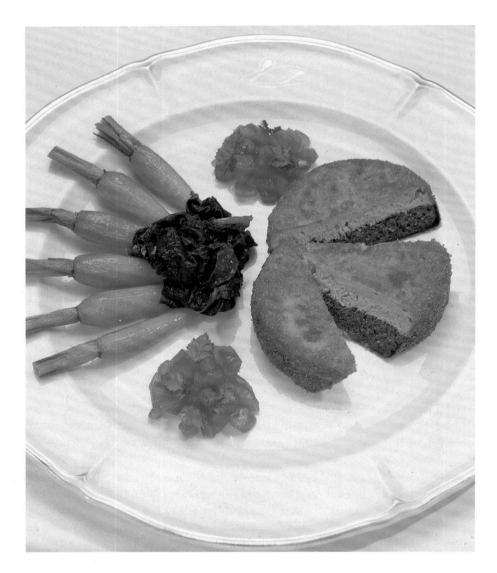

SPINACH AND CARROT TOFU CAKES IN TOMATO SAUCE
"Le Vegetarien"
SWITZERLAND

When executive chef Jean-Claude Bergeret introduced this "gourmet tofu" at the casual Grignotière restaurant in Geneva, he was responding to a general health and fitness awareness among the hotel guests, but he was skeptical about the dish's survival. In fact the crumb-coated, creamy-textured patties—tinted by the spinach and carrot purees that flavor them—became an immediate best-seller and have remained one. The simple tomato coulis *that moistens them has a fruity bite from the raspberry vinegar, which blends surprisingly well with the touch of soy sauce.*

2 pounds firm tofu (may be called Chinese tofu)
¾ pound carrots, peeled
½ teaspoon nutmeg
1 teaspoon salt
2 heaping tablespoons all-purpose flour
One 10-ounce package frozen spinach, defrosted and drained (or 2 pounds fresh spinach, trimmed, blanched and well-drained)

2 pounds canned plum tomatoes (see Note)
About 2 tablespoons soy sauce
2–4 tablespoons raspberry vinegar
About 2 teaspoons sugar
Coating
¾ cup all-purpose flour
3 eggs, beaten to blend
2 cups fine dry bread crumbs
About 6 tablespoons mild olive oil

1. Place the tofu in a wide shallow dish. Set a pan or lid on the tofu and top with a 5–6-pound weight. Let stand for 1–1½ hours. Drain.

2. Meanwhile, simmer the carrots in water to cover until tender, 12–15 minutes. Drain; cut into 1-inch chunks. Puree to a rather smooth texture in a blender or processor. Add *half each* of the tofu, nutmeg, salt, and flour. Whirl to a very fine texture.

3. Press the liquid from the spinach. Puree as fine as possible. Add the remaining tofu, nutmeg, salt, and flour. Puree smooth.

4. Cover a baking sheet with plastic wrap. Oil a round 3½-inch cookie cutter (or use a tunafish can with top and bottom removed) and set on the sheet. Fill to a depth of ½–¾-inch with one-sixth of the carrot mixture; smooth with a spoon. Lift off the ring. Repeat, cleaning the ring as necessary, to make 6 cakes of each mixture.

5. Set in the freezer to harden slightly, about ½ hour. Meanwhile, prepare the sauce. Press the tomatoes through the fine disk of a food mill or puree roughly in a processor or blender and press through a sieve. Add 2 tablespoons soy sauce, 2 tablespoons vinegar, and 2 teaspoons sugar. Boil to reduce to about 2 cups, or until thickened to taste. Adjust the seasonings.

6. Preheat the oven to 400°. Coat the cakes: Coat each cake thoroughly with the flour, then the eggs; roll in the crumbs to cover entirely. Set each cake on a baking sheet as it is completed.

7. Heat 2 tablespoons olive oil in a wide skillet over moderately low heat. Lightly brown 4 cakes at a time, about 1 minute per side. Replace on the baking sheet. Add oil as needed to brown 2 more batches.

8. Bake the cakes in the center of the hot oven for 10 minutes, until sizzling hot. Serve 1 of each cake to each diner, accompanied with the sauce.

Note: *Because this dish is served year-round, and because the quality of tomatoes varies considerably, canned have been used rather than fresh. If sweet, flavorful tomatoes are available, substitute them by all means, and cook down to the desired consistency.*

Advance preparation: *The tofu cakes can be browned, cooled, and refrigerated, then heated in a 400° oven for 15 minutes before serving. Or the uncoated cakes can be wrapped and frozen for months. To finish, defrost slightly, then proceed with Steps 6–8.*

6 SERVINGS AS A MAIN COURSE

VEGETABLE STRUDEL WITH HERBAL CREAM
AUSTRIA

In the sunny Café Am Park that spills out onto a terrace above the rambling city park in Vienna, you can choose from a constantly changing procession of hot desserts and sweet and savory pastries that flow from the hands of Heinrich Wittman, whose remarkable deftness is on display as he works in view of the customers. The burly, bearded gentleman who presides over the pastry kitchen is well known as a teacher throughout Europe and was named World Strudel-Making Champion. The delicacy of his strudels is due partly to the unusual technique he has evolved for forming the sheets of dough— flinging and spinning pizza-style, rather than in the traditional manner—and partly to the restrained seasoning, which gives fruits and vegetables pride of place. Although it is impossible to teach the strudel-dough technique without Chef Wittman's guidance, the home cook can produce a fine version of his unusual vegetable strudel using packaged strudel or phyllo sheets.

¼ pound spinach, stems removed and well washed
¼ pound string beans, trimmed
3 medium carrots, trimmed and peeled
1 medium kohlrabi, leaves removed, peeled, and cut into ½-inch dice
1 medium-small yellow squash, cut into ½-inch squares
¼ cup heavy (or whipping) cream
2 egg yolks
Salt and pepper
1 small package strudel or phyllo leaves (see Note)
3 tablespoons melted butter

1 whole egg blended with 1 tablespoon water for egg wash
Sauce
1 tablespoon butter
2 tablespoons minced shallots
½ cup dry white wine
½ cup veal or chicken stock
1 cup heavy (or whipping) cream
1 tablespoon minced chives
2 tablespoons minced parsley
8 large sorrel leaves, stems removed, leaves slivered fine (about ⅓ cup)
¼ cup minced watercress leaves
Salt, pepper, and lemon juice

1. Preheat the oven to 350°. Drop the spinach leaves into a large pot of boiling salted water; return to a boil. Scoop out the leaves with a strainer; drop into ice water. Drain, then spread flat on toweling.

2. Drop the beans into the boiling water; boil until tender, about 4 minutes; with a slotted spoon transfer to ice water. Quarter one carrot lengthwise, cut the others into ½-inch dice. Drop into the water; boil 1 minute. Add the kohlrabi; boil another minute. Add the squash; boil 30 seconds longer. Pour into a colander to drain, then spread on a towel. Drain and dry the beans; cut in ½-inch lengths.

3. Puree the cooked, quartered carrot in a processor or blender, scraping down the sides. Add the cream and egg yolks; puree fine. Combine with the diced vegetables and toss to coat. Season with salt and pepper.

4. Spread one leaf of strudel on a dish towel, a long side toward you. Brush with melted butter to coat completely. Continue layering and buttering until you have used 7 sheets.

5. Lay the spinach leaves in the center of the phyllo to form a rectangle about 12 × 6 inches, a long side toward you. Spread the vegetable mixture over this. Fold in the short edges of phyllo where they meet the filling, then the long sides. Butter these folded margins. Begin rolling from the long side close to you, using the towel to shape a neat cylinder.

6. Place seam side down on a buttered baking sheet. Brush with the egg wash. Bake in the center of the hot oven for 25–30 minutes, until nicely browned.

7. Meanwhile, make the sauce: Melt the butter in a medium saucepan. Add the shallots; cook over moderately low heat until soft. Add the wine; reduce to almost a syrup. Add the stock and cream; boil to reduce to 1 cup. Add the chives, parsley, sorrel, and watercress. Whiz until frothy in a blender or processor (see Option). Reheat. Season to taste with additional salt, pepper, and lemon juice.

8. Cut the strudel into 12 slices. Distribute the sauce onto 6 warmed plates, then place 2 slices on this. (For an appetizer, cut 16 pieces—one per person—and serve a table-spoon of sauce with each slice.)

Note: *Strudel and phyllo doughs vary in size, but are usually about 12 × 17 inches. Some are more brittle than others, so it is prudent to have on hand more than the 7 sheets required in case of breakage. If the dough looks fragile, cover with a sheet of waxed paper, then a damp towel.*

Because packaged doughs are more brittle than Mr. Wittman's, we have cubed the vegetables instead of cutting them in narrow sticks, which makes the slicing of the strudel somewhat easier. If you use homemade dough, you may prefer to cut ¼-inch bâtonnets, as the chef does; you may also find the egg wash unnecessary, as homemade pastry will color more deeply and evenly.

Option: *If you have one of the handy electric rods with a tiny high-speed blade at the tip that is variously called a hand- or immersion- or stick-blender, place it directly in the sauce pot and whiz to create a lovely froth, as the chef does.*

Advance preparation: *The strudel can be made up to a day ahead and refrigerated. Brush with the egg wash just before baking. Although the sauce can be prepared ahead, it loses its fluffy texture and becomes somewhat heavier and more prominently sorrel-flavored.*

6 SERVINGS AS A MAIN COURSE, 16 AS AN APPETIZER

Vienna's Rôtisserie Prinz Eugen: A Trend-Setting Restaurant in a City That Resists Change

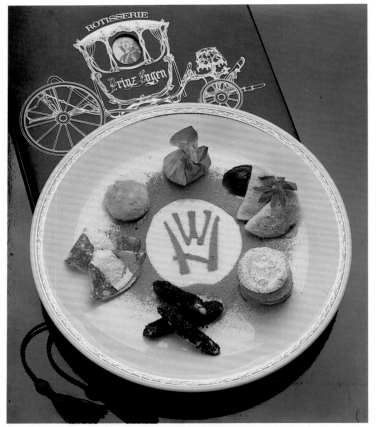

A contemporary presentation of traditional Austrian desserts in miniature, at the Rôtisserie Prinz Eugen

I n a grand-scale trio of authentically and opulently decorated Baroque rooms (named after Prinz Eugen, the military strategist who delivered Austria from Turkish domination), the meals served are as apparently simple as Vienna is ornate. In a city where customs and tastes change slowly and food standards are unusually high, the local elite has singled out (as have *Michelin, Gault et Millau,* and a score of other guides) this deluxe, spacious restaurant as one of the most favored in the city—and the country.

In fact, it was the opening of the Rôtisserie Prinz Eugen in Hilton International's largest European hotel and the influence of its first chef, Werner Matt, that transformed the cuisine of Vienna, beginning a trend now called *Neue Wiener Kuche,* or Nouvelle Cuisine Viennoise. As in most contemporary French cooking, the ingredients of the day's market dictate the dishes that appear on the menu. Lighter than the usual Viennese fare, the larder is adventurous (containing such newcomers as tropical fruits, wild rice, and a wide range of seafood, previously little used in the region), but still stocked with traditional Austrian delicacies, such as plump white asparagus, wild mushrooms, and an abundance of game and organ meats. Gradually, Viennese residents came to trust (and look forward to) the unusual intrusions in their classical *plats;* guests began to expect the imaginative smaller courses and less formal presentations. The dining room became the testing ground for subtle creations that are now a matter of fact.

Eduard Mitsche, sous-chef in the kitchen of 70 that provides for the hotel's five eating places, moved to the position of executive chef and added his own graceful touch. Lean and energetic, sunny and communicative, Mitsche pulls out books to illustrate his points as he speaks. Interested, absorbed, his long fingers understand the qualities of the fruits and vegetables he is showing and describing, automatically sensing the potential of the raw material. An Austrian ("a kitchen in Vienna will not tolerate anything else," he laughs), he has a love for the traditional foods of the country which he interprets in sturdier and more conventional ways for the four other hotel restaurants. Widely traveled, he was the first non-British employee on the *Queen Elizabeth 2,* its VIP chef, then went on to the London Hilton on Park Lane, before returning to Cunard to sail around the world on the same vessel. His experience has led him to prefer a kitchen staff in which cooks of different nationalities meld and clash—a challenge to coordinate and a source of stimulation and information. It seems to be working beautifully as a philosophy in this hotel. And as testament to the kitchen's successful approach, it is interesting to note that at this writing, almost every other fine dining room in Vienna is headed by a chef who worked in the kitchen of the Hilton International Wien somewhere along the line.

While the performance of the dining room staff is as polished and old-world as the array of glittering glasses and formal flower arrangements, when the silver domes are removed from diners' plates (with the simultaneous precision of the violin section of the Vienna State Orchestra), the arrangements within are deceptively simple. An *amuse-gueule,* cute and simple, begins the meal: A miniature money-bag unadorned, perched next to a slim cylinder of tissue-thin strudel dough, tied with a chive, scroll-like. The baglet stuffed with wild rice, the cigarette with salmon, each cuts with the slight pressure of a fork to make two delicate bites. Long slices of soft breast of guinea-hen touched with a hazelnut vinaigrette follow, strewn casually over warm, crisp *haricots verts,* barely but quintessentially dressed. A pure, fresh broth with ribbons of zucchini, carrot, and onion hold a scallop, a shelled lobster claw, a rectangle of turbot and another of red mullet with its silvery crimson-etched skin—each poached to individual perfection, *à point.* A shallow bowl coated with a bare slick of marbled purees of unsweetened kiwi, mango, strawberry, and black currant with a spiral of thin sour cream ("a dialogue of fruit purees") is briskly tart and perfumed, truly a palate refresher. A medallion of pink, pale veal barded with a thin Savoy cabbage leaf is inset with sweetbread and a fine herbed veal *farce,* then daubed with its own juice. A tiny fried potato cornucopia spills baby potato balls, snow peas, slivers of turnip, and carrot *bâtonnets.* For dessert, slices of rosy papaya surround a light honey and ginger ice cream.

Each statement in the meal is clear and subtle. As gifted gardeners instinctively pluck a fruit from a tree just at its peak, so some cooks have a feeling for cooking and seasoning food until it reaches the stage that most naturally underscores the finest qualities of the fish or fowl, fruit or vegetable in question. Such are the dishes that come from the kitchen of the Prinz Eugen.

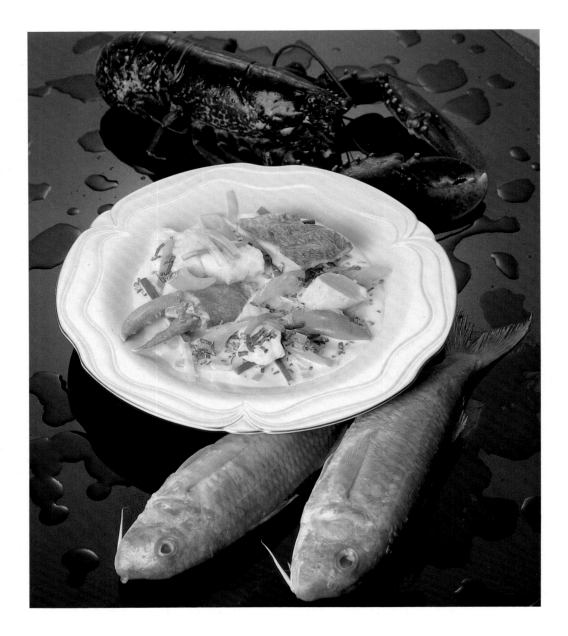

LOBSTER, RED SNAPPER, SCALLOPS, AND FLOUNDER WITH VEGETABLE STRANDS IN LIGHT STOCK

AUSTRIA

The essence of understated luxury: arranged with Japanese simplicity, the finest seafood is presented with no frills, but much care, each ingredient given equal billing in the pale stock. You must be an admirer of this type of pure, light food to make the expense and effort worthwhile. Perfect ingredients and split-second timing are crucial, or you wind up with casual—albeit pleasant—fish soup.

To accompany this quintessential dish, its creator, chef Eduard Mitsche of the Hilton International Wien, suggests a soft leafy salad for the first course and a side dish of wild rice or steamed potatoes for the seafood.

---

1 red mullet, red snapper, or pompano (about 2½ pounds), filleted with skin intact and bones reserved for the stock
½ cup dry white wine or dry vermouth
½ teaspoon bruised peppercorns
½ bay leaf
1 small shallot, chopped
Salt
1 lobster (about 3 pounds)
1 tablespoon butter
2 rather large carrots, peeled and cut into fine julienne about 3 inches long (about 2 cups)
4 tender inner celery ribs, cut in fine julienne about 3 inches long (about 1¼ cups)
1 small leek, dark green tops removed, well washed, and cut into very thin rounds
White pepper
4 large or 8 medium sea scallops
6–8 ounces flounder or sole fillets, cut into 4 pieces
Basil sprigs for garnish

---

1. Halve each fish fillet. Remove the gills and innards; rinse the bones well and cut them small. Combine in a saucepan with 5 cups water, the wine, peppercorns, bay leaf, and shallot. Bring to a boil, skimming. Gently simmer for 20 minutes. Strain the fish stock through dampened cheesecloth; you should have about 3 cups. Season with salt, as desired.

2. Drop the lobster into boiling salted water. Simmer gently for 10 minutes. Remove and cool slightly. Halve the body lengthwise and remove the carapace. Jiggle open the small pincers, then crack and gently remove the shells from the claws. Remove the tail meat. Halve the meat from each in neat diagonals. Remove the meat from the large front legs. Combine all the meat in a saucepan with ½ cup of the fish stock.

3. Heat the butter in a wide skillet; add the carrots, celery, and leek and toss until coated. Add ½ cup fish stock and toss on moderately low heat until just cooked through, 7–8 minutes. Add salt and pepper, as desired.

4. Meanwhile, butter a deep skillet. Spread the snapper fillets in this, skin sides up. Heat the remaining 2 cups fish stock; add it and the scallops and bring to a simmer; add the flounder and cook until barely translucent inside. At the same time, warm the lobster.

5. Divide the seafood evenly into warmed, wide soup plates. Strain the stock into the vegetable mixture and bring to a boil. Divide evenly into the soup plates. Serve immediately, garnished with basil.

4 SERVINGS

FISH TERRINE WITH BASIL

BELGIUM

Remarkably clean and uncomplicated, this terrine is also freshly pretty: a mosaic of red snapper fillets speckled with basil is enclosed between layers of smooth fish puree, the whole wrapped in spinach leaves. The festive, summery slices are sparked by a bright plum-tomato garnish.

The terrine, like most at the Hilton International Brussels, is the creation of Christian Albrecht, the transplanted German sous-chef who, with the French executive chef Michel Theurel, has worked there since the hotel's opening. The unusually long-lived team has been variously described as "the visionary Frenchman and the pragmatic German," "the artist and the technician," "the flexible doer and the perfectionist brainchild" by their colleagues. Both are dedicated teachers and recognized as Master Chefs of Belgium.

¾ **pound skinned red snapper fillets**
2 tablespoons lemon juice
1 medium-large bunch basil (4
   ounces), trimmed and chopped
   (about 1 cup)
¾ **pound smooth spinach leaves,**
   cleaned, stems removed
1 pound skinned sea bass fillets, well
   chilled and cut into 1-inch pieces
1 egg
1¼ **teaspoons salt**
½ **teaspoon white pepper**

1⅔ **cups heavy (or whipping) cream**
Tomato garnish
8 medium plum tomatoes, peeled,
   seeded, and diced (about 1¾ cups)
Salt and pepper
1 tablespoon lemon juice
2 tablespoons olive oil
2 tablespoons peanut oil
About ¼ teaspoon each dried basil,
   thyme, tarragon, and fennel seeds
Basil sprigs for garnish

1. Cut the snapper fillets into strips of more or less equal thickness about 1½ inches wide and 4–5 inches long. Arrange in a nonaluminum dish; sprinkle with the lemon juice and chopped basil; toss to coat. Cover and let stand at room temperature while you prepare the rest of the dish.

2. Drop the spinach into boiling salted water; return to a boil, then drain and drop into ice water. Drain, then spread flat between towels to dry.

3. Preheat the oven to 350°. Line a 9 × 5-inch loaf pan with plastic wrap to overhang somewhat. Line completely with the spinach, placing the leaves so that they hang over the edge a few inches.

4. Chop the sea bass to a fairly fine texture in a food processor. Add the egg, salt, and white pepper; whirl to barely mix. Add the cream and puree fine.

5. Spread one-third of the fish puree in the mold, smoothing some up the side to lightly coat the spinach. Place half the fillets on this, arranging in a single layer. Spread half the remaining puree on this; top with the rest of the fillets. Cover neatly with the remaining puree, smoothing with the back of a spoon. Overlap the spinach to cover the dish, adding a few more leaves if necessary. Fold over the plastic to seal tightly.

6. Set in a pan and pour in boiling water to reach halfway up the mold. Set in the center of the oven and bake for 1 hour. Remove from the water and cool on a rack. Chill well (do not remove the plastic)—at least 6 hours or for up to 1½ days.

7. Combine the tomatoes, salt and pepper to taste, the lemon juice, olive and peanut oils; crumble the herbs and add; chop the fennel seeds and add. Let stand for at least 1 hour at room temperature; adjust the seasoning to taste.

8. Unmold the terrine, remove the plastic, then slice with a serrated knife. Place the slices (2 for a main course, 1 as an appetizer) on each of the serving plates. Spoon the sauce alongside. Garnish with basil sprigs.

Note: *The plastic wrap holds the terrine neatly, keeps juices inside, and gives a shiny finish to the spinach.* Serving: *Simple and attractive, this works beautifully for a buffet, with the slices arranged on a platter and the sauce alongside to spoon over. A cucumber salad makes a nice accompaniment.*

8 SERVINGS AS A MAIN COURSE, 16 AS AN APPETIZER

Fish Fillets in Red Wine Butter Sauce

GERMANY

Executive chef Gerhard Heusing of the Hilton International Düsseldorf (the first German hotel-restaurant to receive a Michelin *star) has an ability to balance flavors unerringly, to contrast textures, temperatures, and flavors in a way that might be considered the culinary equivalent of perfect pitch: a terrine of smooth, cool, goose liver is dabbed with crème fraîche and escorted by apple julienne; a rosette of raw petals of turbot inlaid with salmon and transparently dressed with vinaigrette is caviar-touched; sliced fillet, kidney, and liver of rabbit are accompanied by a velvety black olive puree and fresh herbed noodles; frozen Grand Marnier parfait is set on poufs of unsweetened cream around a pool of bittersweet kumquat sauce.*

Unfortunately, although the presentation of each dish is unaffected, preparation is most often extremely labor-intensive and ingredients are very difficult to obtain, making home-cooking nearly impossible. Thus, we have but one easily realized example of Heusing's provocative work. The sauce is fruity, slightly sweet, thin-bodied, with great depth—and is a most unlikely blueberry-violet-gray. The fish fillets that nearly float in it are coated with a moist layer of taupe-brown mushrooms and crumbs. And somehow, the flavors and colors magnify the beauty of the fish; they do not mask or overwhelm it.

Two 1½–2-pound sea bass (or other firm, small white-fleshed fish), filleted, with skin removed, skeletons and heads reserved
1 medium carrot, chunked
1 small onion, chunked
1 medium celery rib, chunked
¼ teaspoon peppercorns
¾ cup dry red wine
⅓ cup white port

6 tablespoons (3 ounces) butter
¼ pound mushrooms, minced very fine
1 cup soft fresh white bread crumbs
1 tablespoon minced chervil (or parsley with a touch of tarragon)
Salt and pepper
2 tablespoons heavy (or whipping) cream

---

1. Remove and discard the innards and gills; rinse the bones and heads. Combine in a saucepan with the carrot, onion, celery, peppercorns, and about 3 cups water to just barely cover. Simmer gently for 20 minutes, skimming occasionally. Strain out the solids. Skim the fish stock and simmer to reduce to 1¼ cups.

2. Preheat the oven to 400°. Combine 1 cup of the fish stock with the red wine and port in a nonaluminum saucepan. Boil to reduce the sauce to a scant cup.

3. Melt 2 tablespoons butter. Toss with the mushrooms, crumbs, and chervil. Season the fillets and place in a buttered flameproof platter or jelly-roll pan. Distribute the crumb mixture over the fillets, patting firmly to form a neat covering. Spoon the remaining ¼ cup fish stock around the fillets.

4. Set in the upper level of the hot oven. Bake for about 8 minutes, until just cooked through. Meanwhile, heat the sauce. Take it off the heat and whisk in the remaining 4 tablespoons butter, one at a time (see Note). Whisk in the cream. Set over lowest heat.

5. When the fish has cooked through, pour about ¼ cup of sauce into each of 4 warmed serving plates. Set the fillets on this.

Note: *If you have one of the handy electric rods with a tiny high-speed blade at the tip that is variously called a hand- or immersion- or stick-blender, place it directly in the sauce pot and whiz to create a lovely froth, as the chef does.*

Serving: *Plates must be heated for this tender, sauced fish. This is spoon food, (not forks)—unless you have a wonderfully effective "saucespoon," a flat, oval utensil that marries fish knife and spoon in its design.*

Advance preparation: *The sauce can be prepared through Step 2 up to two days ahead and the bread-mushroom topping completed a few hours in advance.*

4 SERVINGS

Brochettes of Monkfish and Salmon with Lime

SWITZERLAND

(continued)

This pastel-pretty, citrusy brochette is a best-seller at the lively Grignotière restaurant of the Hilton International Genève. Monkfish (also called lotte, bellyfish, goosefish, angler) *is particularly favored for its firm flesh in much of Europe, but executive chef Jean-Claude Bergeret suggests halibut as an American alternative; fettuccine or rice soaks up the thin wine cream sauce.*

2 small limes
½ pound boneless, skinned salmon fillet
¾ pound boneless monkfish steak or thick fillet, membranes trimmed
1¾ cups dry white wine

3 tablespoons chopped shallots
4 teaspoons tarragon vinegar
¼ cup heavy (or whipping) cream
8 tablespoons (4 ounces) butter
Salt and white pepper

1. Thinly pare the zest from 1 lime using a vegetable peeler; cut into fine julienne. Remove and discard the white pith. Bring the julienned zest to a boil with water to cover. Drain and cool.

2. Cut all the rind and pith from the other lime; cut the lime in half lengthwise, then across into very thin half-rounds. Cut both types of fish into 1¼-inch squares. Alternate salmon and monkfish on 4 thin wooden skewers about 8 inches long, placing a lime slice between each and beginning and ending with monkfish.

3. Combine the white wine, shallots, and vinegar in a wide nonaluminum saucepan or skillet. Boil to reduce to ½ cup. Strain into a small nonaluminum pot. Add the cream; boil to reduce to ½ cup. Stir in 5 tablespoons butter; remove from the heat. Add salt and pepper to taste, and half of the lime julienne.

4. Melt the remaining 3 tablespoons butter in a wide skillet. Salt and pepper the brochettes. Place them in the pan and cook for about 1½ minutes on each of the two wide sides, or until barely cooked through. Serve with the sauce; sprinkle with the remaining lime julienne.

Note: *Although the colors are pale, the lime flavor is sharp and dominant—so cut down on the quantity of slices on the skewers if you're not a citrus devotee.*

4 SERVINGS

The Hilton International Genève team of Gilles Dupont (left) and Jean-Claude Bergeret on Lake Geneva, hotel bound

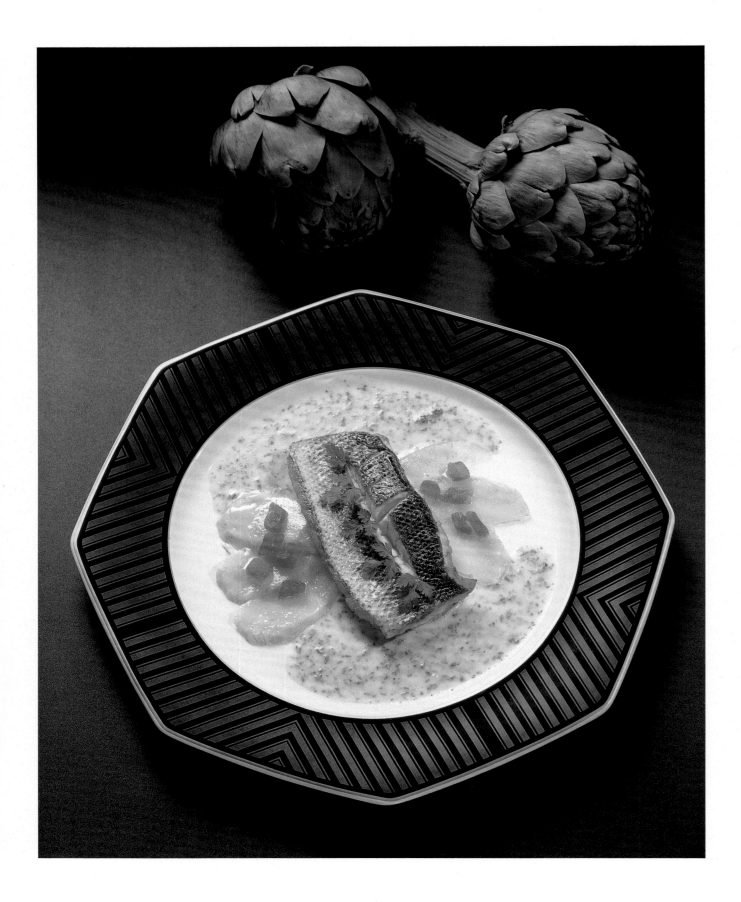

SEA BASS FILLETS WITH ARTICHOKES AND CILANTRO

SWITZERLAND

Gilles Dupont, the young French chef at Le Cygne in the Hilton International Genève, trained in his native country in Annecy, Juan-les-Pins, and Cologny, then went on to Sweden, England, and Canada before joining the Hilton staff in 1980 in Geneva. His inventive combinations, particularly seafood dishes with intensified essential sauces—such as the following harmonious mélange—have drawn numerous accolades from food critics throughout Europe, and two Michelin stars.

Although artichoke hearts and fish are uncommon plate-mates, they have a rare affinity, particularly when underscored by cilantro. The effect is multifaceted, with hints of tastes that are bittersweet, earthy, briny, mushroomy, and acid without being disparate.

Two 1¾-pound sea bass or red snappers, filleted with skin intact, heads and bones reserved
A few peppercorns, bruised
1 bay leaf
1 medium bunch cilantro (about 3 ounces), rinsed
1 cup dry white wine
2 tablespoons chopped shallots

2–3 tablespoons lemon juice
4 large artichokes
1½ cups heavy (or whipping) cream
Salt and pepper
Peanut oil
4 firm medium plum tomatoes, seeded, peeled, and diced (about 1 cup)

---

1. Remove and discard the gills and innards from the skeletons. Rinse the heads and bones well; combine in a saucepan with 6 cups water, the peppercorns, and bay leaf. Simmer for 20 minutes; skim. Strain the fish stock into the saucepan. Chop and add the cilantro stems, white wine, shallots, and 2 tablespoons of lemon juice.

2. Break the stems from the artichokes. Break off the outer leaves until you reach the tender, pale center. Slice across the tops of these leaves to remove about half. Trim off any additional dark leaf parts. Pare away the dark base of the underneath part.

3. Bring the fish stock to a boil. Add the artichoke bottoms; set a dish on top to keep them submerged. Simmer until tender (timing can vary considerably; begin checking at about 25 minutes). Cool slightly in the liquid. Remove the chokes and cut each into 8 wedges.

4. Strain the stock. Return to the saucepan and boil until reduced to ⅓ cup. Add the cream and boil the sauce until reduced to about 1¼ cups and slightly thickened. Add lemon juice to taste. Chop fine enough cilantro leaves to equal 2½ tablespoons (reserve a few sprigs for garnish); add to the sauce. Add salt and pepper to taste.

5. Set a foil-covered broiler rack as close to the heat source as possible and preheat the broiler. Paint the fish fillets on both sides with peanut oil. Broil until just barely cooked, about 5 minutes. *(continued)*

6. At the same time, combine the artichoke hearts and sauce and warm over low heat. Add the tomatoes.

7. Arrange the artichokes and tomatoes on 4 warmed plates with the fish fillets. Garnish with the reserved cilantro sprigs.

Serving: *This lush sauce is lovely with a light grain, particularly a scented rice, such as Basmati, if available, or couscous.*
Advance preparation: *Although this dish is rather labor intensive, it can be almost completely made a few hours in advance—through Step 4.*

4 SERVINGS

MONKFISH FILLET WITH FENNEL AND RED ONION
UNITED KINGDOM

When chef Graham Cadman put together this dish at the Gatwick Hilton International, the ingredients were considered altogether unusual. In fact, when French and English fishermen met in the Channel, monkfish was commonly exchanged for fish more to British taste. Also called goosefish, bellyfish, and angler, only the tail end of this firm-fleshed fish is marketed. Well known in France and Italy (where you will find it as lotte, baudroie, rape), *the fish has just recently become part of the American repertoire.*

The marinating (begun a day before cooking) tenderizes the flesh and adds a gingery Oriental edge to the traditional French white wine sauce, which is brightly verdant from its generous helping of parsley and chives. The garnish of crisp-tender sweet onion and aromatic fennel is particularly pleasant alongside baby new potatoes in their pink jackets.

1¼ pounds monkfish fillet, cut into 16 slices (medallions)
Salt and white pepper
1 tablespoon grated fresh ginger
8 tablespoons olive oil
2 tablespoons butter
2 teaspoons minced shallot
1 tablespoon all-purpose flour, plus flour for dusting the fish
1 cup fish stock (see page 326), or ¾ cup bottled clam juice mixed with ¼ cup water

½ cup dry vermouth
1 pound of fennel bulb, weighed without large stalks
1 large red onion, halved, then thin-sliced
⅓ cup chives cut into 1½-inch lengths
1 tablespoon minced parsley

1. Sprinkle the fish slices on both sides with salt and pepper to taste. Mix the ginger and 4 tablespoons olive oil; spread evenly on both sides of the fish. Cover with plastic; refrigerate for about 24 hours.

2. Preheat the oven to 150–200°. Heat 1 tablespoon butter in a small saucepan. Stir in the shallot and cook until softened over moderately low heat. Add 1 tablespoon flour and cook until slightly colored. Add the fish stock and ¼ cup vermouth; bring to a boil, whisking. Cook over lowest heat for 15 minutes, stirring often. You should have slightly more than ¾ cup of sauce.

3. Meanwhile, trim off the fennel stalks completely, if necessary, saving the small inner leafy parts for garnish. Halve or quarter the bulb(s), as size dictates, then cut across in thin slices. Heat 2 tablespoons olive oil in a medium-large skillet over moderate heat. Add the fennel and cook, tossing often, for 3 minutes, until partly tender. Add the onion and continue cooking until just tender, about 2 minutes. Season to taste. Divide the portions on serving plates and set in the low oven.

4. Heat 1 tablespoon of the remaining oil in a 9-inch nonstick skillet (or use a very good stainless or copper one; the fish sticks) over moderate heat. Dust half the fish slices with flour. Cook until lightly browned on both sides, about 2 minutes. Arrange on the plates with the vegetables. Repeat with the remaining 1 tablespoon oil and fish (or use 2 skillets and cook all at once).

5. Add the remaining ¼ cup vermouth to the pan in which the fish cooked; stir over moderate heat until the brown bits have been loosened. Add to the vermouth sauce. Press through a strainer. Add the chives and parsley; bring to a simmer. Off the heat, stir in the remaining 1 tablespoon butter.

6. Remove the plates from the oven, spoon the sauce around the fish and vegetables. Serve at once.

Advance preparation: *The recipe can be completed through Step 2 a day ahead.*

4 SERVINGS

A Quiet Coup: Graham Cadman at the Gatwick Hilton International

Graham Cadman and his son, Ben, at home

"I can't help it. I was born with an English handicap," says lean, affable Graham Cadman, a native of Sheffield. "My teachers told me that I should change my name if I wanted to get on in the field, that I could never make it." But he has, and so have the restaurants with which he has been affiliated in his 21 years in the business—13 of them with Hilton International. "It's a fluke my being a chef, anyway. My mother, a fine farm cook, made nice jams and bread, but never touched a piece of garlic or other 'strange things.' The closest I ever came to cooking or caring much about it was picking berries." At sixteen, an average student and avid soccer player, he was persuaded by a school counselor to try his hand at cooking. Christmas season being near and hotel kitchen help never sufficient, he found himself peeling mountains of turnips and potatoes—and happy as a lark. "There was steam everywhere, turkeys were tossed through the air, grown men were swearing at each other and running around with pots and platters; it was as much fun as a soccer match."

Cadman apprenticed for four years in England, then went on to Switzerland—where he realized he knew just about nothing, and virtually began again. As a foreigner in a

Swiss kitchen, he managed to achieve the almost unheard of high rank of sous-chef, then decided to glean some international experience. But the giant beach-barbecues and rum-and-Coke atmosphere of the Caribbean where he was transferred were too much of a shock to his system after the chilly precision of Zurich. And, more important, there was *beurre rouge* ("not *beurre blanc,* but a new sauce, a new world to discover")! A friend had sent an innovative menu from Europe—subtle dishes with classic under-pinnings and daring new ingredients and techniques—the burgeoning of Nouvelle Cuisine. "If I stay away from Europe too long, I may never know *beurre rouge,*" proclaimed the brave young sous-chef, and had himself moved to Europe, even though the change meant a lesser position. He learned to make a red wine butter and much more, and became executive chef of the Amsterdam Hilton. A three-year stint in Holland found him a bit homesick, and when an appropriate place became available in England, he relocated to the Gatwick Hilton International.

Just imagine driving out-of-the-way to an airport hotel to have dinner prepared by an English chef—on purpose! Of course, that's just what happened. Cadman's calm, sensitive style, his unflagging enthusiasm, his ability to sense guests' preferences, his seasonal menus based on the fine regional products—simple vegetables, Welsh lamb, Angus beef, perfect turbot and Dover sole, Dublin Bay prawns, remarkable cheeses—and his ability to meld traditional English ingredients with continental ones, resulted in an award-winning restaurant "worth the detour" and loved by locals. "The restaurant started out serving giant portions of English food kept in *bain maries* large enough to swim in, and wound up—with Hilton's blessing, and the help of a remarkable team—with a European kitchen built to produce European food." Candid to the quick, his dark-lashed, sky-blue eyes direct, he says, "I cannot tell you how I love the commitment it takes to be a chef. The involvement of so many people along the line, the fact that you see a product from the beginning to the end. I couldn't dream of doing anything else." From the following "sampler" meal, we should all be grateful for this last statement.

—Smooth, thin slices of burgundy-red, salt-marinated raw duck slicked with olive oil, truffle-topped, served on warm potato slices

—Miniature medallions of golden-sautéed sweetbreads and pine nuts tossed with crunchy stir-fried *bâtonnets* of asparagus and carrots, touched with a mere gloss of balsamic vinegar and lightest walnut oil

—A cool terrine of mixed poultry and wild mushrooms, cut in large morsels, Madeira-touched, served with warm slivers of herb-flecked tawny forest mushrooms

—Tenderest shrimp and baby papaya balls in a thin, fresh chili-spiked sauce of the pureed fruit, shellfish stock, and finished with butter and cream to barely bind

—A small salmon fillet, pan-seared, deglazed with currant-vinegar puree, served on a bed of tart-sweet, diced bell peppers (yellow, red, and green), eggplant, zucchini, and capers

—Two diminutive lamb chops from the rack, mahogany-toned from a light smoking, served with a scant spoon of reduced juices, tiny turned turnips, a miniature carrot flan, and *haricots verts*

—A tulip cookie cup containing strawberry, pear, and mango sherbet surrounded by a marbled fantasy design of cream and sour raspberry puree, escorted by slices of lightly liqueur-macerated strawberries, mango, and pear.

OVERLEAF, TOP: **Monkfish Fillet with Fennel and Red Onion (see page 166 for recipe)** BOTTOM: **Lamb with Minted Red Wine Sauce and Mustard Seeds**

LAMB WITH MINTED RED WINE SAUCE AND MUSTARD SEEDS

UNITED KINGDOM

The origin of some dishes is less poetic than others. In this case Graham Cadman was confronted upon his arrival at the Gatwick Hilton International by a huge supply of mustard seeds, left by his predecessor—who was passionately fond of the spice. A number of weekly specials were thus inspired by inherited mustard seeds.

Try this new approach to lamb with mint sauce: a wine reduction accented with fresh mint leaves moistens long, rosy slivers of loin. The peppery herb comes through with surprising clarity, adding nuance and depth to a sauce that is at once candid and complex.

Bone-in rib roast (rack) of lamb (8 ribs; 2½ pounds), meat removed in one long cylinder, bones and trimmings hacked into small pieces
1 tablespoon vegetable oil
2 small onions, chunked
1 carrot, sliced
½ teaspoon peppercorns, crushed slightly with the blade of a knife
½ bay leaf

1 garlic clove
¼ cup lightly packed cleaned peppermint leaves
2 cups dry red wine
1 large shallot, minced (about ¼ cup)
5 tablespoons butter
Salt and pepper
About 1 teaspoon mustard seeds, crushed slightly with a knife blade
Mint sprigs for garnish

---

1. Discard the fat from the lamb trimmings and bones. Heat the oil in a very wide skillet over high heat; add the bones and trimmings, onions, and carrot and toss until well browned, about 15 minutes, pouring off the fat as it accumulates. Add the peppercorns, bay leaf, and garlic; toss for 5 minutes longer. Add 2 cups water and bring to a boil slowly. Boil, stirring occasionally, to reduce the liquid to 1¼ cups, 10–15 minutes. Pour the lamb stock into a container. Spoon off the fat.

2. Preheat the oven to 400°. Combine the lamb stock, mint, wine, and shallots in a saucepan. Boil until the sauce is reduced to ¾ cup.

3. Meanwhile, heat 1 tablespoon butter in a skillet with an ovenproof handle. Sprinkle the meat with salt and pepper; brown it lightly on both sides. Set in the hot oven for 6–10 minutes for rare, or until a thermometer registers 125°. Set on a cutting board to rest for 5 minutes or so, lightly covered with foil to keep warm.

4. Add the reduced sauce to the pan with any juices that have accumulated from the meat. Boil to reduce to ½ cup. Strain into a small saucepan. Bring to a boil. Remove from the heat and stir in the remaining 4 tablespoons butter and 1 teaspoon mustard seeds. Season to taste, adding more mustard seeds, if desired.

5. Cut the meat into about 24 slices. Spoon 3 tablespoons of the sauce onto each of 4 heated plates. Arrange the meat over, garnish with mint sprigs, and serve at once.

Note: *If you like meat very rare, there is no need to roast it in the oven. Simply cook over direct heat.*
Advance preparation: *The lamb stock and wine reduction can be made 2–3 days ahead.*

4 SERVINGS

SWEETBREADS WITH HONEY SAUCE AND MELON

BELGIUM

This finely tuned and understated dish comes from Michel Theurel of La Maison de Boeuf in Brussels, where it is served with Chinese rice noodles, glazed pearl onions, a snippet of lime zest, and mint sprigs. It is one of those inventions in which the sum equals far more than the parts. The melons are no mere fanciful garnish, but lend their sweetness and acid to the gingery-meaty sauce which burnishes the pale sweetbreads.

---

1 pair veal sweetbreads (about 1½ pounds)
½ small ripe honeydew, *or* a whole Cavaillon or Galia melon
½ ripe cantaloupe, orange melon, or an equivalent amount of another orange-fleshed melon

Salt and white pepper
3 tablespoons butter
2 tablespoons light fragrant honey
3 tablespoons sherry vinegar
⅔ cup chicken or veal stock
½ teaspoon very finely grated fresh ginger

---

1. Soak the sweetbreads in a bowl of water in the refrigerator for about 24 hours, changing the water 4–8 times, as convenient; all blood spots should be soaked clean.

2. Slip the sweetbreads into a pan of simmering salted water to cover. Simmer for 10 minutes. Drain and cool slightly. Set the sweetbreads in a pan; place a dish and a 5–6-pound weight on top. Let stand for ½–1 hour. Trim and discard the heavy membranes.

3. Preheat the oven to 150–200°. Scoop out and reserve the melon seeds and attached fibers. With a 1-inch melon ball cutter, scoop about 20 balls of each melon; cut each of these in half. Scrape both seeds and enough remaining ripe flesh from each melon to make about ⅔ cup.

4. Sprinkle the sweetbreads with salt and pepper. Heat 1½ tablespoons butter in a medium skillet over moderately low heat. Cook the sweetbreads until golden on both sides, about 5 minutes. Spoon the honey over the sweetbreads; lower the heat and cook for about 10 minutes, basting and turning often, until the sweetbreads are richly browned and glazed. Set on a dish in the warm oven.

5. Pour the vinegar into the skillet in which you glazed the sweetbreads; stir over high heat for a moment until the steam dies down. Add the reserved melon seeds and pulp and the stock. Bring to a boil, stirring; boil for 1 minute. Strain into a small pan.

6. Boil the sauce to reduce it until it becomes slightly shiny and sticky—about ¼ cup. Add the ginger and the remaining 1½ tablespoons butter; pour in the juice that has accumulated from the sweetbreads.

7. Cut the sweetbreads into diagonal slices. Spoon the sauce onto 4 warmed plates. Arrange the sweetbreads on it. Shake the melon balls in a skillet over high heat for a moment to heat through. Distribute over and around the sweetbreads.

Advance preparation: *The sweetbreads can be soaked, poached, and flattened in advance.*

4 SERVINGS

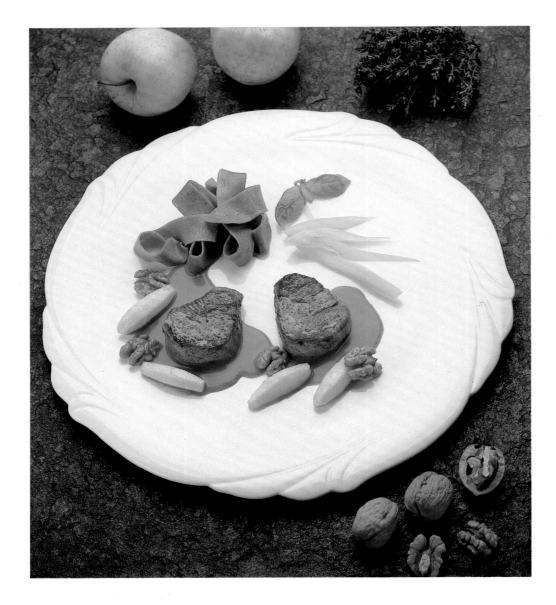

VEAL MEDALLIONS WITH APPLES AND WALNUTS

SWITZERLAND

Franz Kuhne, executive chef at the Hilton International Basel, and Marcel Roth, food and beverage manager, have been at the hotel since its opening in 1975. Both native Swiss, they work together with Rolex precision. Meticulous craftsmen, they stress a traditional education and are dedicated to the training of young chefs. They are not of the wild individual school of cooking, but rather advocate more subdued personal expression, rooted in the classics.

This dish then, of tender veal morsels in a generous gilding of glossy sauce is (reluctantly spoken by chef Kuhne) "a creation," but based on beloved Swiss ingredients—palest meat, walnuts, and apples—in a classic veal reduction.

5-pound veal rib roast (6 chops), meat removed in one long cylinder, bones and trimming hacked into small pieces
2 medium carrots, peeled and cut into thick slices
3 medium onions, peeled and chunked
1 celery rib, cut into thick slices
½ teaspoon crushed white peppercorns
Salt and white pepper
¼ cup all-purpose flour

4 tablespoons butter
1 cup dry white wine, preferably Swiss (Dézalay or Fendant) or a dry Riesling
1 cup heavy (or whipping) cream
2 tablespoons Calvados or apple brandy
3 Golden Delicious apples, peeled and cored
1 tablespoon lemon juice
1 cup (4 ounces) walnuts
Basil sprigs for garnish

1. Preheat the oven to 400°. Cut the meat into 12 equal medallions. Spread the bones and trimmings in a wide roasting pan. Set in the preheated oven and roast for 30 minutes, until well browned. Add the carrots, onions, celery, and peppercorns. Roast for 30–40 minutes longer, until well browned. Pour off the fat. Transfer the contents of the pan to a stockpot. Add 1 quart of water to the roasting pan and bring to a boil over high heat, stirring. Pour into the stockpot. Bring to a boil with an additional 1 quart of water. Simmer, uncovered, for about 1½ hours. Strain out the solids, then boil the stock to reduce it to 1 cup.

2. Preheat the oven to 200°. Sprinkle the veal with salt and pepper; dust evenly with the flour. Heat 1 tablespoon butter in a very wide skillet over moderate heat; add half the veal; cook until lightly browned on both sides, about 2 minutes. Transfer to a platter in the warm oven. Repeat with the remaining veal, using another tablespoon of butter. Pour out the fat.

3. Add the wine to the pan; stir over high heat until reduced to a syrupy consistency. Add the cream and reduced veal stock; boil, stirring, until reduced to about 1⅓ cups. Add the Calvados and salt and pepper to taste. Remove from the heat; add another tablespoon of butter.

4. Cut each apple into 12 wedges; toss with the lemon juice. Heat the remaining 1 tablespoon butter in a wide skillet. Add the apples; sauté until nicely colored on both sides, about 3 minutes. Add the walnuts; toss for 2 minutes. Arrange with the veal on the platter. Spoon some sauce over the meat. Garnish with basil sprigs.

Serving: *Accompany with noodles, or the snipped Swiss noodles,* spätzli, *or rounded* knöpfli *(little buttons). Serve the remaining sauce alongside.*

6 SERVINGS

SQUAB AND ENDIVE WITH SALAD GREENS

FRANCE

The Maison du Boeuf in the Hilton International Strasbourg began as a showcase for the finest American meat. It seemed foolhardy for an American hotel chain to compete with the many celebrated restaurants in this much-starred Alsatian food town. However, when Dominique Michou began to make his imprint, he not only managed to attract the tourists, but the critical locals—and a Michelin *star. Grilled and roasted meats were gradually replaced with trendy versions of local specialties, such as this dish.*

The gamy flavor and deep-rose color of squab are well suited to the bittersweet Belgian endive, barely butter-braised, and jewel-bright mâche and radicchio combination.

---

4 squab (each about ¾ pound)
Salt and pepper
2 tablespoons sherry vinegar
¼ cup hazelnut oil
1 pound Belgian endives
6 tablespoons butter

1 small head of radicchio (about 6 ounces), rinsed and dried and torn into bite-size pieces
1 large bunch of mâche (corn salad) *or* 1 small head of imported curly chicory *(chicorée frisée)*, rinsed and dried

---

1. Cut the leg-thigh pieces from the squab. Cut off the wings (leave the first joint of the wings intact), then remove the breast meat from the bird. (Save the wings, carcasses, giblets, etc. for future stock-making). Sprinkle with salt and pepper.

2. Mix together the vinegar and salt and pepper to taste; blend in the oil.

3. Halve the endives and trim out the cores. Rinse and pat dry. Cut crosswise on a slant into 3 sections, if large, 2 if small.

4. Heat 3 tablespoons butter in a very wide skillet (see Note) over moderately high heat. Cook the squab pieces until deep pink within, about 2 minutes on each side. Set on a cutting surface and cover lightly to keep warm.

5. Heat the remaining 3 tablespoons butter in a wide, rather deep skillet or sauté pan over moderately high heat. Add the Belgian endive leaves; toss until they lose their raw crunch, about 3 minutes. Season with salt and pepper.

6. Toss the salad greens with the dressing; divide onto one side of 4 large serving plates. Arrange the endive next to this. Quickly slice the breasts lengthwise; cut apart the leg-thigh sections. Arrange the squab over the endive. Serve at once.

Note: *If you cook the squab in a black cast-iron pan it will brown more thoroughly and the skin will be crisper.*
Serving/Presentation: *This compound salad will be most attractive served on very large plates, especially dark-colored ones.*

4 SERVINGS

DUCK IN TWO ACTS:
CRACKLING SALAD AND SLICED DUCK WITH SPRING VEGETABLES IN BROTH
UNITED KINGDOM

British chef Graham Cadman is reluctant to call a dish his invention or confess to personal preferences, but he does allow that this creation is his ("although based on the classic boeuf à la ficelle*"), a response to the overload of richness in most haute cuisine preparations.*

A new way of looking at duck, this recipe supplies both salad and main course for four with one bird. Satiny Belgian endive and radicchio are tumbled with crunchy strips of duck skin for an appetizer salad, then the meat is served with a bouquet of springtime vegetables in a modicum of full-flavored broth. Not a soup, not a stew, the combination is clean, light, Japanese in feeling; a natural, pure ensemble of rewarding simplicity.

5–6-pound duck
1 large onion, cut in chunks
1 large carrot, cut in chunks
6 cups cold unsalted chicken (or duck) stock
4 small red potatoes, scrubbed and sliced ¼ inch thick
6 ounces *haricots verts* (or tiny stringbeans), trimmed
4 medium carrots, quartered lengthwise, cut into 1½-inch lengths
½ pound (3 small) turnips, cut the same size as the carrots

¼ pound snow peas, strings removed
Salt and pepper
1½ tablespoons red wine vinegar
3 tablespoons olive oil
1 medium head radicchio (about 5 ounces), cored, rinsed, and cut bite-size
2 medium Belgian endives, halved, cored, and sliced across
2 tablespoons minced parsley
1 tablespoon fine-sliced chives
2 teaspoons soy sauce

---

1. Prepare the duck stock: Cut the leg-thigh pieces from the duck; trim neatly. Cut off the wings (leave the first joint of the wing attached). Halve the breast down the center and remove the 2 pieces from the carcass with the wing joints. Trim these, saving the trimmings. Cut up enough fat to yield about 1 cup (discard the remainder). Heat in a very wide skillet over moderate heat. Chop the carcass, wings, and neck into small chunks and add to the pan. Cook over moderate heat until browned, about 15 minutes, turning occasionally; pour off fat as it accumulates. Add the onion and large carrot; stir now and then until well browned, about 10 minutes. Remove from the heat; tip the pan so the fat runs to one side; let stand for a few minutes. Pour off the fat. Add the chicken stock; bring to a boil. Simmer until reduced to 3½ cups, 25–30 minutes.

2. Preheat the oven to 425°. Prepare the vegetables: Drop the potatoes into a large pot of boiling, salted water. Boil for 30 seconds. Add the *haricots verts* and carrots; boil for 1½ minutes, until half-cooked. Add the turnips and snow peas; boil for 1½ minutes longer, until all the vegetables are just cooked through. Drain; drop into ice water. Drain again.

3. Cook the duck: Heat 1 tablespoon of duck fat or oil in a clean ovenproof skillet. Salt and pepper the breast and thigh pieces and place skin-side down in the pan. Brown lightly, then turn and sear the meat. Pour off the fat. Set the breast pieces on a plate. Place the pan with the thighs in the hot oven for 15 minutes. Add the breast; roast about 10 minutes longer, until the meat is pink within. Transfer to a cutting board. Pour the fat from the pan.

4. Prepare the salad: Add the vinegar to the skillet; stir over low heat for 30 seconds to deglaze the pan. Strain; pour into a small bowl. Whisk in salt, pepper, then olive oil to make a dressing. Remove the duck skin/fat from the roasted pieces; cut this into thin, even strips. Toss in a medium skillet over moderate heat until golden and crisp. Toss the radicchio and endive with the dressing, then top with the duck skin and serve as a first course.

5. To prepare the main course: Combine the duck stock, parsley, chives, and soy sauce in a wide saucepan. Bring to a simmer, covered. Add the blanched vegetables; return to a simmer. Taste; adjust seasoning and herbs. Meanwhile, cut the duck meat into thin strips. Spoon the vegetables into 4 wide, heated serving bowls. Top with the duck meat, dividing breast and leg-thigh meat equally. Pour the hot stock over all.

Serving: *You can also serve the two dishes together, as is done at the Gatwick Hilton International.*
Advance preparation: *The duck stock and blanched vegetables can be prepared in advance. If you don't want to make the dish ahead of time, the vegetables can be blanched, drained, and added to the hot stock at serving time.*

4 SERVINGS, AS BOTH SALAD COURSE AND MAIN COURSE

OVERLEAF: **An innovative meal for four from one duck: Sliced Duck with Spring Vegetables in Broth (left); Crackling Salad (right—with a few crisp bits in the foreground)**

Breast of Hen with Green Beans in Hazelnut Dressing

AUSTRIA

Executive chef Eduard Mitsche in Vienna is partial to salads of lightly cooked warm fish or poultry nestled against a toss of tender greens touched with nut-oil dressings (as is Dominique Michou, in Strasbourg). He serves the following as an appetizer course (with breasts of guinea hens substituted for the Rock Cornish hens), but for home cooks this is more likely to be a featured main course. As with all of Mitsche's dishes, there is no hiding place: the simple flavors are the focus, so ingredients must be perfect.

2 Rock Cornish hens
8–10 ounces *haricots verts* (or tiny stringbeans)
2 tablespoons balsamic vinegar
1 teaspoon sherry vinegar
Salt and pepper
¼ cup hazelnut oil

¼ cup plus 2 tablespoons olive oil
1 tablespoon minced shallots
1 medium head of soft lettuce, such as oakleaf, rinsed and dried
4 quail eggs (optional, but desirable)
12 cherry tomatoes, halved

1. Preheat the oven to 350°. Cut the leg-thigh sections from the hens, then the breasts. Remove the wings from the breasts and the bones from both breast and leg-thigh pieces (freeze and reserve these for stock).

2. Trim the beans and drop into boiling salted water; boil until barely tender, about 3 minutes. Drain, cool in ice water; drain and dry. Blend the 2 vinegars and salt and pepper; whisk in the hazelnut oil and ¼ cup of the olive oil; add the shallots. Toss the beans with half the dressing.

3. Sprinkle the hens with salt and pepper. Heat the remaining 2 tablespoons olive oil in a wide skillet over moderate heat. Place the leg-thigh pieces in the pan and brown lightly on both sides. Leave these in the pan and add the breasts, skin side down. Cook until golden; tip the pan and spoon the fat over the meat. Set the pan in the oven for 10 minutes, or until just barely cooked.

4. Drop the quail eggs into boiling water; boil for just under 2 minutes. Drop into cold water to cool slightly; gently crack shells and remove them. The eggs should be warm.

5. Arrange the lettuce and beans on 4 large plates. Cut the thigh pieces into fairly thick slices on a diagonal. Place these on the lettuce. Cut the breasts into thin, long slices and arrange these on the plate. Stir the dressing and spoon over hens and lettuce.

6. Garnish with the cherry tomatoes. Halve the eggs and set on the plates. Serve at once.

4 SERVINGS AS A MAIN COURSE

CHICKEN BREASTS WITH RED PEPPER SAUCE
SWITZERLAND

La Grignotière, a casual restaurant at the stunning Hilton International Genève, spills out onto a broad terrace once the weather warms. This is not surprising, as the view may be one of the most beautiful any restaurant can claim: Right on the shore of the glittering lake, one can see as far as Mont Blanc and as near as the graceful swans that sail along the shore below.

Although a "fast-food" restaurant in comparison to Le Cygne (the luxury dining room of the hotel), La Grignotière, supervised by executive chef Jean-Claude Bergeret, a tough, handsome Hilton International veteran of 23 years standing, is by no means standard— as is clear from the following recipe for a best-seller of juicy chicken served with a tart-sweet, vividly orange bell pepper sauce and egg noodles.

---

4 chicken breast halves with wings
  (6–7 ounces each)
Salt and pepper
3 tablespoons butter
1½ cups chicken stock
2 large, meaty red bell peppers,
  halved and coarsely diced

2–3 tablespoons raspberry vinegar
2–3 teaspoons sugar
1 large green bell pepper, halved
¼ cup dry white wine

---

1. Preheat the oven to 375°. Trim the wing tip and attached joint from each piece (reserve for stock-making); sprinkle breasts with salt and pepper. Heat the butter in a wide ovenproof skillet until foaming; add the chicken breasts, skin side down. Cook over moderate heat until browned, about 5 minutes. Turn to barely color, about 1 minute. Cover; transfer to the hot oven. Roast until cooked through, about 15 minutes.

2. Meanwhile, combine the stock and red peppers in a saucepan. Simmer until tender, about 10 minutes. Puree in a blender or processor. Add 2 tablespoons of the vinegar and 2 teaspoons sugar; puree fine. Add sugar, salt, pepper, and vinegar to taste. Bring to a boil and cook for a minute or two.

3. Drop the green bell pepper into boiling, salted water. Return to a boil. Refresh in ice water. Dry and cut into very fine strips.

4. Transfer chicken to a platter (remove breast bones, if desired); cover with foil.

5. Boil the liquid in the roasting skillet until the fat rises to the top and the particles beneath are browned. Pour off the fat. Add the wine to the pan and bring to a boil, scraping the pan bottom. Simmer for 2 minutes on low heat. Strain into the pepper puree. Bring to a simmer.

6. Serve the chicken and sauce garnished with the green pepper.

Note: *For velvety sauce, grill and peel the peppers before simmering.*

4 SERVINGS

CHICKEN BREASTS STUFFED WITH LIVER IN LIGHT BASIL CREAM SAUCE

UNITED KINGDOM

This recipe is slightly adapted from the version developed by chef Graham Cadman and served at the Gatwick Hilton International, where chicken is stored and cooked in vacuum-sealed pouches that maintain freshness and yield a flavorful, moist finished product. The presentation resembles a miniature ballottine: *pale chicken breasts wrapped in spinach leaves are centered with rosy livers. The warm slices are arranged on an ivory* sauce suprême *sparked with a generous amount of basil.*

---

3 tablespoons butter
2 tablespoons all-purpose flour
2 cups chicken stock
½ cup heavy (or whipping) cream
¼ cup finely minced basil leaves
4 medium chicken livers, cleaned
   and halved (about 6 ounces)

Salt and pepper
About ½ pound spinach leaves, as
   smooth and flat as possible;
   cleaned, with stems removed
4 boned and skinned chicken breast
   halves (4 ounces each)

---

1. Heat 2 tablespoons butter over low heat in a small saucepan. Add the flour and stir for 2 minutes; do not brown. Add the stock, whisking. Bring to a boil, stirring, then simmer gently for 15 minutes, or until reduced to 1⅓ cups. Add the cream; simmer gently until reduced to 1¼ cups. Add the basil. Remove from the heat.

2. Heat the remaining 1 tablespoon butter in a small skillet over moderate heat. Season the livers with salt and pepper, then sear on both sides. Set aside to cool.

3. Drop the spinach into boiling salted water; return to a boil. Drain; refresh in ice water. Spread about 6 overlapping leaves on paper towels to form a rectangle the size of each breast piece. Form 4 of these. Spread out the remaining leaves to dry on towels.

4. Enclose each liver piece in a leaf of spinach. Cut a pocket running the length of each chicken breast piece; insert 2 spinach-wrapped liver packets. Place each chicken piece on a spinach rectangle; sprinkle with salt and pepper. Enclose each breast in the spinach (adding additional leaves as needed), to cover completely.

5. Wrap each chicken packet in buttered foil to make a neat cylinder, leaving the ends open. Place the packets on a steamer rack set over boiling water. Steam for 10 minutes, until just cooked through; the liver will still be slightly pink. Let cool for 5 minutes.

6. Slice the chicken into rounds and arrange on a warm platter. Gently rewarm the sauce, then spoon a little over the slices; serve the rest separately.

Option: *The chicken can also be chilled, sliced, and served with basil mayonnaise as a cold hors d'oeuvre.*

4 SERVINGS

Rabbit and Endive in Cream with Walnut Dressing

FRANCE

Most of the diners who spend the evening at La Maison de Boeuf in the Hilton International Strasbourg are locals. They have come to expect meals that depend on the day's market, and on the creative whims of chef Dominique Michou—rather than a traditional fixed menu. Michou is particularly fond of warm, lightly cooked fish or meat, arranged around salad greens tossed with nut oil and sherry vinegar. Here, creamy endive shreds accompany port-scented rabbit slices brushed with walnut-sherry dressing. While the presentation of this dish is simpler than most of Michou's, the flavors are characteristically subtle. You'll need to plan on marinating the rabbit for about a day.

Two 2½-pound rabbits
1¼ cups heavy (or whipping) cream
⅓ cup port
2 tablespoons light vegetable oil
5 large Belgian endives (about 1½ pounds)

2 tablespoons butter
2 tablespoons walnut oil
1 teaspoon sherry vinegar
Salt and pepper
1 very small head of oakleaf or other soft lettuce, rinsed and well dried

1. Remove the hindquarters, then the forelegs from the rabbits. Bone the loin/breast section carefully, so that it remains in one piece. (If you are less than practiced, you might ask the butcher to take over.) Roll and tie this large piece to form a cylinder. Bone the hind quarters (keep the forelegs, bones, and trimmings for future stock-making). Combine ¾ cup cream and the port in a nonaluminum dish. Turn the rabbit pieces around in the cream; cover, and refrigerate for 12–24 hours.

2. Preheat the oven to 350°. Remove the meat from the dish, scraping off some of the marinade. Heat the oil in a wide gratin pan or skillet with ovenproof handle. Lightly brown the rabbit on both sides. Set in the hot oven for 30 minutes, or until tender. Let stand for 5 minutes before slicing.

3. Meanwhile, halve the endives and trim out the cores. Cut across into thin slices. Heat the butter in an 11–12-inch skillet. Add the endive and toss over high heat until most of the juice has exuded, about 2 minutes. Add the remaining ½ cup cream. Toss frequently over high heat until the cream has thickened to a slick.

4. Blend together the walnut oil and sherry vinegar with salt and pepper to taste. Arrange the lettuce on 4 plates.

5. Divide the endive over the lettuce. Slice the rabbit and arrange around the two. Brush the meat with the walnut dressing and sprinkle a little on the lettuce. Serve at once.

Serving: *The aromatic, bone-dry white wines of Alsace are the natural accompaniment to this creamy dish. A Riesling or Tokay, if available, will serve beautifully.*

4 SERVINGS

Hilton International Brussels:
From Vegetarian Club Sandwiches
to Foie Gras on Rose Petal Gelée,
a Kitchen That Stays in Tune

Residents of Brussels are knowledgeable—and passionate—about fine food, and so are most of their cosmopolitan visitors. In the city that is home for NATO and the European Parliament, heads of state wind up meetings on time to keep their reservations in the many prestigious eating establishments. In fact, for anyone attempting to choose a dining spot, whether casual or formal, the abundance of restaurants is almost daunting. It is therefore quite remarkable that the three large restaurants of a deluxe, modern American hotel, which handles 1,200 meals on an average day (banquet service included), should all be highly rated in numerous European restaurant guides and that 85 percent of the clientele is local.

In the glassed-in terrace of the Cafe d'Egmont (overlooking the château of the count of Egmont, inspiration to Goethe and Beethoven) you can order a quick snack or meal anytime. Enjoy crunchy rolls and fine croissants for a continental breakfast (or try the Belgian-style sweet *pain perdu* with a glass of buttermilk into which large brown sugar crystals are stirred). After noon, listen to the pleasant hum of Swiss-German, French, Dutch, and English as businessmen, tourists, and sleek ladies-who-lunch fill the tables. Gloved and veiled dowagers take over with their dachshunds and poodles at tea time, downing copious quantities of tartes and tortes, coupes and creams, coffee and chocolate. Evening finds a menu of seasonal specials that changes weekly—such as the silky white May asparagus, in a mousse of eel and basil, or in a gamut of salads and soups, or in puff pastry with watercress mousseline alongside, or with rabbit in mustard.

Lunch or dine any day of the year in the easy atmosphere of La Maison du Boeuf (like the restaurant of the same name in Strasbourg and the San Francisco Grill in Düsseldorf, beef was once the raison d'être of these restaurants, which have now come to feature light, creative cuisine as well). A floor above the cafe, over the same cool, wooded park, the comfortable room is frequented by regulars. Genial Willy Rayemakers, one of the three long-term maîtres d's, greets many guests by name. Luxuriate in the imaginative, constantly changing menu: bosky wild mushrooms in cream, steamed goujonettes of sole and ribbons of endive in pale butter with chives, sweetbreads in a slick of ginger-tinged honey essence with tiny melon rounds, traditional (but lightened) veal kidneys *liégeoise* (with juniper sauce), a full-flavored orange and bitter chocolate parfait with a thin, fresh *coulis* of pears, or crunchy *tulipes* filled with wild strawberries and almond ice cream.

The place to go for special occasions is En Plein Ciel (In Mid-Sky), from where you can look out onto the twinkling city from the 27th floor. There the accomplished captain,

Chef Michel Theurel (left) with Marc Roger, his produce supplier, at the spotless wholesale market in Brussels

Jacques Ingerhoets, takes charge amid the candles, flowers, and couples in formal dress dancing to live music sung in a dozen tongues. While the atmosphere is festive, the food is altogether serious—in the best gastronomical sense. A menu will speak for itself:

—Tuna and salmon tartare with lime (barely marinated slivers, sea-breeze fresh, with a few pale salmon eggs, fine radish julienne, and snippets of chive)

—A slice of the freshest goose liver set on a mirror of cool gelée made of an infusion of rosebuds in which are suspended mere threads of pink and yellow petals

—Langoustines, halved, cooked with only a little butter and pink peppercorns, served with slivers of deep-fried Belgian endive and a julienne of zucchini

—Red mullet fillets, their gaudy skin intact, lightly crumbed and browned, accompanied with a deep-dark puree of purple onions set against a pale fennel foam

—Fanned slices of duck breast around a shallow flan of pears in a peppery, minted custard, alongside a paper-thin basket of deep-fried celery root cradling baby favas and mushrooms

—Ovals of iced nougat cream and kiwi sorbet set in a pool of vividly bright, sour raspberry *coulis.*

To create such variety you need a devoted group, with a wide range of talents. The 190 in the food staff at this hotel have shown unusual constancy and devotion: Christian Albrecht, head sous-chef (and himself a *maître cuisinier de Belgique*) has spent 20 years in the same kitchen, the technical strength that supports many of the creative efforts. Other sous-chefs, the butcher, and pastry chef, have been part of the team for 10 years; the maîtres d'hotel have been there longer, as have many of the 46 on the kitchen team. Most agree that it is the captain of the team who sets the pace and the standards.

Michel Theurel—*chef des cuisines, maître cuisinier de Belgique,* a strong-minded, vigorous, humorous man—has been at the helm since the hotel's opening in 1967. From the Vegetarian Club Sandwich in the cafe (three layers of fine-grained warm toast, grated carrot and paper-thin apple slices, tomato, cucumber, and slivered Belgian endive, all lightly mayo-ed) to the *soufflé du soir,* from birthday party to embassy banquet, he is the man in charge. He thanks and blames his maternal grandmother for his energy and gregarious nature: "She kindled the spark that became my career and my pleasure. Although widowed early and living alone, she loved the garden and kitchen dearly. She would cook all day to feed 50 even if there were never that many." The favorite grandchild of four, he spent days with her watching the progress in the garden, rabbit hutches, and chicken yard. They put up the winter produce together, neatly layering conserves and pickles, *confits* and terrines ("I still wish I knew how she made that incredible rabbit terrine!"). A confident, organized Lyonnais who bops into the kitchen in sweatpants in a city where it seems appropriate to wear a tie and jacket to bed, this chef champions the camaraderie of the job, loves the challenge of working with other stimulating chefs and the process of choosing and developing new talent. In fact, all the fine hotel kitchens in Brussels are headed by his disciples.

Layered Orange and Chocolate Parfait with Pear Sauce (recipe on next page)

Layered Orange and Chocolate Parfait with Pear Sauce

BELGIUM

At the Hilton International Brussels, this dessert is frozen in 3-inch timbales, then un-molded onto the pear sauce, which is scattered with white and milk chocolate shavings and bright, sour airelles *(like tiny cranberries). The creamy dessert, which fluffs as it softens, is the result of the combined efforts of Michel Theurel, executive chef, and Jacky Chartier, the sous-chef who runs En Plein Ciel, the more formal of the hotel's restaurants. Although a labor-intensive dish, the result is elegant, unusual, and serves a goodly number of guests.*

Orange parfait mixture
2 medium juice oranges
½ cup plus 6 tablespoons sugar
2 eggs, at room temperature and
  separated
⅛ teaspoon lemon juice
Pinch of salt
1 cup heavy (or whipping) cream
Chocolate parfait mixture
3 ounces bittersweet chocolate,
  broken into small bits
3 eggs, at room temperature and
  separated thoroughly (no white
  should remain in the yolks)

⅓ cup sugar
Pinch of salt
1 cup heavy (or whipping) cream
Sauce
3 tablespoons honey
1–2 tablespoons lemon juice
3 medium-large very ripe pears
  (about 1½ pounds)
¼ vanilla bean pod, halved lengthwise
Orange zest for garnish

1. Prepare the orange parfait mixture: Remove the orange zest with a peeler, avoiding all the bitter white pith beneath. Combine the zest in a food processor with ½ cup of the sugar; whiz the rind into small particles. Scrape into a very small, heavy pot. Squeeze the juice from the oranges to make ½ cup. Add to the orange sugar; bring to a boil, stirring. Lower the heat; simmer until the syrup reduces to a syrupy texture—slightly less than ½ cup—about 10 minutes. Strain.

2. Beat the egg yolks in a small bowl with an electric mixer; gradually add the hot syrup, beating until the eggs form a thick, slowly dissolving ribbon when the beater is lifted, about 5 minutes.

3. Combine the egg whites, lemon juice, salt, and the remaining 6 tablespoons sugar. Beat until soft peaks form; when you dip a finger in the meringue and hold it up, the mixture should form a soft hook, not a firm peak. Beat the cream until softly mounded, not stiff. Transfer the egg yolk mixture to a larger bowl; stir in one-third of the meringue mixture to blend well. Delicately fold in the remainder. Gently fold in the cream. Cover and refrigerate.

4. Prepare the chocolate mixture: Melt the chocolate over hot, but not simmering, water; it should be about body temperature. Remove from the heat; stir in the yolks, one at a time. Beat the egg whites, sugar, and salt to form firm but not stiff peaks. Whip the cream to form soft peaks; blend into the whites. Scrape the chocolate into a mixing bowl. Scoop ¼ of the cream-egg white mixture into the chocolate; blend well. Add the remainder and fold in gently.

5. Line a pan (see Options) with plastic wrap. Spoon in half the chocolate mixture, smoothing lightly. Top with half the orange; gently distribute the remaining chocolate over this, then the rest of the orange. Fold over the plastic; freeze for at least 6 hours.

6. Meanwhile, make the pear sauce: Combine the honey, ⅔ cup water, and 1 tablespoon lemon juice in a nonaluminum saucepan. Bring to a boil. Meanwhile, peel, quarter, and core the pears, placing them directly in the syrup. Cover and simmer for 10–15 minutes, until soft. Puree in a blender or processor. Scrape in the vanilla seeds to taste. Cover and chill.

7. To serve: Slip the loaf from the pan and unwrap the plastic. Gently cut slices, rinsing the knife with warm water between each cut. Place on chilled dessert plates. Spoon 2–3 tablespoons sauce alongside each serving (if the sauce has thickened, add a little water or pear liqueur). Sprinkle with the orange zest.

Options: *You can mold the dessert in any fairly smooth form of about 6-cup capacity: a long narrow terrine, a* rehrücken *mold, melon mold, triangular ice cream mold, or simple 9×5-inch loaf pan or dish.*

ABOUT 12 SERVINGS

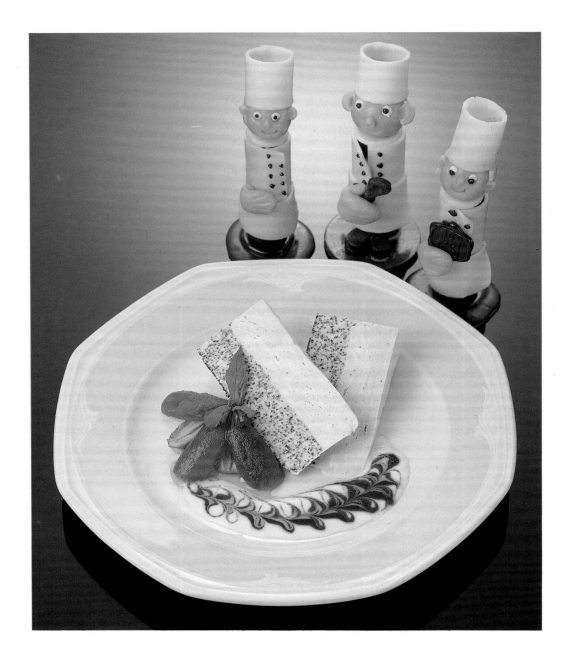

Frozen Poppy Seed and Cinnamon Parfait with Rum Dates
AUSTRIA

A traditional European ingredient—poppy seeds—distinguishes this creamily soft con-
fection, from the Hilton International Wien. The tiny, black, oily seeds are little known
in the United States except as a topping for dinner rolls. Here, they present a visual and

textural contrast to the cinnamon-scented parfait mixture. Oozingly rich, the sweetness intensified by the dates in rum, this is a dessert to be savored in small portions.

¼ **cup poppy seeds (see Note)**
½ **cup milk**
3 **cinnamon sticks, broken into small splinters**
1¾ **cups heavy (or whipping) cream**
4 **egg yolks**

2 **whole eggs**
⅔ **cup sugar**
12 **pitted dates (about ¾ pound; see Note)**
¾ **cup dark rum**

1. Gently simmer the poppy seeds and milk in a small pan until almost all of the milk has evaporated. Stir often as the mixture becomes thick.

2. Meanwhile, combine the cinnamon in a tiny pot with ¼ cup cream. Cook over *lowest* heat (or all the liquid will cook off), tightly covered, for 5 minutes. Let steep, covered, off the heat.

3. Combine the egg yolks, whole eggs, and sugar in a heatproof bowl. Whisk to blend. Set in a pan of simmering water and whisk constantly until meringue-like, thick and shiny; when the whisk is lifted the egg mixture should leave slowly dissolving ribbons on the surface. Remove from the heat, set in a pan of ice water, and whisk until cooled.

4. Whip the remaining 1½ cups cream to form firm peaks; add it gently to the eggs, folding with a spatula. Scoop the poppy seeds into a mixing bowl; stir in a few spoons of the egg-cream to lighten the texture, then fold in a little less than half of the remaining mixture. Strain the cinnamon cream into the unflavored egg-cream mixture, scraping off as much as you can from the shards of cinnamon; fold to mix well.

5. Scoop about ½ cup of the poppy seed mixture into each of six 1–1½-cup ramekins, bowls, or other fairly straight-sided, smooth molds. Top with the cinnamon mixture, dividing evenly. Cover with plastic and freeze for at least 6 hours.

6. Meanwhile, halve the dates lengthwise. Combine with the rum in a saucepan. Bring to a simmer over low heat. Scoop into a bowl, cover, and let stand until serving time (there is no need to refrigerate).

7. To serve, dip the base of each mold into hot water for 15 seconds; run a knife around the edge, then unmold onto icy-cold plates. Garnish each with 4 of the date halves. Serve immediately.

Note: *Poppy seeds have a very high oil content and become rancid quickly. Taste before you use them, to be sure they are not musty.*

Although dates were the chef's choice, we found prunes to be an effective, somewhat less sugary complement.

6 SERVINGS

HONEY-GINGER ICE CREAM WITH PAPAYA AND MANGO

AUSTRIA

Eduard Mitsche, executive chef at the Hilton International Wien, serves this honeyed dessert, more gelato *than ice cream, with sunset-pink papaya slices. If papayas are less than fragrant, substitute mangos, nectarines, or peaches. But* do *find a special fruit, for the smooth, intense frozen cream needs the contrast, both for taste and visual effect.*

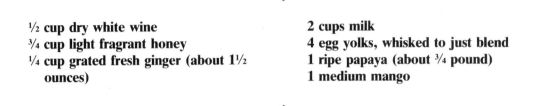

½ **cup dry white wine**
¾ **cup light fragrant honey**
¼ **cup grated fresh ginger (about 1½ ounces)**

2 cups milk
4 egg yolks, whisked to just blend
1 ripe papaya (about ¾ pound)
1 medium mango

1. Combine the white wine, ½ cup honey, and the ginger in a small nonaluminum saucepan. Boil to reduce to ⅔ cup. Strain and reserve.

2. In the top of a double boiler, heat the milk. Measure out a cupful and whisk slowly into the egg yolks; add this mixture to the remaining milk.

3. Set the pan over simmering water. Stir for about 5 minutes, until the mixture coats the back of a metal spoon, leaving a path when you draw your finger down it (it will be about 175°). Remove from the heat at once, strain into a bowl set in ice water.

4. Cool the custard, stirring often. Add the strained honey-ginger mixture and the remaining ¼ cup honey.

5. Pour into the container of an ice cream maker. Freeze according to the manufacturer's directions. Pack into a container; place in the freezer for at least 12 hours.

6. Halve, seed, and peel the papaya. Cut into thin diagonal slices. Do the same to the mango. Arrange on 6 plates. Place a ball of the ice cream on each.

Note: *As the ice cream is particularly concentrated and sweet, this small quantity is sufficient to serve 6 in combination with the fruit. However, if you prefer to make a large amount, the recipe can be doubled to make about 1½ quarts, then stored for a week.*

6 SERVINGS (SEE NOTE)

Ice Cream with Melon and Jasmine Tea Sabayon

GERMANY

Another unusual concept from flamboyant Pierre Pfister of the Hilton International Mainz: a strong infusion of jasmine tea tints and flavors the warm, barely sweet sabayon sauce that clings to the ice cream and floats over the summery melon balls.

1 pint vanilla ice cream
1 very small ripe honeydew, orange
   melon, large Galia or Cavaillon
   (about 2 pounds)
⅓ cup boiling water

3 tablespoons jasmine tea leaves
1 whole egg
1 egg yolk
2 tablespoons sugar

1. Using a large scoop, form the ice cream into 4 neat balls; place on 4 dessert plates. Set in the freezer.

2. Halve and seed the melon. With a melon ball cutter, scoop out about forty 1½-inch rounds. Set these in the refrigerator.

3. Pour the boiling water over the tea leaves and infuse for 4 minutes; strain, pressing lightly.

4. When you are ready to serve the dessert, distribute the melon balls equally around the ice cream. Return to the freezer.

5. Combine the whole egg, egg yolk, and sugar in the top of a double boiler or in a bowl set over a pot of simmering water. With a portable electric mixer, beat in the tea gradually. Continue beating until very pale, fluffy and creamy, and quite warm—3–4 minutes.

6. Remove from the heat, beating. Spoon the sauce over the ice cream, and serve at once.

Advance preparation: *Steps 1–3 can be done ahead.*

4 SERVINGS

CHAMPAGNE SORBET WITH CAMPARI

SWITZERLAND

The popular French Kir royale *(a rosy quaff of Champagne and black currant syrup) has an Italian cousin of sparkling wine flavored and colored with the vividly red, bitter* aperitivo, *Campari. Chef Franz Kuhne of the Hilton International Basel adapted it to sorbet form, lightening the Campari to a mere hint that barely modifies the flavor of the bubbly base and transforms the color to an innocent blush.*

---

1 cup sugar
1 packet unflavored gelatine
1¾ cups boiling water
2½ cups Champagne or other
   sparkling dry white wine

3 tablespoons Campari
2–3 tablespoons lemon juice

---

1. Combine the sugar and gelatine in a bowl; add the boiling water and stir to dissolve the granules. Set in a container of ice water.

2. Add the Champagne, Campari, and lemon juice to taste. Cool the mixture, stirring now and then. Pour into a metal pan.

3. Set in the coldest part of the freezer (0° F or less) until frozen almost solid, but still mushy in the center.

4. Scoop into the bowl and beat with an electric mixer until rather fluffy, but not liquefied. Immediately return to the metal pan and freeze almost solid, about 2 hours (although timing varies).

5. Beat the sorbet until soft and homogenized in texture. Scoop into a storage container, cover tightly, and freeze until firm, for at least 4 hours or up to 3 days.

Note: *If you have an ice cream maker that contains its own freezing unit, this ice can be made quickly and will have a finer, silkier texture, closer to the snowy sherbet served by Chef Kuhne.*

ABOUT 1½ QUARTS

ENGADINE NUT CAKE

SWITZERLAND

Grisons, the northeastern canton of Switzerland that juts into Austria, is celebrated, among other things, for its pastry cooks and its walnuts. The tuorta de nusch Engiadinaisa, *made of shortbread dough packed with caramelized nuts, is a confection for serious sweet lovers. Each slice is more like a toffee bar wrapped in cookie crust than a cake.*

Crust	*Filling*
2¼ sticks (9 ounces) butter, at room temperature	1½ cups sugar
¾ cup sugar	1⅔ cups heavy (or whipping) cream
¼ teaspoon salt	⅓ cup (3½ ounces) honey
1 egg	4 cups (13½ ounces) walnuts, coarsely chopped
2½ cups (12 ounces) all-purpose flour	1 egg beaten lightly with 1 tablespoon water for egg wash

1. Prepare the crust: Combine the butter, sugar, and salt in the small bowl of an electric mixer. Beat until very light and creamy. Add the egg. On lowest speed, add the flour, mixing until barely incorporated. Divide the dough into 2 disks, making one slightly larger than the other. Wrap and chill for 1 hour or more.

2. For the filling: Combine the sugar and ⅓ cup hot water in a heavy medium saucepan and let stand for a few minutes to moisten evenly. Cook over medium-low heat until the sugar dissolves completely; cover and cook over low heat for 1 minute to be sure all the crystals have washed down the sides. Raise the heat and swirl the uncovered pan until the syrup turns medium-deep amber.

3. Remove from the heat and stir in the cream, keeping clear of the considerable splatters (don't worry when the caramel lumps: it will smooth out). Return to the heat and bring the mixture to a boil, stirring. Add the honey and walnuts. Let cool.

4. Soften pastry for 15 minutes at room temperature. Preheat oven to 375°. Roll out the larger round on a lightly floured board to form a 12–13-inch circle. Ease into a 9-inch springform pan. If the pastry breaks, patch as necessary. Press it up the sides to make a wall about 2 inches high; even it by pressing downward to form a slight lip.

5. Pour in the filling. Roll out the remaining dough to form a 10-inch circle. From this cut a 9-inch circle. Paint the rim of the lower pastry with the egg wash; lay the top crust on this (it will be easy if you have another 9-inch tart or cake pan bottom to use as a spatula). Press lightly. Paint the crust generously with egg wash. Seal the edge with a fork, then incise a pattern on the surface.

6. Bake in the center of the oven for 30 minutes, until nicely browned. Set on a rack to cool for at least 30 minutes. Slowly slip a knife around the edge of the pan, then remove the side. Without covering the cake, let stand overnight before serving.

10 SERVINGS

FLAMED BLACKBERRIES WITH PERNOD AND ICE CREAM

SWITZERLAND

Deft tableside preparation of spectacular desserts is one of the pleasures of the Hilton International in Geneva, from where this recipe comes. If you have a chafing dish, the effect and efficiency are well worth the effort of assembling the ingredients and performing for your guests, for the luscious dessert truly takes minutes to prepare. It is important to shake the pan throughout the brief cooking, but do not be tempted to stir the mixture, which will become runny.

The warm berries swell and create a dramatically garnet sauce that is lightly syrupy and coats the ice cream (here set in a tulipe cup). The fruit flavor dominates, while the tart-sweet sauce adds its liquorish punch.

1 pint blackberries	**1 teaspoon lemon juice**
1 pint vanilla ice cream	**5 tablespoons Pernod**
¼ cup sugar	**3 tablespoons dry red wine**
1 tablespoon butter	**3 tablespoons Cointreau**
1 tablespoon orange juice	

1. Pour the berries into a bowl of water; gently scoop out and spread on a soft, absorbent towel; pick up the corners of the towel to roll the berries gently until dry (if they are garden-fresh, ignore the washing). Scoop 4 large balls of vanilla ice cream and place on a sheet of waxed paper in the freezer.

2. Measure and set out all the remaining ingredients.

3. Sprinkle the sugar evenly in a 9–10-inch skillet or sauté pan. Over moderate heat tip the pan as the sugar melts to dissolve it fairly evenly. When the sugar has melted, lower the heat and tip for a minute or two until the syrup turns amber. Add the butter and stir to blend.

4. Add the blackberries and gently shake the pan (do not stir the berries) until some juice seeps out, about 30 seconds. Add the orange and lemon juices and shake the pan.

5. Pour in the Pernod, then ignite. Shake the pan gently until the flame is extinguished. Add the red wine and Cointreau and return to a simmer. Remove from the heat.

6. Immediately divide the berries and juices onto 4 large dessert plates. Place a scoop of ice cream on top of each. Serve at once.

4 SERVINGS

GATEAU DEVIDAL
(Chocolate Mousse Cake)
SWITZERLAND

Looking over light-encircled Lake Geneva from a dining room paneled in mirror-finish Brazilian rosewood, there is little question about being in one of the most comfortable laps that luxury can provide. When the dessert course arrives at Le Cygne restaurant in the Hilton International Genève, six trolleys (silver-serviced, flower-bedecked) bear the burden of sweets offered as an end to a memorable meal. The sleek chocolate confection that is a favorite of the pastry chef, Régis Devidal, seems almost austere among the cascade of choices. No buttery embellishments, no triumvirate of sauces: just fine chocolate lightened with cream and egg to a mousse consistency, melded to rum-moistened chocolate génoise. Simple and very special.

Génoise
3 whole eggs
½ cup sugar
½ cup all-purpose flour (2½ ounces)
3 tablespoons (½ ounce) unsweetened cocoa powder
1 tablespoon melted butter, lukewarm
Rum Syrup
2 tablespoons sugar
¼ cup dark rum

Chocolate Cream
9 ounces bittersweet chocolate
  (with cocoa butter content of 50
  percent or more; check the label)
2 cups heavy (or whipping) cream
2 egg yolks
Final Assembly
1½ ounces bittersweet chocolate
About 2 tablespoons unsweetened
  cocoa powder

1. Prepare the génoise: Preheat the oven to 350°. Grease a 9-inch springform cake pan. Line the bottom with parchment or waxed paper. Grease this, then flour the pan.

2. Place the whole eggs and sugar in a mixing bowl; set over simmering water, whisking until the sugar dissolves and the mixture is barely lukewarm—about 100°. Remove from the heat and set in a stand mixer. Beat on high speed until tripled in volume, about 4 minutes.

3. Sift together the flour and cocoa powder. Gradually add to the eggs, beating on lowest speed until not quite incorporated. Add the melted butter and beat for another moment, until barely mixed in.

4. Pour at once into the prepared pan; smooth the top with a rubber spatula. Tap the pan gently on the counter to release air bubbles.

5. Bake in the lower third of the oven until the cake begins to pull away from the sides and the center feels moistly spongy, not liquid, when pressed (do not open the oven before almost baked), 25–30 minutes.

6. Place on a rack to cool for 5–10 minutes. Run a thin knife around the pan to release the cake, then remove the side of the pan. Invert on the rack, remove the bottom, then the paper. Cool completely.

(continued)

One of the dessert trolleys at Le Cygne in Geneva, with the signature Gateau Devidal in the foreground

7. Prepare the rum syrup: Combine the sugar and 2 tablespoons water in a tiny pan; bring to a boil, swirling. Off heat, stir in the rum. Cut the cake into 2 equal layers with a long serrated knife (wrap and freeze one layer for future cake-making). Set one layer, cut side up, back in the springform pan on a round of waxed paper. Paint evenly with the rum syrup.

8. Make the chocolate cream: Break up the chocolate in small pieces and set in a bowl over hot, but not simmering, water. When barely melted (chocolate should be only about body temperature) remove from the heat. Whip 1⅔ cups cream until thickened and fluffy, but not firm enough to mound; it should be slightly liquid. Blend together the remaining ⅓ cup cream and the egg yolks; pour this into the chocolate all at once, then stir lightly but rapidly with a rubber spatula to blend. Pour the whipped cream over this and blend in gently. Scoop the chocolate cream onto the cake; smooth with a spatula. Chill for at least 4 hours (see Advance Preparation).

9. Final assembly: Run a knife around the rim of the pan, then carefully remove the side. Grate the chocolate on the medium holes of a standing grater. Press this gently onto the side of the cake to coat evenly. Sift the cocoa over the top.

Advance preparation: *The génoise base can be made a day ahead of assembling and refrigerated (or weeks ahead and frozen). The cake can be finished through Step 8 up to 48 hours in advance.*

8 SERVINGS

Thurgau Apple Cake

SWITZERLAND

The canton of Thurgau, in northeast Switzerland, is notable for its apples, which appear in cider and a wide range of cakes and tarts. Among the more casual and simple of the baked goods, this light, lemony, slightly sweet cake is easy to make and pretty: a snowfall of sugar dusts overlapping crescents of apple inlaid in a puffed golden batter that rises between the slices.

7 tablespoons (3½ ounces) butter,
   at room temperature
11 tablespoons granulated sugar
4 eggs, separated
⅛ teaspoon salt
1 teaspoon grated lemon zest
2 tablespoons lemon juice

1 cup (5 ounces) all-purpose flour
1 teaspoon baking powder
3 medium-large apples, preferably
   Golden Delicious
Confectioners' sugar
Whipped cream (optional)

Thurgau Apple Cake (sugar-dusted) and caramel-rich Engadine Nut Cake (see page 199 for recipe)

1. Preheat the oven to 375°. Butter a 10-inch springform pan. In the small bowl of an electric mixer, beat the butter with 3 tablespoons granulated sugar until light. Beat in the egg yolks, one at a time; add the salt, lemon zest, and lemon juice (do not worry if the mixture curdles).

2. Beat the egg whites until soft peaks form; gradually beat in 7 tablespoons granulated sugar, whipping until firm. Blend one-third of the whites thoroughly with the butter-yolk mixture; gradually incorporate the remainder with a rubber spatula.

3. Sift the flour and baking powder into the mixture, folding gently. Scoop into the prepared springform pan.

4. Peel, halve, and core the apples. Cut into thin crosswise slices. Arrange them overlapping closely to cover the cake, pressing lightly into the batter. Sprinkle with the remaining 1 tablespoon granulated sugar.

5. Bake in the center of the oven for about 45 minutes, or until a straw or needle poked into the center comes out clean. Cool briefly on a rack, then unmold.

6. Serve the cake warm, lightly sprinkled with confectioners' sugar. Offer whipped cream alongside, if you like.

Serving: *Do not reheat the cake or prepare far in advance, as it will dry out, as do most baking powder cakes. Enjoy it warm and soft as breakfast, brunch, or tea/coffeecake, with or without cream, or with a glass of apple brandy or sherry alongside.*
Option: *This simple coffeecake can withstand plenty of variation: Play with the design of apple slices so that the batter squeezes up between them. Experiment with other fruit—such as peeled peaches, apricots, cherries, or tender pears.*

8 SERVINGS

BAKED APPLE CUSTARD WITH CARAMEL PEPPER SAUCE

GERMANY

Every fall the Hilton International München holds a game festival to celebrate the bounty of its forests—with hare, chamois, red deer, elk, and more. Among the desserts suggested as finales for these specials are rose cream, chestnut mousse, blueberry pancakes, and this tender egg custard topped with a fan of hot apples and doused with a chilled, peppery caramel sauce—a unique complement to the creamy-fruity flan.

Sauce
⅔ cup sugar
½ cup heavy (or whipping) cream
1 teaspoon freshly ground black
   pepper
2 tablespoons Calvados or other
   apple brandy

Apple Custard
4 medium-large Golden Delicious
   apples
3 eggs
1 cup milk
½ cup heavy (or whipping) cream
1 teaspoon vanilla extract
2 tablespoons plus 2 teaspoons sugar
½ teaspoon ground cinnamon

1. Prepare the sauce: Combine the sugar and 3 tablespoons hot water in a small heavy saucepan: let stand a few minutes to moisten evenly. Cook over medium-low heat until the sugar dissolves completely; cover and cook over low heat for 1 minute to be sure all crystals have washed down the sides. Raise the heat and swirl the uncovered pan until the syrup turns medium amber. Remove from the heat and drizzle in 3 tablespoons hot water, keeping clear of considerable splatters. Return to the heat and stir a moment until the caramel has completely dissolved. Add the cream and pepper and simmer for 2 minutes. Cool to lukewarm. Strain through a sieve; add the Calvados. Chill (see Note).

2. Make the custard: Preheat the oven to 300°. With a corer, remove the core and seeds from the apples; then peel and halve them lengthwise. Cut crosswise into thin slices. Arrange 1 apple in an overlapping flower pattern in a shallow gratin or baking dish about 6-inches in diameter. Repeat to fill 3 more dishes.

3. Blend together the eggs, milk, cream, vanilla, and 2 tablespoons sugar. Spoon gently over the apples, distributing evenly. Mix the remaining 2 teaspoons sugar with the cinnamon. Sprinkle evenly over the apples, coating lightly.

4. Arrange the dishes in a roasting pan. Set in the center of the oven and pour in boiling water to reach halfway up the sides of the molds. Bake until the custard has just set in the center, 30–35 minutes.

5. Serve warm with the sauce alongside.

Note: *If the sauce is chilled, the pepper flavor becomes pleasantly pronounced; however, if served at room temperature, it helps retain the appealing warmth of the custard.*

4 SERVINGS

DIALOGUE OF FRUIT PUREES

AUSTRIA

A lengthy, elegant meal at the Rôtisserie Prinz Eugen in Vienna is served with the kind of exquisite attention one would expect from a host of footmen at a royal home—which is what this spacious, darkly handsome trio of rooms is modeled on.

Surprisingly, the free-form "painting" of this stunning, unusually tart palate-freshener seems altogether appropriate in the regal library setting. At a more modest meal than Chef Mitsche's you would probably wish to enjoy the mélange as a dessert. However it is offered, it is imperative that the fruit be in peak condition, as there is no sweetening or additional flavoring. Consider ripe apricots or mangos as alternatives to the peaches, if they are in finer form.

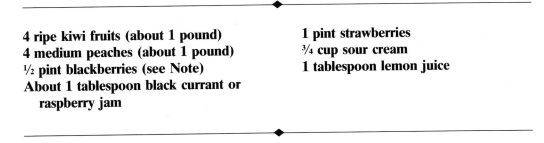

4 ripe kiwi fruits (about 1 pound)
4 medium peaches (about 1 pound)
½ pint blackberries (see Note)
About 1 tablespoon black currant or
raspberry jam

1 pint strawberries
¾ cup sour cream
1 tablespoon lemon juice

1. Remove the kiwi skins with a swivel peeler. Slice the fruit and press through the fine disk of a stainless-steel food mill into a bowl.

2. Drop the peaches into boiling water; return to a boil. Drop into cold water, drain, and dry. Remove the skins and pits. Press through the fine disk of the food mill.

3. Press the blackberries through the disk with 1 tablespoon jam; taste and add more jam if desired. Press the strawberries through the mill into another bowl.

4. Stir together the sour cream and lemon juice. Thin with about 1 tablespoon water to the texture of heavy cream.

5. Spoon about one-quarter of each of the purees and the cream gently into wide plates to make 5 wedge-shaped puddles that almost touch. Shake the plate slightly so that they run together. With a chopstick or wooden skewer, swirl the purees slightly to give them a somewhat marbled appearance; do not mix.

Note: *Mr. Mitsche uses fresh black currants to make the puree, but they are virtually unavailable in the American marketplace.*

This is the kind of dish that will be different every time you make it, depending upon the quality of the fruit. Try for a balance of sweet and sour and contrasting colors. Enjoy the palette of colors and play with the food, dipping, dotting, and marbling at whim.

Advance preparation: *All of the purees can be prepared in advance and refrigerated, covered, in separate bowls.*

4 SERVINGS

Prune Terrine with Sabayon Cream

SWITZERLAND

Although this lacquer-brown loaf of winy prunes and chewy nuts is based on a traditional recipe from an old cookbook ("it has been a Swiss grandmother's dish forever," says Franz Kuhne, executive chef of the Hilton International Basel), this elegant version, graced by a billowy sauce, is suited to the most contemporary dining room. As fragrant as fruitcake, the dessert seems spicy and very rich, even though it is neither. (In the Wettstein Grill where this is featured, a small scoop of cinnamon ice cream completes the picture.) A unique, satisfying sweet that is easy to prepare.

1½ cups dry red wine
1 packet unflavored gelatine
¼ cup sugar
1¾ pounds pitted "tenderized" prunes
¼ cup (1 ounce) shelled unsalted pistachio nuts
¼ cup Armagnac or brandy
⅓ cup (1 ounce) walnuts, chopped

¼ cup (1 ounce) pine nuts (pignolia)
1 navel orange
Sauce
⅓ cup sugar
4 egg yolks
¼ cup dry white wine
¼ cup Armagnac or brandy
1 cup heavy (or whipping) cream

1. Combine ¼ cup water and ¼ cup of the red wine in a cup; sprinkle the gelatine over this and let stand to soften. Combine the remaining 1¼ cups wine with the sugar and prunes in a nonaluminum saucepan; bring to a simmer, stirring. Cover and simmer until tender, about 5 minutes. Add the gelatine mixture and bring to a simmer, stirring gently so as not to break up the fruit. Remove from the heat.

2. Drop the pistachios into a small pan of boiling water; return to a boil. Drain, then rub in a towel to remove the husks. Add to the prunes with the Armagnac, walnuts, and pine nuts. Cut the rind and membrane from the orange. Cut between the interior membranes to section out the pulp; cut into ½-inch pieces. Add to the prunes.

3. Rinse a 9×5-inch glass or ceramic loaf dish with cold water. Pour in the prune mixture. Press down firmly so that the solids are covered by the liquid. Cool completely, then cover and refrigerate for at least 4 hours, preferably overnight.

4. Make the sauce: Combine the sugar and 2 tablespoons water in a small pot and bring to a boil, swirling. Whisk the egg yolks in a bowl to blend well. Whisk in the hot syrup gradually. Set the bowl in barely simmering water and whisk (or use a small portable mixer) until hot and thickened to the consistency of soft whipped cream. Remove from the heat and continue whisking until cooled and pale. Whisk in the white wine and Armagnac. Whip the cream to form soft peaks. Pour the egg sauce over it. Fold together gently with a rubber spatula. Serve at once, or chill, covered, for up to 5 hours before serving.

5. To serve, dip the loaf dish into warm water for 15 seconds; slip a knife gently around the side of the loaf to release it. Invert onto a cutting board. Ladle ¼ cup of sauce onto each dessert plate; tip to distribute neatly. Using a very sharp or serrated knife carefully cut the terrine, placing a slice on each puddle of sauce. Serve at once.

Advance preparation: *The terrine can be prepared a day in advance, the sauce up to 5 hours ahead.*

12 SERVINGS

BERRIES PERFUMED WITH KÜMMEL

FRANCE

Here is one example from the hundreds of problems that arise when converting chefs' recipes for home use: The Food Research Center received a recipe from chef Dominique Michou—"Soup of Berries Perfumed with Kümmel"—that called for four kinds of berries, honey, and Kümmel (caraway liqueur). The directions read: "Heat the Kümmel. Add the honey. Place the fruits in a bowl. Pour the Kümmel onto the berries." We tried to test it by feel, guessing how many it was meant to serve, whether it should be hot or chilled, whether the Kümmel was sweet or dry, what we should substitute for bilberries, whether the strawberries were small wild ones or large cultivated ones, how to arrange the berries, why it was called "soup" with only 4 tablespoons liquid specified. In short: Dieter Hannig came up with his own version.

Later, there was the opportunity to taste the "original" in Strasbourg: Thin slices of fresh figs were pressed against the sides of an enormous balloon glass overflowing with whole strawberries, raspberries, an abundance of passion fruit, and topped with fresh strawberry sorbet, mint leaves, and a julienne of candied orange peel. A soupçon of Kümmel perfumed the accumulated juices. When asked about the recipe we had "tested," Michou explained that it had been inspired by a dessert from the Crémaillère d'Orléans where he had worked previously, and that of course *dishes were different every time you made them, no? Pinning down specifics with a fine chef may be compared to trapping lightning. It is worth the trip to Strasbourg to sample Michou's "Soup" of the day. In the interest of simplicity, Mr. Hannig's version follows—a beautiful, effortless finale.*

½ **pint raspberries**
1 pint strawberries, rinsed and hulled
½ **pint blackberries or blueberries,**
   gently rinsed and tenderly patted

dry (or untouched, if fresh from
   the garden)
¾ **cup Kümmel (see Note)**
¼ **cup honey**

---

1. In each of 4 shallow soup dishes or deep plates arrange the raspberries in a ring around the outer edge. Quarter or halve the strawberries and place them inside the circle; arrange the blackberries or blueberries in the center. (Or place the berries in a single layer in any design that suits your taste.)

2. Combine Kümmel and honey in a small pot; bring to a boil. Spoon ¼ cup of hot liquid over each of the plates of fruit. Cover with plastic; chill 2 hours or more.

Note: *Of the several varieties of dry-to-sweet Kümmel (the word means caraway in German and Dutch), those most frequently sold in the United States are quite sweet.*
Serving/presentation: *Try this clean, light "soup" as an appetizer for a multi-course meal or brunch dish.* Advance preparation *is a must, as some mellowing time must be allowed for the full flavor to develop. An hour is sufficient, about 12 maximum. The longer it stands, the pinker the pale syrup becomes.*

4 SERVINGS

PREVIOUS PAGE: Executive chef Dominique Michou with a typical *menu dégustation* in La Maison du Boeuf in the Hilton International Strasbourg

RECIPES

APPETIZERS

Herbed Shrimp Terrine in Aspic *(Australia)* 219
Marinated Raw Salmon with Cilantro-Green Peppercorn Sauce *(Australia)* 220
Oysters Wrapped in Raw Beef with Horseradish Vinaigrette *(Australia)* 223
Pork, Shrimp, and Vegetable-Filled Rolled Crêpes *(Philippines)* 224
Terrine of Mixed Fresh Mushrooms *(Japan)* 226
Lobster Ravioli with Sea Urchin Sauce *(Japan)* 229
Spiced Red Snapper with Herbs *en Papillote (United Arab Emirates)* 231

SALADS

Shrimp Salad with Cucumbers, Chili, Garlic, Mint, and Lemon Grass *(Thailand)* 232
Hot and Spicy Glass Noodle, Shrimp, and Pork Salad *(Thailand)* 236
Salad of Pepper-Seared Beef Fillet *(Japan)* 241

SOUPS

Squab Consommé with Quail Eggs *(Singapore)* 246
Oyster Consommé with Seaweed Twists *(Australia)* 250
Chicken Broth with Cilantro Wontons *(Thailand)* 252
Thai Soup of Mixed Oriental Vegetables and Shrimp *(Thailand)* 254
Red Bean Soup with Ginger *(Indonesia)* 256
Clear Shrimp Soup with Lemon Grass *(Indonesia)* 258

VEGETABLES, GRAINS, AND PASTA

Asparagus with Thai Sauce *(Thailand)* 263
Stuffed Tofu with Shrimp *(Taiwan)* 264
Roasted Root Vegetable Strips with Caraway *(Australia)* 265
Aromatic Rice with Nuts, Raisins, and Shallots *(Indonesia and Malaysia)* 266
Fried Egg Noodles with Mixed Vegetables *(Indonesia)* 268
Spaghetti Sakura *(Japan)* 270
Spiced Chick-Peas with Fresh White Cheese *(India)* 271

PREVIOUS PAGE: **The floating market at Damnoen Saduak, outside of Bangkok**

SEAFOOD

Shrimp in Coconut-Chili Sauce *(Indonesia)* 277
Shrimp in Papaya Sauce *(Singapore)* 278
Fillet of Sole with Sour Turmeric Sauce *(Indonesia)* 280
Pompano with Ginger Fragrance *(Singapore)* 283
Fancy-Cut Squid Stir-Fried with Asparagus *(Taiwan)* 284
Salmon Fillets with Vinegar Sauce on Diced Vegetables *(Singapore)* 286

MEAT AND POULTRY

Beef Steaks with Mustard Cream *(Japan)* 292
Buffalo Fillets with Pumpkin Sauce and Goat Cheese *(Australia)* 295
Smoked Duck Breast Salad, Javanese-Style *(Indonesia)* 297
Pork Loin with Quince *(Australia)* 298
Stir-Fried Pork and Cashew Nuts *(Thailand)* 300
Hainanese Chicken-Rice Dinner *(Singapore, China, and Taiwan)* 302
Chicken Terrine with Coconut-Chili Sauce *(Indonesia)* 304
Chicken Stir-Fried with Tree Ears and Ginger Julienne *(Thailand)* 307
Chicken and Cashews with Chinese Mustard Greens *(Taiwan)* 310
Braised and Grilled Chicken in Coconut and Javanese Spices *(Indonesia)* 312

DESSERTS

Cucumber-Ginger Granita *(Indonesia)* 314
Strawberry and Yogurt Mousse with Grand Marnier Sauce *(Singapore)* 315
Guava Fritters and Mango with Blueberry Tofu Cream *(Taiwan)* 316
Dried Fruit Bread *(Australia)* 321
Dampers *(Australia)* 323

HERBED SHRIMP TERRINE IN ASPIC
(Adaptation of Potted Moreton Bay Bugs)
AUSTRALIA

Of the many colorfully-named crustaceans that inhabit the waters in and around Australia, Moreton Bay bugs, a species of small, flat marine lobster, are among the sweetest and meatiest. They are served in an appetizer terrine at the darkly handsome Victoria's, a sleek restaurant done up in silken dusky plum, the luxury dining room of the shining new Hilton International Brisbane. The terrine is thickly studded with the tender lobster meat, dotted with yellow and white chopped egg, cilantro leaves, red bell pepper, chive snippets, and sharpened with green peppercorns. The dressing, similar in color and texture to the terrine, is mellowed with creamed Caboolture cheese, a cottage cheese made in an area north of Brisbane that is renowned for its dairy products. Serve one of the many fine Australian Chardonnays to complement the fresh-flavored dish.

---

6 cups fish stock (see page 326)
3 eggs
2 small red bell peppers (about 7 ounces)
Salt
1 ¼ pounds raw medium shrimp in the shell (see Note)
5 teaspoons unflavored gelatine
⅓ cup dry vermouth
½ cup firmly packed cilantro leaves (no stems)
1 tablespoon drained green peppercorns, coarse-chopped

3 tablespoons thin-sliced chives
Dressing
1 pound firm, sweet-ripe tomatoes, peeled, seeded, and cut into tiny dice
¼ cup sliced chives
¼ cup cider vinegar
Salt and pepper
¾ cup olive oil
⅓–½ cup small-curd creamed cottage cheese

---

1. Gently pour the stock through a sieve lined with several layers of dampened fine cheesecloth, being careful to avoid any sediment that may have accumulated. Simmer the stock, skimming as necessary, until reduced to 2¾ cups.

2. Meanwhile, place the eggs in a pan of boiling water. Simmer for 12 minutes. Place under cold running water, tap the shells to crack them all over; leave to cool completely.

3. Boil the red peppers for 2 minutes, turning occasionally. Halve, seed, and cut into tiny dice; spread on paper towels. Peel and halve the eggs; chill briefly.

4. Bring 4 cups water and 1 tablespoon salt to a boil; add the shrimp. Cover and bring to a simmer over highest heat. Remove from the stove; drain. Remove the shells, halve each shrimp lengthwise, then remove the veins as needed. Cut each half into 2–3 pieces. Chill. *(continued)*

5. Sprinkle the gelatine over ½ cup water; let stand 2–3 minutes. Combine with the hot stock over moderate heat. Stir to dissolve completely, scraping the bottom. Stir in the vermouth. Add salt, as desired. Pour ½ cup of the aspic into a narrow terrine mold about 11 x 3½ x 3½ inches. Chill briefly until set, but not hard. Chill the remaining aspic until cold, but not set.

6. Meanwhile, cut the cilantro leaves into coarse slivers. Mince the egg and yolks separately, then combine in a bowl with the red peppers, cilantro, green peppercorns, and chives. Gently toss to mix.

7. Spread half the egg mixture on the aspic layer, then press down firmly with a spatula. Arrange half the shrimp on this, then the remaining egg mixture, then shrimp, leaving a small margin of uncovered aspic all around. Slowly pour the remaining liquid aspic into the terrine. Chill for at least 12 hours.

8. Make the sauce: Combine the tomatoes, chives, and cider vinegar. Add salt and pepper to taste. Stir in the olive oil; chill.

9. To unmold, dip the base of the mold in hot water, then run a knife gently around the edge to release the loaf. Invert onto a cutting board, rapping sharply. Immediately return to the refrigerator for a few minutes to firm any melting exterior aspic.

10. Add the cottage cheese to the tomato dressing, adjusting the quantity to taste. With a serrated knife, gently cut the shrimp loaf into 1-inch slices. Serve the sauce alongside.

Note: *If you have access to cooked, picked crayfish, it is a superior substitute for Moreton Bay bugs. Fourteen to 15 ounces of cleaned meat should be used. Or you can substitute rock lobster tails, or a combination of shellfish, all cut in smallish pieces.*

8–10 SERVINGS

Marinated Raw Salmon with Cilantro-Green Peppercorn Sauce

AUSTRALIA

Adapted from the silky appetizer developed by Gerard Taye, executive chef of the Hilton International Adelaide, this sumptuous course requires waiting time for its preparation, but little labor. The tangy, pleasantly biting sauce is laced with cilantro leaves and green peppercorns, and bound with tomato, mustard, and grapeseed oil. If this pale, delicate oil is not easily found, substitute another mild, light oil, such as sunflower seed.

2-pound salmon fillet (with skin)
¼ cup coarse kosher salt
1 teaspoon coarse-ground black
 pepper
½ cup thin-sliced shallots
1 cup cilantro (fresh coriander)
 leaves, lightly packed (1 medium
 bunch)
½ cup dry, light white wine
Sauce
1 tomato (5–6 ounces), peeled,
 seeded, and chunked

1 tablespoon drained green peppercorns
⅓ cup cilantro leaves (no stems),
 lightly packed
1 tablespoon Dijon mustard
¾ cup grapeseed oil
Lemon juice
Cilantro sprigs

1. With tweezers or fine pliers, pull out any small bones that may remain in the salmon fillet. Trim off any fatty or membranous areas. Place the fish skin side down in a heavy plastic bag. Rub with the salt to coat evenly. Close the bag; refrigerate for 12–24 hours, turning once.

2. Rinse the fish well. Pat dry. Coat with the pepper. Spread half the shallots and half the cilantro in a dish just large enough to hold the fish. Place the salmon on top, skin side up. Cover with the remaining shallots and cilantro leaves. Pour over the wine; cover closely with plastic.

3. Refrigerate for 2 days, turning occasionally.

4. Remove from the marinade and scrape clean. Wrap tightly in plastic and refrigerate until serving time.

5. Prepare the sauce: Combine the tomato, green peppercorns, cilantro leaves, and mustard in the container of a blender or processor. Whirl to form a smooth puree, scraping down the sides. With the motor running, gradually add the oil; whirl until as smooth as possible. Add lemon juice to taste. Chill until serving time.

6. Cut the salmon on the bias into thin slices. Either lay flat, or coil to form rose shapes, as they do at the restaurant. Ladle a pool of sauce alongside. Garnish with cilantro sprigs.

8–10 SERVINGS

Oysters Wrapped in Raw Beef with Horseradish Vinaigrette

AUSTRALIA

This trendy recipe comes from chef Herbert Franceschini of the Hilton International Brisbane, who devised the hors d'oeuvre with one of the local specialties, rock oysters. These are so small that one can be wrapped in beef, set on a lettuce nest, crowned with marinated pear slivers—and still fit into a teaspoon, which is the way the appetizer is presented in Australia, five per serving. For the United States, where almost all oysters are larger, we suggest placing the rosy beef packages on pale leaves of Bibb set into oyster shells.

The lush oysters and soft meat topped with the crisp pear and crunchy sesame create an effect that is mainly textural, with a flavor far less complicated than the list of ingredients indicates.

5–6 ounces fillet of beef
3–4 tablespoons fresh-grated horse-radish (or prepared horseradish in vinegar, squeezed dry, to equal that amount)
1 tablespoon minced shallot
2 teaspoons Dijon mustard
2 tablespoons raspberry red wine vinegar (or simple red wine vinegar)
1 tablespoon dry white wine or vermouth
½ teaspoon pepper

¼ teaspoon minced garlic
⅔ cup light olive oil
Salt
20 medium oysters on the half-shell
1 or 2 heads of Bibb lettuce (20 leaves)
2 medium firm-ripe pears; cored, peeled, and cut into finest julienne about 1½ inches long
2 tablespoons hulled white sesame seeds
20 cilantro sprigs

---

1. Set the beef fillet in the freezer until not quite frozen solid (timing will depend on your freezer). Meanwhile, prepare the dressing: Combine 2 tablespoons of the horse-radish, the shallot, mustard, vinegar, wine, pepper, and garlic in a small bowl; whisk to blend. Gradually whisk in the oil. Add salt to taste. Set aside.

2. Remove the oysters from their shells and set them aside in a strainer. Rinse the shells; set 4 on each of 5 serving plates and place a lettuce leaf, trimmed to fit if necessary, in each shell. Toss the pears with a scant ¼ cup dressing and set aside. Stir the sesame for a few minutes in a skillet over low heat, until golden.

(continued)

3. Let the frozen beef stand for a few minutes, then cut into 20 thin slices (see Note). Place between layers of plastic wrap and flatten with the side of a cleaver or meat pounder. Distribute the remaining horseradish (1–2 tablespoons, to taste) over the meat. Place an oyster in the center of each slice; roll up neatly. Set in a shell.

4. Top each roll with a little of the pear julienne; drizzle the remaining dressing over each. Top with the sesame, then a cilantro sprig.

Note: *For paper-thin slices, cut the fillet on a meat slicer or have the butcher do this, then pack between sheets of plastic.*
Serving/presentation: *Although finger food, these appetizers are a bit unwieldy for stand-up service. Instead, offer them as a first course to be enjoyed while seated. Try them for brunch, with sparkling wine. In Australia the packets are tied with chives.*
Advance preparation: *The dressing can be prepared and the meat cut, pounded, layered between sheets of plastic, and refrigerated.*

5 SERVINGS AS AN APPETIZER

PORK, SHRIMP, AND VEGETABLE-FILLED ROLLED CRÊPES
(Lumpia Ubod)
PHILIPPINES

The Filipino wrappers (lumpia) *that here enclose crisp shreds of iceberg lettuce, shrimp, and pork bits (although sweet fillings are as common as savory) are soft as chamois and pale as ivory. The size and shape of smallish egg rolls, these traditional delicacies are dipped into a lightly thickened, sweetened soy sauce and topped with paper-thin fried garlic chips.*

1 cup (5 ounces) all-purpose flour
²⁄₃ cup (3 ounces) cornstarch plus 1½ tablespoons for sauce
3 eggs, beaten to blend
About 3 tablespoons peanut oil
¾ pound raw shrimp in the shell
5 ounces whole, drained bamboo shoot (see Note)
¾ pound pork loin, cut into ¼-inch dice
⅓ cup fish stock (see page 326), or bottled clam juice

½ teaspoon granulated sugar
3 tablespoons lightly packed brown sugar
2 tablespoons soy sauce
1²⁄₃ cups chicken stock
½ head of garlic, peeled and thin-sliced (about ⅓ cup)
About 3½ cups thinly slivered iceberg lettuce

1. With a whisk, blend together the flour and ⅔ cup of the cornstarch. Gradually whisk in 3¼ cups water, then add the eggs.

2. Heat a 6-inch crêpe pan (or nonstick skillet) over moderately low heat. Brush with a little oil. Remove from the heat. Taking a scant 3 tablespoons (1 ounce) portion at a time, ladle the batter into the center of the pan; immediately tip and shake to distribute the thin batter evenly. Cook only until the sides of the *lumpia* separate from the pan, about 30 seconds (do not brown or turn). Gently transfer to a working surface, baked side down. Continue making pancakes, stirring the batter often, and placing each crêpe separately on the work surface (see Advance Preparation).

3. Shell and devein the shrimp as needed; cut into ½-inch pieces. Cut the bamboo shoot into fine dice (there should be 1 cup). Heat a wok over high heat; pour 1 tablespoon oil around the rim and tip to distribute. Add the pork and toss for 2 minutes. Add the bamboo and toss for 2 minutes longer. Add the fish stock; toss for 1 minute. Add the granulated sugar; toss for another minute or so, until the liquid has evaporated. Add the shrimp; toss just until pink. Set aside to cool.

4. Prepare the sauce: Blend together the remaining 1½ tablespoons cornstarch and the brown sugar. Add the soy and mix; add the chicken stock. Heat 2 tablespoons oil in a small saucepan. Add the garlic and cook over moderately low heat until golden-brown. Remove with a slotted spoon and reserve. Pour the stock mixture into the oil and stir over moderate heat until thick. Pour into a small bowl and cool to room temperature.

5. Spread a heaping tablespoon of lettuce shreds in the center of each pancake; spread a heaping tablespoon of the filling over this. Turn in the sides slightly over the filling, then roll each gently but firmly. Place seam side down on a serving dish. Accompany with the garlic and sauce.

Note: *Canned, whole bamboo shoots are available in all Oriental groceries and some supermarkets.*
Serving/presentation: *Either pick up the rolls with your fingers and dip in the sauce. Or place a few on each diner's plate and pour the sauce alongside, then eat with fork and knife. Sprinkle over garlic slivers to taste. If you have time to spare, tie each roll with a length of narrow scallion. The* lumpia *work beautifully as a summer buffet or hors d'oeuvre. Or for a spa-style lunch, serve 4 rolls per person along with a clear soup and fresh fruit mélange.*
Advance preparation: *You can prepare the pancakes 3–4 hours ahead, stack them, and cover with a paper towel. Stuffing and sauce can be made far ahead and brought to room temperature. The rolls can be assembled about 2 hours in advance.*

36–40 ROLLS

TERRINE OF MIXED FRESH MUSHROOMS
(Terrine Forestière)
JAPAN

Light but sumptuous, this creamy beige terrine is thickly studded with woodsy mushrooms in different shapes and sizes and punctuated by confetti of chives, parsley, and tomato dice. The work of Siegfried Jaeger, executive chef of the vast Tokyo Hilton International, this is the type of dish favored by Japanese diners in the primarily Western restaurant of the hotel, the Imari: top quality ingredients presented in more-or-less traditional guise, no fussy garnishes, direct but subtle flavors.

8 fresh medium *shiitake* (4–5 ounces), stems removed and reserved for another use, caps cut into ½-inch slices

¾ cup dry white wine

¾ pound medium button mushrooms, cleaned and quartered

12 fresh small morels (about 1 ounce), halved and rinsed (see Note)

¼ pound small oyster mushrooms, trimmed of heavy stems

2 envelopes unflavored gelatine

1½ cups heavy (or whipping) cream

1 teaspoon salt

¼ teaspoon white pepper

¼ cup thin-sliced chives

¼ cup minced parsley

2 tablespoons Cognac, Armagnac, or brandy

2 medium plum tomatoes, peeled, seeded, and diced (about ½ cup)

⅛ teaspoon nutmeg

Relish

5 medium plum tomatoes, peeled, seeded, and diced (about 1¼ cups)

Minced chervil or parsley

Salt and pepper

Lemon juice

1. Combine the *shiitake* and ½ cup of the wine in a nonaluminum pot; bring to a boil, covered. Simmer gently until soft, about 10 minutes. Add the button mushrooms, morels, and oyster mushrooms. Cover and simmer until tender, about 8 minutes. With a slotted spoon transfer the fungi to a mixing bowl. Boil the liquid to reduce to 2 tablespoons. Add to the mushrooms.

2. Combine ¼ cup water with the remaining ¼ cup wine in a small pan; sprinkle the gelatine over this; let soften for a few minutes. Add ½ cup cream and the salt and pepper and bring to a simmer, stirring, over low heat. Pour this over the mushrooms. Add the remaining 1 cup cream, the chives, parsley, Cognac, tomatoes, and nutmeg. Set in a larger bowl of ice water. Stir often until jelled.

3. Line a mold of about 4½-cup capacity, preferably about 3½ by 11 inches (or use a 9 × 5-inch loaf pan—although the slices will be less trim), with plastic wrap. Pour in the mushroom mixture. Cover and chill for at least 4 hours or up to 24.

4. Meanwhile, prepare the relish: Combine the plum tomatoes, chervil, and salt, pepper, and lemon juice to taste. Refrigerate until serving time.

5. Let the terrine stand at room temperature for about ½ hour before slicing. Serve with the tomato relish spooned alongside.

Note: *If you cannot find fresh morels, use dried ones. Select 12 tiny ones, soak in warm water until barely cuttable, a matter of a few minutes. Trim off any heavy base parts. Halve the mushrooms lengthwise and rinse lightly. Add to the cooking liquid at the same time you would the fresh morels—and expect a stronger, smokier flavor.*

8–10 SERVINGS

Lobster Ravioli with Sea Urchin Sauce

JAPAN

Thin rounds of pasta (wonton wrappers) filled with herbed lobster sail in a golden, buttery sea urchin cream sauce. The Japanese who dine at the polished, low-key Imari restaurant in the Tokyo Hilton International are partial to lobster, pasta, and sea urchin—which is why chef Siegfried Jaeger assembled this dish. It exemplifies the style of luxurious Western haute cuisine, Japanese-tinged, that comes from his kitchen. Interestingly, although eating habits in that country are based on awareness of the lightest, healthiest foods, this extraordinarily rich dish is a best-seller. Perhaps it represents the quintessential indulgence?

Lobster Ravioli
2 lobsters (each about 1¼ pounds; see Note)
1½ tablespoons butter
1 tablespoon minced shallots
3 tablespoons dry white wine
½ cup heavy (or whipping) cream
1 tablespoon minced parsley
1 tablespoon minced basil
Salt and pepper
36 wonton wrappers (see Note)
1 egg beaten with 1 teaspoon water

Sauce
6–10 sea urchins (to equal about ⅓ cup; see Note)
2 tablespoons softened butter
1 teaspoon minced shallot
¼ cup dry white wine
⅓ cup dry vermouth
1¼ cups heavy (or whipping) cream
Salt and white pepper
About 2 teaspoons lemon juice
Basil sprigs for garnish

1. Prepare the lobster ravioli: Place the lobsters on a rack over boiling water; cover and steam for 8 minutes (or drop into boiling water for 5). Cool until you can handle them, then cut off the claws where they attach to the body. Twist off the tail; snip the cartilage with a scissor; remove the meat and chop coarsely. Cut the claws from the attached joints; halve these joints lengthwise, pull out the meat and chop coarsely. Jiggle the small pincers on the claws to pull out the cartilage; then crack the heavy shell with the dull side of a knife or a lobster cracker. Gently withdraw the lobster meat; cut in neat lengthwise slices. Set aside in a saucepan with liquid from the steamer to partly cover (refrigerate if you won't be using within the hour).

2. Heat the butter in a skillet over moderate heat. Add the shallots and toss for a minute. Add the wine and cream and boil until thick, or reduced to about ⅓ cup. Add the chopped lobster meat and toss to coat. Off the heat, add the minced herbs. Season with salt and pepper. Cool and chill. *(continued)*

3. Place 18 wonton rounds on a work surface. Place a heaping tablespoon of the lobster filling in the center of each. Paint the surrounding area with the beaten egg. Place a round of the remaining dough on top of each, press to flatten the filling a bit, then tamp down the edges to seal tightly.

4. Prepare the sauce: Combine the sea urchins in a sieve with 1 tablespoon of the softened butter. Press through, scraping every bit into a bowl. Heat the remaining 1 tablespoon butter in a small skillet. Add the shallot; stir over low heat to soften slightly, but not to color. Add the wine and vermouth; boil to reduce to ⅓ cup. Add the cream; boil, stirring, to reduce to 1 cup. Season with salt and white pepper. Remove from the heat.

5. Slip the ravioli into a large, wide pan of boiling water. Simmer until soft, about 2 minutes. Meanwhile, heat the lobster claw meat. Drain the ravioli carefully. At once warm the cream reduction; remove from the heat and stir in the sea urchin butter and the lemon juice to taste.

6. Place 3 ravioli on each of 6 plates, spoon over the sauce, garnish with the drained lobster meat and basil sprigs.

Note: *If you do not wish to cook and clean lobsters, you can buy 6–7 ounces (or 1⅓ cups) fresh chunk lobster meat and forgo the garnish of claws.*

Round skins for boiled dumplings, about 3½ inches in diameter, are available in Oriental noodle shops. Square wonton skins the same dimension are easily found in many supermarkets and all Oriental groceries. To use these, cut circles with a 3½-inch cookie cutter or impress a circle on each skin and cut off the excess.

Cleaned fresh sea urchin roe can be purchased in some sushi shops and in Japanese markets, neatly packed in little boxes. If you buy the sea urchin in the shell from a fish market, be sure that there is no off odor and that the spines stick straight out, porcupine-fashion, with no flattened or tired looking stickers. Holding a sea urchin with a pot holder or in a thick glove, insert the point of a scissor into the soft depression in one side, cutting out a round lid of about one-third of the shell. Gently rinse the interior, then carefully spoon out the ochre roe, avoiding the dark membranes. The roe should be rather strong smelling, but sea-like, not unpleasant.
Advance preparation: *The ravioli (or just the filling, if you like) can be made up to a day ahead, then tightly wrapped in a single layer, and refrigerated.*

6 SERVINGS AS A FIRST COURSE

Spiced Red Snapper with Herbs en Papillote

UNITED ARAB EMIRATES

At the Hilton International Dubai, a rainbow of fishes from the Persian Gulf takes pride of place at the Al Fahidi Grill, under the guidance of executive chef John Dolan. Among the various best-sellers on the menu are Poached Paupiette of Baby Hammour, *Fried Fillet of* Gaian, *Baked Fillet of* Khen, Moussa *with Apricot Essence,* Beiah *with Fine Vegetables, and* Nagrour *with Pistachio. Fortunately, there is also a fish we can recognize: red snapper.*

Unlike most red snapper recipes, this one is hot, spicy, with a big, brash bouquet. The intensity makes it a more likely candidate for a first course than a main one, but if you double the quantity of fish (two fillets in each pouch), keeping spicing the same, it will be fine in the latter role. Do not be put off by the long list of ingredients, which are simply seasonings, called collectively, "Arabic Spice" in recipes from the area.

½ teaspoon pepper
½ teaspoon ground cumin
½ teaspoon ground paprika
¼ teaspoon ground cloves
¼ teaspoon ground cinnamon
¼ teaspoon ground coriander
¼ teaspoon salt
Large pinch of ground cardamom (optional)

1 lime
1 tablespoon minced cilantro leaves
¼ cup minced parsley
1 tablespoon olive oil
4 red snapper fillets with skin (each about 3 ounces; or substitute another firm, white-fleshed fish)
2 tablespoons butter, cut into small pieces

1. Preheat the oven to 400°. Combine the pepper, cumin, paprika, cloves, cinnamon, coriander, salt, and cardamom. Peel the zest from the lime and cut into very fine julienne; add ½ teaspoon to the spices. Squeeze the juice from the lime and add to the spices with the cilantro and parsley. Rub the fish with the mixture, dividing evenly.

2. Cut four 11-inch circles of aluminum foil. Paint with the oil. Place a fillet, skin side down, on one-half of each circle, dot with the butter; fold the other half of the foil as you would a turnover. Crimp together the edges.

3. Set the packets on a baking sheet in the lower third of the oven. Bake for 8 minutes, until just cooked through. Serve the remaining lime zest in a tiny dish, so each diner can sprinkle some on his fish as he cuts open the aromatic package.

Serving: A cucumber-yogurt sauce alongside is a refreshing complement. You might follow this with a room-temperature vegetable entrée, then a cooling fruit dessert.

4 SERVINGS AS A FIRST COURSE

SHRIMP SALAD WITH CUCUMBERS, CHILI, GARLIC, MINT, AND LEMON GRASS
(Goong Plar)
THAILAND

A traditional hot/aromatic Thai dish interpreted by Viboon Roongrojpanawan, sous-chef of the Hilton International Bangkok. This easy assembly embraces the primary flavors of the sultry country: garlic, chili, lemon grass, nam pla, and seafood—which should be just barely cooked through in this recipe. Fiery and garlicky is the Thai rule of thumb and the strength on which the balance depends, so you might wish to experiment to the hilt for the full impact. But if you are timid-tongued, cut down on chili and garlic.

32 medium shrimp in the shell (about 2 pounds)
3 medium stalks lemon grass (see Note)
¼ cup *nam pla* (see Note)
¼ cup lemon juice
1 tablespoon minced garlic

About 1 tablespoon fine-sliced hot green chili-pepper (such as Cayenne), seeds and veins removed
⅓ cup sliced small shallots
½–1 cup small mint leaves (removed from stems), plus a few sprigs
2 medium-small cucumbers
4 ripe plum tomatoes, quartered lengthwise

1. Pour boiling salted water over the shrimp in a wide skillet. Bring to a simmer. Remove from the liquid and let cool just until they can be handled. Remove the shells; devein shrimp, as necessary. Cool completely. (But do not chill.)

2. Meanwhile, remove the upper leaves, heavy outer leaves, and thick base tip from the lemon grass. Halve the stalks lengthwise, cut out any tough core, then cut across into the finest slices possible. (You should have ⅔ cup.) Mix together ⅓ cup of the lemon grass, the *nam pla*, lemon juice, garlic, 2 teaspoons of the sliced chili-pepper, the shallots, and ½ cup mint leaves, crushing lightly with a spoon. Add the shrimp and taste for seasoning, adding mint and lemon grass if not sufficiently assertive.

3. Rinse the cucumbers and remove alternating strips of peel lengthwise. Cut into very thin slices. Arrange these around 4 serving plates. Divide the salad into the centers. Top with tomato wedges and mint sprigs.

Note: *Long stalks of greyish-green fresh lemon grass can be found in Southeast Asian markets and some supermarkets. It adds a subtle, inimitable lemon pungency.*

Nam pla *(Thai) or* nuoc mam *(Vietnamese) is a thin, fermented sauce somewhat like light soy sauce with a fishy taste. It is easily obtained in all Oriental markets.*

Serving and presentation: *With half the quantity of shrimp and dressing, this becomes a versatile appetizer. Or prepare a large platter and serve the dish buffet-style for a party.*

Do not be tempted to serve the dish cold, as the shrimp becomes too firm and the strong flavors of the sauce quickly overpower the delicate seafood if left to marinate.

In Bangkok unpeeled cucumbers are cut in thinnest lengthwise strips, to make wide ribbons. These are folded in half to form a flower-like design around the central shrimp. If you have a mandoline or other slicing device to cut the full length of the cucumber in thin slices, present the salad this way.

4 SERVINGS AS A MAIN COURSE; 6–8 AS AN APPETIZER

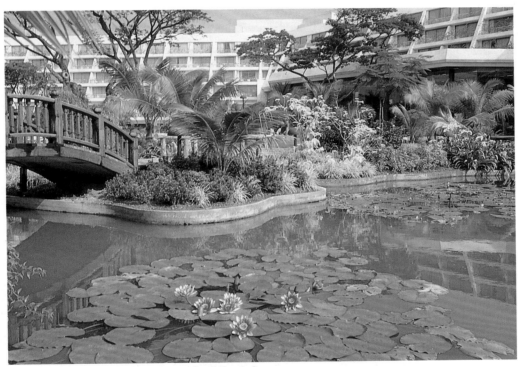

The water lily pond at the Hilton International Bangkok

Floating atop the world's largest water lily species, in the pond of the Hilton International Bangkok, is a selection of the flavors that characterize Thai cuisine: mint, kaffir lime leaves, chili-peppers, shallots, and stalks of lemon grass. In the center, presented as it is made at the hotel's garden restaurant Suan Saranrom, is the pungent Shrimp Salad with Cucumbers, Chili, Garlic, Mint, and Lemon Grass.

HOT AND SPICY GLASS NOODLE, SHRIMP, AND PORK SALAD
(Yum Woon Sen)
THAILAND

This pretty salad seems right at home in the sunny three-story, glass-walled restaurant, Suan Saranrom, which looks into the tropical foliage of Nai Lert Park, in which the Hilton International Bangkok is located. Rattan chairs upholstered in apricot and pistachio, and peach-clad young serving personnel (commented one American: "waitresses from paradise in the City of Angels," as Bangkok is known) add to the breezy summerhouse effect.

Although an ordinary family dish in Thailand, this will be quite out-of-the-ordinary for Westerners: a clean, assertive, hot and citrusy taste (there is no oil in the dressing) in a tumble of feathery yellow celery leaves, crunchy black tree ears, red chili-pepper slivers, chewy-translucent glass noodles, crisp and strong onion, scallion, and shallot mellowed by sweet pork and shrimp.

---

6 large dried tree ears (about ¾ ounce; see Note)

7–8 ounces glass noodles (see Note)

3 tablespoons vegetable oil

¼ cup dried shrimp (see Note)

¾ pound coarsely ground or hand-chopped lean pork

⅓ cup sliced small shallots

1 medium onion, cut in quarters and thin-sliced

⅓ cup thinly sliced scallion greens

⅔ cup small, tender inner leaves of celery

⅓ cup *nam pla* (see Note)

⅓ cup lemon juice

1½ teaspoons sugar

4 teaspoons (or to taste) minced hot red chili-peppers, such as Cayenne (seeds removed)

½ cup cilantro leaves

Lettuce

16 cooked shrimp, peeled and deveined as needed

---

1. Soak the tree ears in about 2 cups warm water until supple, about 15 minutes. Rinse lightly; cut off any knotty parts. Slice in thin strips. Pour boiling water over the noodles and let stand until tender to taste, about 5 minutes. Snip the noodles into 3–4-inch sections with scissors. Drain, rinse in cold water, and drain again.

2. Heat 2 tablespoons of the oil in a small pan; fry the dried shrimp until just crisp. Drain and reserve. Heat the remaining 1 tablespoon oil in a medium pan; toss the pork over high heat until cooked through. Drain.

3. Combine the shallots, onion, scallion, celery leaves, and tree ears in a bowl and toss. Mix together the *nam pla,* lemon juice, and sugar; add to the bowl along with the drained noodles, dried shrimp, pork, and 1 tablespoon chili slivers, or to taste. Cut the shrimp in thirds, diagonally, reserving 4 whole ones for garnish. Toss and season heavily, adding the remaining 1 teaspoon chili, and lemon juice and *nam pla* to taste. Toss with the cilantro leaves.

4. Arrange on a lettuce-covered platter or 4 plates. Serve at room temperature, garnished with the whole shrimp.

Note: *Tree ears (also called* cloud ears, wood ears, mo-ehr, *black fungus) are thin, black and grey dried mushrooms that have little flavor but a delightful textural crunch, once soaked.*

Glass noodles (also called silver noodles, cellophane noodles, bean threads, and mung bean noodles) are white, thin dried strands sold in oval skeins, like yarn. Depending upon which brand you buy, the skeins will weigh 2, 3⁷/₈, or 8 ounces.

Miniature brined, dried shrimps are a pungent seasoning used in Chinese and Southeast Asian cooking. Comparatively large ones provide more flavor and meatiness.

Nam pla *(called* nuoc mam *in Vietnamese) is a thin, fermented sauce somewhat like soy, but with a fishy flavor.*

All the above are available in most Oriental markets.

Serving and presentation: *Scallions that have been trimmed, then brush-cut and soaked in ice water make a festive garnish, as do petal-cut red and green chili-peppers.*

Advance preparation: *This salad works beautifully if prepared up to a day ahead of time, since it retains its colors and texture. The flavors blend and become slightly more assertive. Serve chilled, or allow to return to room temperature, as desired.*

4 SERVINGS AS A MAIN COURSE

OVERLEAF: **Hot and Spicy Glass Noodle, Shrimp, and Pork Salad on a plate of folded palm leaves, wreathed in fragrant ceremonial garlands**

Salad of Pepper-Seared Beef Fillet

JAPAN

Gentle murmurs are the loudest sound in the Imari of the Tokyo Hilton International, where the Japanese take dining seriously—and often silently. Raw dishes, particularly the bright-rose beef of Kobe and Matsuzaka (astronomically-priced and much in demand in fine restaurants) are among the favored first courses and luncheon dishes. This unusual treatment from executive chef Siegfried Jaeger produces meltingly soft slices that are black-seared without, raw within, somewhere between carpaccio and pepper steak in appearance. (It is imperative that you buy beautifully marbled prime beef for this dish, or the point is lost.) Ever-so-slightly dressed with a soy-sesame sauce and combined with a trio of leaves of various chicories, the flavors are Oriental-Italian.

2 tablespoons black peppercorns
1½ teaspoons coarse kosher salt
1¼ pounds trimmed prime beef fillet
1 tablespoon vegetable oil
2 tablespoons lemon juice
3 tablespoons olive oil
Additional salt and pepper
1½ tablespoons chicken or beef broth
1½ tablespoons soy sauce
1 tablespoon rice or white wine vinegar
¾ teaspoon sugar

2 teaspoons dark (Oriental) sesame oil
2 medium Belgian endives, trimmed, rinsed, and dried
1 small head of radicchio (about 3 ounces), trimmed, rinsed, and dried
1 very small head of imported curly chicory (*chicorée frisée*) or ½ bunch watercress, trimmed, rinsed, and dried

1. Crush the peppercorns with a heavy knife blade or meat pounder. Combine with the salt. Coat the fillet with the mixture. Let stand at room temperature for 1–2 hours.

2. Heat a skillet until very hot over moderate heat. Add the vegetable oil, then the beef. Sear over highest heat until just browned all over (do not cook through). Cool, then chill, lightly covered, for several hours or longer.

3. Mix together the lemon juice and olive oil with salt and pepper to taste. In a separate bowl blend the chicken broth, soy sauce, vinegar, and sugar. Add the sesame oil.

4. Toss the cleaned salad leaves with the olive oil dressing; divide onto 4 serving plates. Cut the meat into about 24 slices and arrange alongside the greens, very slightly over-lapping. Stir the sesame dressing and spoon evenly and sparingly over the meat.

Serving and presentation: *Several alternative presentations are part of the repertoire of the Imari: The beef may be accompanied by a few thin onion rings and watercress alone, or by several asparagus and* kaiware *(daikon or Oriental radish sprouts). Or paper-thin slices of completely raw fillet (no pepper, no searing) are served as an appetizer with 4 endive spears, a small bunch of cress in the center, and long chive stalks atop each beef slice.*

4 SERVINGS AS A MAIN COURSE; 8 AS A FIRST COURSE

A World Tour, Luxury Class, at the Tokyo Hilton International

In the world's most populous city, living space is minuscule, home kitchens often nonexistent, and dining out simply a way of life. In fact, eating in Tokyo is both a recreational and business pastime, with as many secretaries and salesmen likely to spend a large chunk of their paychecks on dinners and afternoon cakes and tea as bank presidents. After a time of postwar isolationism and relative conservatism, the last 15 years or so have seen a volcanic rise in the variety of cuisines and number of restaurants in the city.

At the Tokyo Hilton International, three to four thousand meals are served daily, about 85 percent of these to Japanese. Among the world's most demanding and knowledgeable diners, and contrary to the ideas of most Westerners, the Japanese also happen to be among the most open-minded and adventurous eaters on the globe. With the city itself and the hotel in particular as indications, the desire for new tastes seems boundless. Provided that service is absolutely exquisite (and the Tokyo Hilton International is frequently cited as having the finest in Asia), presentation superb and never fussy, and ingredients beyond compare, money is no object.

Because no single approach could begin to satisfy the Japanese appetite for the unknown, the food outlets at the Tokyo Hilton International, already diverse in styles, offer ever-changing menus based on a score of national cuisines and on strictly seasonal products. The Imari, for example, the hotel's showcase of creative haute cuisine, adds a spate of weekly specials—such as meals by foreign chefs, desserts of American cherries, oyster dishes, fresh caviar—to its already extensive Continental menu. With caviar prices ranging from 7,800 yen ($52, at the time of writing) for a tasting portion to 12,000 ($80) for a regular one, you can imagine the willingness to eat well. The immaculate service and individual attention in this hushed and spacious room are the kind allotted to royalty. The display cases of museum-quality porcelain ware and the picture-perfect seafood still-life wheeled to each table as a show-and-tell of the day's specials set the tone for a dining room that is serious about food: Rounds of raw beef without equal are barely touched with sesame and soy; a custard of vibrant orange bell peppers set on velvet avocado cream has no distracting interference from outside seasonings; tissue-thin packets of lobster meat float in a pale ochre pool of sea urchin butter; crisp-sautéed red snapper is decked with fresh *shiitake* slivers; fanned slices of lean duck breast with a black currant reduction are escorted by stuffed baby turnip halves; a symphony of fresh fruits and fruit sorbets follows; then, bonbons set on wildly misting dry ice that engulfs the diners in the theatrical finale—for restaurant is theater in Japan.

Meanwhile, around the corner, the Dynasty room is in full swing. This classical Chinese restaurant with 200-plus dishes that represent the regions of China has a kitchen

A quartet of culinary gems from an elegant *kaiseki ryori* dinner presented at the Musashino restaurant in the Tokyo Hilton International

staff that does the same. As if such a range were not sufficient, constantly shifting menu schemes for specialties—such as cold noodle dishes, seasonal shellfish, new liqueurs—keep the insatiable diners on their toes.

The casual coffee shop Sakura offers a mixed menu of hamburgers, spaghetti Bolognese, Indian chicken samosas, Indonesian *nasi goreng*—then takes a monthly detour to Switzerland, Thailand, Hungary, a world of Hollywood soda fountain extravaganzas, or an American Thanksgiving.

The clubby, British St. George Bar in the lobby, handsomely turned out in green marble, brass, leather, and plushy dark chairs, is the regular home of roast beef, other carvery items, and salads, but at a moment's notice can become the backdrop for an Oktoberfest or Swiss food buffet.

In the morning, the sleek, modern Marble Lounge in the lobby, its colossal, dappled cream columns creating intimate conversational oases, is the scene of the power breakfast. By noon the popular Continental lunch buffet, its platters refreshed at such a rate that each guest is virtually the first to serve himself, takes over the same comfortable area. At 2:30 the place is peacefully packed with women—from teenagers to dowagers, who in a two-hour period may pack in (without adding a centimeter to their delicate frames) a pastel profusion of 80 cakes, 20 monumental platters of French pastry, and 50 quarts of ice cream from the Austrian-style dessert buffet. Come early evening, snacks and drinks take over (in that order, for Japanese request first food, then alcohol), and the lively lobby keeps hopping into the night.

Behind the scenes, spread out in numerous private rooms, are the banquets, meals usually containing six or more courses—fresh goose liver from France, lobster from North America, and Japan's fillet of beef are *de rigueur*—whether for a fashionable society ball or wedding (both the hotel's Shinto and Christian chapels are booked for an average of eight marriages every day).

Who better to oversee the execution of this multinational carnival than Siegfried Jaeger, an Austrian chef who grew up speaking French, German, and English, moved from Switzerland and England to a position on round-the-world cruisers, landed in Bombay, then took on Singapore, Manila, Seoul, and, finally, opened the mammoth food operations of the award-winning new Tokyo Hilton International? While familiar with a wide range of cuisines, he is particularly at ease with Japanese aesthetics, sensibilities, and work ethics. "I don't like messy or fussy food, and neither do the cooks I work with," he explained. "Nor do I like wasting time. Once you show a Japanese cook how to do a recipe—that's it. It will never vary. You don't need to check; you can relax, knowing it will always be produced as agreed." The lanky chef lopes around the kitchen, towering over most of the staff and grazing all the door frames, even as he stoops to accommodate. "Nowhere have I encountered such an appreciation of quality as here in Japan. Every fruit and vegetable is examined and evaluated," he marvels. Bespectacled and trimly mustachioed, his imperial fingers calmly designating various tasks throughout the kitchen, he looks more the part of a chief surgeon or scientist in a secret laboratory than the man in charge of a food staff of 550.

Perfection is the password at this smoothly-run operation, and no detail is too small to warrant attention. Each food outlet has a training manual that specifies virtually every move to be made by each employee—and the reasons why. Eight steps are required to explain the proper way to change a tablecloth in The Imari; four pages describe the correct serving of various desserts—a page each for cakes, pastries with sauces, ice creams and coupes, and fruits. The service of tea requires two pages, and French bread must be sliced on a 45° angle, four to five centimeters thick, while German rye needs a vertical cut only one centimeter wide.

Imagine the scrutiny to which a sumptuous Japanese restaurant in the only American-run hotel in the city is subjected, how flawless it must be! The Tokyo Hilton's Musashino—in effect a collection of restaurants housed in a single, gleaming space, the areas divided by brass-edged screens of bevelled glass—provides the lover of true Japanese dishes with happy choices: The sushi room, where ingredients and execution are religiously pristine, vies with the finest in the country; famed Matsuzaka beef and peak-quality vegetables are cooked to order with balletic precision on the grills of the *teppan-yaki* room; the tempura area opposite, graced with an arrangement of the day's most stunning produce, offers a seasonal cast of characters that may include minute eggplants and okra pods, plumpest baby shrimps and gingko nuts, tiny shining fish, and the mushrooms of the moment. For a menu composed from the gamut of raw, deep-fried, simmered, grilled, vinegared foods, and soup and pickles that make up the more formal *kaiseki-ryori* dinners, move to the small dining rooms and tatami rooms for memorable feasts, each course displayed in unique dishes by kimono-clad beauties as graceful as the porcelain, glass, and ceramic accoutrements. Among the parade of unique presentations are a free-form, ice-filled carved crystal bowl (too heavy to lift with one hand) that bears a chrysanthemum on which rest furled petals of raw tuna and red snapper; squares of silver flying-fish enclosing slices of fragrant *matsutake* (pine mushrooms) are sandwiched between scented cedar shingles (the packet is untied at the table, its aromas unleashed for the guest) and served with shoots of pale-pink fresh ginger; an iced Champagne coupe holds a puree of sweet-sharp Asian pear crowned with emerald cubes of *suizen-ji nori* (lake algae), baby bay scallops, carved cucumber ovals and red-tipped white radish shreds—and on and on as long as you enjoy the flow of perfectly executed art that streams from the kitchen of chef Matsuda.

Squab Consommé with Quail Eggs

SINGAPORE

A hallmark of quality in many fine dining rooms, this deep-flavored amber essence (developed by chef Peter Knipp of Shanghai when he was a sous-chef in Singapore) is a luxury to be savored as one would fine wine. The tender squab breast and poached quail egg must be prepared at the last minute, to the exact degree of doneness, or they will cloud and cool the sparkling liquid. For connoisseurs and comfortable cooks.

3 squabs (about 2¼ pounds total
   weight)
1 celery rib, sliced
1 medium carrot, sliced
½ small onion, sliced
Top green part of 1 small leek,
   sliced
10 peppercorns, roughly crushed

1 small bay leaf
1 teaspoon fresh thyme
2 egg whites
2½ quarts cold, *very* strong homemade chicken stock (see Note)
Salt and pepper
2 tablespoons butter
12 quail eggs

1. With a boning knife, cut the breast meat from the squabs; remove and discard the skin. Trim any fat or membranes from the meat; cover tightly and refrigerate. Chop the rest of the birds into small pieces.

2. Combine the squab pieces in a stockpot with the celery, carrot, onion, leek, peppercorns, bay leaf, and thyme. Whisk together the egg whites with a few cups of cold chicken stock. Add to the stockpot with the remaining stock. Whisk to blend very thoroughly.

3. Bring to a simmer over moderately low heat. As soon as the stock begins to simmer, turn the heat so low that only an occasional bubble floats to the surface. Do not stir or in any way disturb the foamy crust that floats atop the stock or the essence will not be clear. Keep at this level, uncovered, for about 3½ hours. The flavor should be pronounced and full.

4. Carefully remove the crust. Ladle the soup gently through a cheesecloth-lined sieve. (You should have about 6 cups of consommé.) Cool; cover, and refrigerate.

5. At serving time, skim off all fat particles; place the consommé over low heat. Set 6 shallow, wide soup plates in a warm oven to heat. Season the breast pieces with salt and pepper. Melt the butter in a medium skillet over moderate heat. Sear the squab for 1 minute on each side, to medium-rare. Place between towels for about 5 minutes.

6. Meanwhile, tap a quail egg sharply with a knife to break it in half. Drop into a small cup or dish, then slip into a skillet of not-quite-simmering water (or preferably, light stock). Continue until all the eggs are in the water. They will be poached in a matter of minutes, as you finish the slicing of the breasts.

7. Cut each piece of breast meat in long, narrow slices. Arrange in a fan in a heated soup plate. Place 2 quail eggs in the dish. When all the squab and eggs have been arranged, bring to the table. Immediately divide the hot consommé over each, about 1 cup per person.

Note: *The excellence of this intense consommé depends upon the quality of the stock, which should be strong and fat-free.*

6 SERVINGS

The famed rock oysters of Australia—petite, buttery, plump—star in this pristine soup, here set on a background of black coral. Should you be in the country of the dish's origin when you're preparing it, use 3-year-old Sydney rock oysters, as chef Herbert Franceschini specifies (recipe appears on next page)

Oyster Consommé with Seaweed Twists

AUSTRALIA

Sparkling fish stock is garnished with plump oysters, leaves of Chinese cabbage and spinach, tomato dice, and ginger julienne in this Nouvelle-Oriental presentation from Herbert Franceschini of the Hilton International Brisbane. (Should you prepare the dish on its home turf, use three-year-old Sydney rock oysters, as the chef specifies.) Puff pastry sticks swirled with seaweed, candy-cane fashion, are the unusual accompaniment.

4 cups cold fish stock (see page 326)
1 very small leek, white part only, well rinsed
½ medium celery rib
1 small carrot
1 cilantro stalk with root
2-inch knob fresh ginger, peeled
6 peppercorns
3-ounce fish fillet, cut into 1-inch pieces
2 egg whites

1 bay leaf
2 cloves
⅛ teaspoon dried tarragon
Salt
1 small Chinese cabbage
12 very small spinach leaves
12 large oysters, shucked with their liquor reserved
⅓ cup dry white wine
1½ tablespoons finest ginger julienne
1 tomato, peeled, seeded, and cut into tiny dice

1. Reserve ½ cup fish stock. Cut the leek, celery, carrot, cilantro and knob of ginger into chunks. With the motor running, drop these into a processor container with the peppercorns. Chop to a coarse texture. Add the fish fillet; process to a medium texture. Add the egg whites; whirl to a puree.

2. Combine the puree with the 3½ cups fish stock in a nonaluminum saucepan, blending thoroughly. Add the bay leaf, cloves, and tarragon. Bring to a simmer over low heat. Reduce the heat to its lowest point. Cook for 15–20 minutes, until the "crust" begins to crack and separate from the sides of the pot. Very gently lift the crust from the soup. Carefully ladle the consommé through a sieve lined with dampened cheesecloth. Add salt, as desired.

3. Remove the smallest central leaves from the cabbage. Rinse, then trim as needed, to yield 12 small leaves. Combine with the reserved ½ cup stock in a small nonaluminum saucepan. Simmer gently, covered, until just tender, 4–5 minutes. With a slotted spoon transfer the cabbage into 4 heated soup bowls. Divide the spinach leaves over these.

4. To the stock in the saucepan add the oysters, their liquor, and the wine. Poach over low heat until just plumped, 1 minute. Strain the liquid into the consommé. Arrange 4 oysters in each bowl. Bring the consommé to a simmer; divide into the bowls.

5. Arrange the ginger julienne and tomato dice over each. Serve with the Seaweed Twists (recipe follows).

Advance preparation: *The stock can be prepared and clarified in advance.*

4 SERVINGS

Seaweed Twists

Traditional puff pastry sticks are dramatically swirled with green-black seaweed.

½ **pound prepared puff pastry (see Note), chilled**
1 egg blended with 1 tablespoon water

1 sheet *nori* **(dried, pressed seaweed), about 7½ × 8½ inches (see Note)**

1. Preheat the oven to 400°. Roll the pastry on a lightly floured surface to form a 16 × 9-inch rectangle. Brush with the egg. Cover half the pastry with the *nori*, then fold over the remaining half of the dough to enclose it neatly. Press lightly to seal.

2. Using a pastry cutter held against a ruler, trim the 3 open edges of the dough to form an 8-inch square. Using the ruler to form straight lines, cut a strip about ⅜ inch wide. Gently twist to form a neat spiral. Place on an ungreased heavy baking sheet.

3. Repeat until you have cut all the dough to yield about 21 twists, setting them quite close together, but not touching. Set in the center of the preheated oven. Bake for 11–12 minutes, until golden. Cool completely before serving.

Note: *Store-bought or homemade puff pastry can be used.*
    Nori is available in all Oriental markets and many specialty stores.

MAKES 21

CHICKEN BROTH WITH CILANTRO WONTONS

THAILAND

When Thailand's government undertook a program of agricultural expansion in Chiang Mai, in the north of the country, the Hilton International Bangkok featured an herb promotion to familiarize Thais with Western herbs, and foreigners with the Eastern ones.

Sous-chef Martin Gerber developed this fresh first-course soup that he felt would be intriguing to both Oriental and Occidental diners. Light and clean, the pastel flurry of vegetable julienne contributes crunch and sweetness, the silky wontons add a burst of assertive cilantro (also known as fresh coriander, Chinese or Mexican parsley) and an edge of red pepper hotness.

1 skinned and boned chicken breast half (about 4 ounces), cleaned of all membrane and tendon
2 tablespoons sliced cilantro leaves
1 teaspoon soy sauce
Salt, pepper, and ground red pepper
16 wonton wrappers, about 3½ inches square (see Note)
1 tablespoon all-purpose flour blended with 2 tablespoons water

1 small carrot
Trimmed pale green and white part of ½ small leek
1 medium tender inner celery rib, strings removed
1 small turnip
4 cups chicken stock
Cilantro sprigs for garnish

1. Cut the chicken breast into small pieces, then chop medium-fine with a cleaver or large knife. Combine in a bowl with the sliced cilantro, soy sauce, and salt, pepper, and ground red pepper to taste.

2. Place about 1 teaspoon of the chicken mixture on each of the wonton skins. Paint the edges with the flour mixture and fold to form a neat triangle. Paint the 2 points of the triangle that are farthest apart, then paste together to form a bishop's hat shape.

3. Clean the carrot, leek, celery, and turnip, then cut into fine julienne. You should have a total of about 1½ cups.

4. Drop the vegetables and wontons into a large pot of boiling water. Cover and return to a boil on highest heat. Uncover and boil another minute or so, until just tender. Drain.

5. Meanwhile, bring the chicken stock to a boil. Divide the wontons and vegetables into 4 soup bowls, then ladle in the stock. Decorate with the cilantro sprigs.

Note: *Wonton skins this size are available in many supermarkets and all Oriental groceries.*
Serving/presentation: *If you prefer, simply pour the drained vegetables and wontons into the hot broth, then serve in a tureen.*

4 SERVINGS AS A FIRST COURSE

Thai Soup of Mixed Oriental Vegetables and Shrimp
(Gaeng Lieng)
THAILAND

Viboon Roongrojpanawan, who prepared this unusual soup, explained that it is well known to Thais, who relish it at home and in a few fine local restaurants, but that it seldom appears on a hotel menu. Happily, the Hilton International Bangkok, where Mr. Roongrojpanawan is sous-chef, is an exception, and the light, mellow soup (neither oniony nor fishy, as one might expect from the ingredients) has become a popular round-the-clock item there. A colorful pick-me-up, the broth is at once salty, sweet, and peppery, the vegetables crisp and diverse, the shrimp barely poached and tender—and the whole subtle concoction takes just minutes to prepare.

⅓ cup dried shrimp (see Note)

½ cup peeled whole small shallots

1 teaspoon white pepper

2 teaspoons fish paste (optional; see Note)

4 cups unsalted chicken broth

½ pound hard orange-fleshed squash (such as acorn, sweet dumpling, pumpkin, butternut, *kabocha*), peeled, seeded, and cut into ½-inch dice (to equal 1 cup)

About 10 ears baby corn (see Note), cut into 1-inch lengths (to equal ¾ cup)

6 ounces (1 medium) angled loofa (see Note), peeled and cut into ½-inch pieces

2–3 ounces small mushrooms, cut into ½-inch dice (to equal ¾ cup)

2–3 ounces yard-long beans (see Note), cut into 2-inch lengths (to equal ¾ cup)

2 tablespoons *nam pla* (see Note), or to taste

½ teaspoon sugar

About 3 ounces small-leafed spinach, stems removed and rinsed (to equal 1 cup packed leaves)

8 medium raw shrimp (6–7 ounces), peeled and halved diagonally

1 cup lightly packed small basil leaves (about 1 large bunch), stems removed

1. Whirl the dried shrimp to a medium texture in a food processor. With the motor running, add the shallots. Whiz to a medium puree. Add the white pepper, fish paste, and ½ cup chicken broth; continue processing for about 1 minute.

2. Add the puree to the remaining 3½ cups chicken broth in a large saucepan. Bring to a boil, skimming. Add the squash; boil for 1 minute, skimming. Add the corn, loofa, mushrooms, and beans; boil until barely tender, 2–3 minutes.

3. Add the *nam pla* and sugar. Stir in the spinach, raw shrimp, then the basil leaves. Remove from the heat at once and serve.

Note: *Dried, salted shrimp are available in almost any store that carries Oriental ingredients. Choose comparatively large ones.*

Shrimp paste, also called shrimp sauce, terasi, *or* balachan, *is a greyish-pink fermented puree of shrimp and salt, produced thoughout Southeast Asia. Although strong-smelling, its effects are subtle.*

Baby ears of ready-to-eat corn are sold in jars and cans in Oriental groceries and many supermarkets. If fresh ears of baby corn are obtainable, cook them before adding to the soup.

Loofa, luffa, Chinese okra, or sze gwa is a tapered, lightweight sharply ridged green vegetable 1–2 inches in diameter and 8 inches to 2 feet long. It is found in all Oriental vegetable markets and has a mild, grassy-fresh flavor. Peel the ribs before cutting up. Or substitute 4 ounces small zucchini.

Yard-long beans are pencil-slim, flexible dark to medium-green beans (and yes, yard-long) available in most Oriental markets. If you cannot obtain them, substitute firm, thin string beans.

Nam pla (nuoc mam, fish's gravy, fish sauce) is a thin, brown fermented sauce similar to light soy, but with a fishy taste.

4 SERVINGS

RED BEAN SOUP WITH GINGER
(Sop Kacang Merah)
INDONESIA

Executive chef Detlef Skrobanek of the Jakarta Hilton International explained that in all regions of Indonesia red beans appear in salads, soups, and desserts. However, purees such as the following are not traditional; solid ingredients remain intact in soups, and are not removed from the liquid. The flavors here are typically betawi (the adjective used to describe something from Jakarta) derived from the word Batavia, as the city was called by the conquering Dutch.

A smooth, slightly thick consistency and rose-beige color will invite the curious diner, but few will be prepared for the mysterious aroma and truly exotique taste of this silky puree which hints of frankincense and myrrh, ginger and chili, coconut and cedar. The most powerful and unusual ingredient, galingale (see Note below), may seem a bit "medicinal" to those not yet familiar with the cooking of Southeast Asia. Do not overdo it—or the fiery peppers.

2 slices (quarter-size) dried galingale (see Note)
1½ tablespoons peanut oil
¾ cup chopped onion
¾ cup chopped shallots
¼ cup tightly packed *chopped* fresh ginger
2 teaspoons minced garlic
2¼ cups cooked, drained red kidney beans

3⅓ cups chicken stock
½ cup unsweetened coconut milk (see Note)
Salt and pepper
1 tablespoon finest julienne of hot red chili-pepper (such as Cayenne), seeded and deveined
1 tablespoon very fine fresh ginger julienne
4 sprigs cilantro

1. Combine the galingale and ½ cup water in a small pot; simmer for 2 minutes. Cover; let stand for at least 15 minutes. Drain and reserve the liquid; chop the root.

2. Heat the peanut oil in a saucepan; add the onion, shallots, chopped ginger, and garlic. Cook over low heat until soft, but not browned—10–15 minutes—stirring often. Add 1¾ cups kidney beans to the saucepan; toss for 2 minutes. Add the stock, galingale, and reserved liquid.

3. Bring to a boil, then turn down heat and simmer, covered, until vegetables are very soft—about 15 minutes.

4. With a slotted spoon, transfer the solids from the saucepan to a blender or processor. Puree until smooth, gradually adding the liquid. Press through a sieve.

5. Return the soup to the saucepan; add the coconut milk and simmer for 5 minutes. Season with salt and pepper.

6. Distribute the remaining ½ cup beans among 4 small bowls. Ladle in the soup. Sprinkle a few chili and ginger julienne over each (serve the remainder separately in a small dish). Garnish each bowl with a coriander sprig.

Note: *Galingale, galangal, laos root, lang uas or lengkuas is a word used to describe several rhizomes of the ginger family that are popular in Asian cooking. It is available fresh in some Southeast Asian markets, but is more likely to be found in dried form (in powder or dried slices) in most Oriental markets. Its powerful and unusual flavor suggests ginger, camphor, and cardamom.*

Coconut milk is available in canned or bottled form in stores that carry ingredients from South America or Asia. If you cannot buy it, make your own, following the directions on page 325.

Serving: *The potent bouquet of flavors is too intense to consider as a main course but serves brilliantly as a meal opener. Follow with grilled fish or poultry.*

Advance preparation: *The soup can be made ahead and reheated.*

4 SERVINGS

CLEAR SHRIMP SOUP WITH LEMON GRASS
(Sop Pelangi Pagi)
INDONESIA

A sparkling example of chef Detlef Skrobanek's marriage of Asian ingredients to the techniques of European haute cuisine. The name of the soup in Bahasa, the primary Indonesian language, is "rainbow of morning"—and a glance will tell you why: curled peach-colored shrimp, pearly lavender and green lemon grass stalks, pale yellow ears of baby corn, and sharp-cut tomato strips in a shining broth, the whole as bright and as natural as a bird-of-paradise. The flavors, while unfamiliar to some Western palates, are fresh and innocent, soft as a breeze.

½ **pound medium-large raw shrimp in the shell**
1-pound red snapper, filleted (bones and head reserved; see Note)
1 small carrot, peeled and cut into thick slices
1 very small leek, cleaned and cut into thick slices
2 medium garlic cloves, peeled
1 lemon grass stalk, upper leaves cut apart from bulb (see Note)
2 egg whites

1 bay leaf
About ¼ teaspoon Tabasco or other chili-pepper sauce
2 teaspoons tamarind concentrate or paste (see Note)
Salt and pepper
4 ears baby corn (see Note)
2 medium tomatoes, peeled, seeded, and cut into thin strips or diamonds
12 basil leaves

1. Remove and reserve the shrimp shells; devein the shrimp. Clean any gills and innards from the fish. Rinse the bones, head, and shrimp shells and combine in a pot with 4 cups water. Simmer gently, uncovered, for 20 minutes. Add the shrimp; barely simmer for 1 minute. Remove the shrimp and set aside for later; strain the stock. If there is more than 3¼ cups, simmer to reduce to that amount. Set in ice water to chill.

2. Cut the fish into small pieces. With the motor running, drop the carrot, leek, and garlic into a processor; chop to a coarse texture. Add the fish fillet; whirl to a medium-fine texture. Mince the upper part of the lemon grass; blend with the egg whites, bay leaf, and Tabasco. Mix a few spoons of the cold stock with the tamarind; add this to the egg white mixture, then blend into the fish puree.

3. Whisk together the fish mixture and stock to blend. Bring to a simmer over low heat. Reduce the heat to its lowest point (no bubbles should rise) and cook until the "crust" begins to crack and separate from the sides of the pot, 15–20 minutes.

4. Gently remove crust and ladle liquid through a cheesecloth-lined sieve. Season with additional Tabasco and salt and pepper to taste. Reheat to boiling.

5. Meanwhile, trim the lemon grass bulb, then carefully quarter lengthwise. Cut the shrimp and corn in diagonal ¾-inch slices. Arrange with the tomato and basil in 4 small, heated soup bowls. Pour in boiling liquid and serve at once, with the lemon grass.

Note: *Sea bass or another smallish, lean fish can be substituted for the red snapper, if desired.*

Long stalks of stiff, grey-green fresh lemon grass, found in Southeast Asian markets and some supermarkets, add an inimitable lemony pungency. Although sliced, dried lemon grass (takrai or sereh) can be substituted for the chopped upper leaves (in approximately the same quantity as fresh), it is lighter and more tea-like in flavor. Add a bit of lemon zest and juice with the dried, if fresh is not obtainable.

Dark tamarind concentrate or paste, its flavor reminiscent of very sour apricots, is sold in Middle Eastern, Southeast Asian, and some Caribbean shops, and can be added directly to foods. Other forms of the fruit must have pods, seeds, and fibers removed before being used. If solid or dry, the pulp must be mixed with a little boiling water to remove fibers and to soften to the texture of fruit butter.

Ready-to-eat ears of baby corn are sold in jars and cans in Oriental groceries and many supermarkets. If fresh ears of baby corn are obtainable, cook them before adding to the soup.

Presentation: *For a more elaborate look (although a bit difficult to eat tidily) arrange as in photograph.*

4 SERVINGS

Hilton International Bangkok:
The East Through Rose-Colored Glasses

Vending snacks in the rural floating market of Damnoen Saduk, a half-day excursion outside of Bangkok

Outside: careening three-wheeled motorcycle-carriages called *tuc-tucs*, steaming air, a marketplace overflowing with vendors hawking edibles from snakes to lotus seeds, golden temples alongside shanties, bustling boulevards, clogged *klongs* (canals that comprise the secondary transportation system of Bangkok), sharply beeping high-pitched horns, miniature spirit houses alongside every building— even gas stations, heavy pollution, a sprawling crazy-quilt of slums and palaces. Inside: a soft-toned dream of endless space; silence save for the gentlest plashing of waterfalls, the delicate jingle of a bell swinging from the sign carried by a handsome pastel-clad young page, alerting guests to phone calls as they sip tangerine juice in the marble lobby or exotic coolers in the cushioned lounge.

A five-story architectural gala of soaring atriums and sunlit dining areas, two central halls the size of rice fields, terraced interior pools shining with a rainbow of Oriental fish, the Hilton International Bangkok forms a crescent around manicured Nai Lert Park. A botanist's and hedonist's dream, this is a green oasis of frangipani, jasmine, weeping fig, papyrus, the Royal water lily (the world's largest), rose apple, mangosteen, and almost every other kind of fruit and flowering tree that will grow in the country. The scent of omnipresent orchids wafts through the cooled air of open corridors. The decor is modified Thai: subdued silks cover low banquettes; an airy teak *sala* (an ornately carved gazebo with a peaked roof) occupies a corner of the lobby where one can relax to a chamber ensemble playing Bach, or stretch out to people-watch, for this luxurious space houses a rich cross-section of Eastern and Western faces.

This is a theater of hospitality, a fulfillment of the fantasy that blossoms with the mere phrase "the kingdom of Thailand," a place where one expects royal treatment. Here is the idealization of the East, a tamed version of the wild, an armchair traveler's hopes come to life. To keep the show in shape, a cast of 645 players tends to the 342 rooms and food and drink outlets (polishing the marble, cleaning the brass fittings on the silky teak banisters, and generally tidying the public areas requires a 24-hour staff of 20). One thousand roses are arranged each day, along with uncountable orchids. Twenty-odd ice carvings are fashioned in the same period of time, and 90 pounds of fruit are turned into exquisite sculptures: Gardenias are made from watermelons, tulips from turnips, dragon boats from papaya. Pummelo segments arranged in spirals with petal-cut pineapple pieces overflow wooden baskets and banquet displays. Napkins are folded into pleated and swirled swans and angular artichokes that adorn the buffets and cradle the silver finger bowls in which rose petals float.

The food maintains the tone: Muted Thai specialties, nippy with hot-pepper, aromatized with lemon grass, sweet with baby garlic and tender new ginger, are the rule in the tropical Suan Saranrom (garden restaurant) of the hotel, where water trickling down a wall of ferns forms a backdrop for the buffet of glistening-fresh dishes and sculpted fruits and vegetables. (In the outside world the food, sensational in another way, is most often breathtakingly chili-laced and richly redolent of fermented fish sauce and healthy doses of raw garlic, onion, and shallot.)

It is French cuisine that graces Ma Maison, a serene, stylized representation of an elegant Thai home. A glass wall abuts the garden, admitting moonlight through the tossing palms or a view of sun-struck butterflies—all hidden in this green enclave from the tumultuous city beyond. A taste of the untamed may sneak into the classical menu, such as a bevy of Thai game birds—wild pigeon broth with foie gras croutons, wild duck with juniper brown sauce, or orange-braised hill doves—but the preparation will not jar the cultivated European palate. Asparagus arrives with velvety hollandaise or herbal vinaigrette—or a musky Thai sauce with undertones of smoky fish and pungent native lime leaves. The tart young green tamarind makes an appearance in subtly mellowed form, as ice cream.

Foods from both worlds are heaped in profusion alongside the free-form, palm-encircled garden pool for the nightly buffet. Torches flicker in the sultry dark; ice by the ton serves as a base for the display of some 18 barbecue candidates, from skewered local straw mushrooms and lobsters from the Gulf of Thailand to cervelat sausage and New Zealand lamb. A hot stand features spicy Thai soups and fragrant noodles dishes—as well as baked potatoes with all the trimmings. Condiments run the gamut from garlic toast, through Oriental pickles, to pummelo segments, while the salad bar ranges from Chinese cabbage to radicchio. Desserts, cooled by shining ice sculptures, may be as European as cream puffs or *Sachertorte,* or as Thai as *ruam mitr,* a popular sweet of vivid green and pink jellies and fruits swimming in coconut milk.

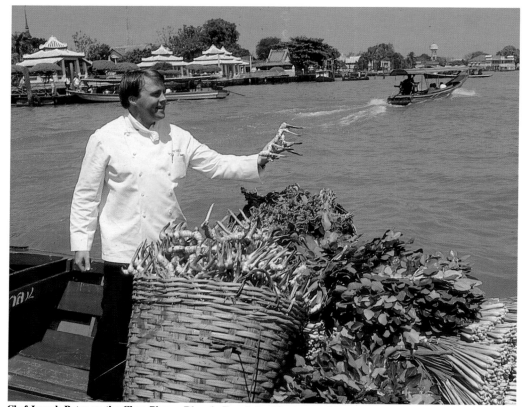

Chef Joseph Peter on the Chao Phraya River in Bangkok with a cargo of lemon grass

The two cultures are presented in refined essentials—discreet and luxurious—everywhere in the hotel . . . or almost everywhere. At a far corner of the compound, near the back entrance, is the shrine of a spirit goddess Tuptim (Pomegranate), who is visited daily by many of the hotel employees and others on whom she has bestowed favors, or who hope for the same. Here, in glorious Technicolor, are a jumble of offerings: heaps of rice, corn, dumplings, (even sandwiches), smoking incense, lotus buds, figurines, and hundreds—probably thousands—of giant male fertility symbols tied with shocking pink and chartreuse scarves. Stacked like logs in a woodpile amid the growth of tangled vines and jasmine wreaths, they contrast dramatically with the stream of white Mercedes that glides in and out of the parking lot alongside.

ASPARAGUS WITH THAI SAUCE

THAILAND

Chiang Mai is a center for the arts—wood carving, painting, umbrella and parasol fabrication—and for a developing agricultural program. The asparagus from the area are green and delicate, like those available in the United States. The unusual sauce— meaty, fishy, buttery, citrusy, herbal, salty—is quite uncharacterizable. Although it looks creamy and innocently pale tan, it is very concentrated and intense in flavor. Derived from a Thai sauce for steamed chicken, it was first altered by a Japanese chef, Otaki, then subsequently adapted by the kitchen staff of Ma Maison at the Hilton International Bangkok. There, the asparagus are offered with a choice of vinaigrette and hollandaise sauces, as well, for those with more traditional tastes.

---

2 cups strong veal or chicken stock
5 dried kaffir lime leaves (see Note)
¼ cup finely grated fresh ginger
3 tablespoons butter
3½ tablespoons Vietnamese or Thai soybean paste (see Note)

¼ cup lemon juice
1 teaspoon *nam pla* (see Note)
¼ teaspoon white pepper
1½ pounds slim asparagus (40 spears), trimmed and peeled

---

1. Boil the stock in a small saucepan to reduce to ½ cup. Soak the lime leaves in warm water to cover. Meanwhile, blend together the ginger with 3 tablespoons water, pour into a sieve, then press hard with a spoon to extract the ginger juice (you should have 2 tablespoons).

2. Melt the butter in a small pan over low heat. Stir in the soybean paste; set aside. Cut the lime leaves into thin strips and add them to the stock; then add the ginger juice, lemon juice, *nam pla,* and pepper. Simmer until reduced to ½ cup. Remove from the heat. Stir in the butter mixture.

3. Cook the asparagus in a large skillet of salted water until just tender. Drain, then spread on a towel to dry. Cut into 2–3-inch diagonals. (Do not chill.) Arrange on serving plates.

4. Pour the warm or room temperature sauce into a small dish or sauceboat. Pour very sparingly over the asparagus.

Note: *Strange and wildly aromatic kaffir lime leaves* (makrut, daun djeruk purut) *which are sold dried, in cellophane packages (or fresh, if you are very fortunate) can be obtained in stores that handle Southeast Asian products.*

Fermented soybean paste from Thailand or Vietnam, a thick, but pourable salt-sweet brew, will be available in the same places as lime leaves, as will nam pla *(also called* nuoc mam, *fish sauce, or fish's gravy), which will also be found in any store that carries Oriental groceries.*

Serving and presentation: *In Bangkok, at Ma Maison, the asparagus are served in long spears with sauces ladled alongside, in traditional European fashion. However, we found it more practical to cut up the asparagus Oriental-style, which also alerts diners to their non-Western seasoning.*

4 SERVINGS AS A SALAD OR APPETIZER COURSE

STUFFED TOFU WITH SHRIMP

TAIWAN

Chefs Yu Wen-Shen and Huang Hsien of the Hilton International Taipei worked together on this version of a Chinese classic that is light and restrained—but releases a powerful perfume of ginger, chilis, and cilantro as you spoon hot oil over the assembled ingredients. Although quick and easy to make, the visual impact is considerable: white tofu rectangles swimming in dark soy sauce are topped with balls of pink shrimp and shreds of red chili, yellow ginger, scallion, and frilly cilantro leaves.

10 ounces medium-small raw shrimp in the shell
1 egg white
⅛ teaspoon salt
Pepper
1 pound medium tofu (also called regular or Japanese tofu) in one block (see Note)
2 tablespoons Chinese dark soy sauce (see Note)

1 medium scallion green, cut into thin 2-inch strips
1 tablespoon very fine julienne-cut fresh ginger
1 teaspoon very fine julienne-cut hot red chili-pepper (such as Cayenne), ribs and seeds removed
16 cilantro sprigs
¼ cup peanut oil

1. Shell the shrimp and set aside 8 of them. Mince the remainder. Whisk the egg white lightly to break it up; measure one half of it, then discard the rest. Blend with the minced shrimp, salt, and pepper.

2. Cut the tofu into 8 rectangles by first halving the block lengthwise, then cutting in 4 crosswise. With a melon ball cutter or teaspoon, scoop a well in the center of each piece to go about halfway through (see Options). Mound a heaping teaspoon of the shrimp filling in each well. Set on a dish to fit on a steamer rack.

3. Place the dish in the steamer over boiling water. Cover and steam for 5 minutes. Set the whole shrimp alongside the tofu; cook for 1–2 minutes longer, until pink. (Drain liquid from the plates if there seems to be an excess.)

4. Spoon the soy sauce onto a heated serving dish. Carefully transfer the tofu to the dish. Set a shrimp on each. Sprinkle with the scallion, ginger, and chili; top with the cilantro. Heat the oil in a small pan; pour evenly over all (beware of splatters).

Note: *The freshly made tofu blocks available in Oriental groceries will have more flavor and delicacy than the packaged varieties—although these will do nicely, as well.*
　Chinese dark, thick, or black soy sauce is available in all Oriental markets and many supermarkets.
Advance preparation: *The dish can be readied through Step 2 and the vegetables julienned, then all refrigerated until 10–15 minutes before serving time.*
Options: *The small balls scooped from the tofu can be steamed alongside the tofu blocks—or nibbled by the cook.*

SERVES 4 AS A MAIN COURSE; 8 AS AN APPETIZER

ROASTED ROOT VEGETABLE STRIPS WITH CARAWAY
AUSTRALIA

Although considerably simplified from chef Herbert Franceschini's original presentation in which a medley of shaped vegetables were set on a trellis of puff pastry, the flavors here are much the same. Colorful and earthy-sweet, this casual version of an elaborate dish is, nevertheless, attractive and unusual. The recipe was developed as an accompaniment to the Buffalo Fillets with Pumpkin Sauce and Goat Cheese (page 295), served at the Hilton International Brisbane.

4 medium-small beets (about 1 pound, weighed without leaves)
1 small rutabaga (about 1 pound), peeled
2 large carrots (about 10 ounces), peeled
2 medium sweet potatoes (about 1 pound)

2 medium potatoes (1 pound)
Salt
2 tablespoons butter
1½ tablespoons vegetable oil
1 teaspoon coarse kosher salt
1 teaspoon caraway seeds
½ teaspoon grated nutmeg
About ¼ teaspoon pepper

1. Preheat the oven to 475°. Drop the beets into a pot of boiling, salted water. Boil until not quite tender, 15–20 minutes. Rinse in cool water; slip off the skins and trim.

2. Meanwhile, bring a very large pot of water to a boil. Cut the rutabaga into strips about 2 inches long and ½ inch thick. Do the same to the carrots. Peel the sweet potatoes and cut to the same size. Do the same with the potatoes.

3. Add salt to the pot of boiling water; drop the vegetable strips in the water, cover, and return to a full boil. (The strips should be barely half-cooked, not tender; you'll need to cook more or less time, depending upon how effective your stove is.)

4. Drain the vegetables well. Heat a wide roasting pan (about 12 by 18 inches) with the butter and 1 tablespoon vegetable oil. Add the vegetables, then sprinkle with the coarse salt, caraway, nutmeg, and pepper. Toss to coat.

5. Place in the upper level of the hot oven. Bake for about 35 minutes, until browned and slightly crisp, tossing gently every 10 minutes or so. Meanwhile, cut the beets into strips the same size as the other vegetables. Combine them in a cake pan with the remaining ½ tablespoon oil. Bake about 15 minutes, until tender and lightly browned. Scoop the mixed vegetables onto a serving platter. Surround with the beets.

4–6 SERVINGS

AROMATIC RICE WITH NUTS, RAISINS, AND SHALLOTS
(Nasi Beryani)
INDONESIA AND MALAYSIA

This traditional dish is a ceremonial one, served only at special banquets and on Fridays (the Muslim sabbath) at the Jakarta Hilton International and the Kuala Lumpur Hilton. For Malaysian and Indonesian dinners of importance, four or five dishes and soup are set out on the table, followed by the plates, onto which is spooned rice (nasi)—which may be plain white, or flavored with coconut, tomato, turmeric, and a number of other variations, such as the following, of Indian Moghul origin. But the flowery incense that blooms forth from the bouquet of aromatics distinguishes the recipe as one transplanted to the Spice Islands.

---

8 tablespoons (4 ounces) butter
1 cup minced onion
½ cup minced shallots
⅓ cup minced peeled fresh ginger
1 tablespoon minced garlic
2 small cinnamon sticks, broken into tiny pieces
10 cardamom pods, crushed, seeds removed, and pods discarded
10 cloves
3 cups long-grain white rice
3½ cups chicken stock

1 cup milk
About 2 teaspoons rose water
12 medium basil leaves (see Note)
1 teaspoon salt
½ cup raisins
½ teaspoon saffron threads mixed with 3 tablespoons hot water
¾ cup roasted *kemiri* (candlenuts), macadamia, or cashew nuts
Fried shallots (see recipe for Hainanese Chicken, page 302)

---

1. Heat the butter in a large heavy saucepan over moderate heat. Stir in the onion, shallots, ginger, and garlic: cook until light brown, stirring often.

2. Add the cinnamon, cardamom seeds, and cloves; toss for 2 minutes longer. Add the rice and stir for 1 minute. Add the chicken stock, milk, 2 teaspoons rose water, the basil, and salt; bring to a boil, stirring.

3. Cover the pot and cook over lowest heat for 20 minutes. Remove from the heat and let stand, covered, for 10–20 minutes, as convenient. Toss together with the raisins in a warm serving dish. Let stand, covered, for 5 minutes. Drizzle the saffron water over the top. Add the nuts and fried shallots. Serve hot.

Note: *Basil leaves have been substituted for* pandanus *(screw pine). If the latter are available to you, use 6 of them instead.*

8 SERVINGS AS A SIDE DISH

FRIED EGG NOODLES WITH MIXED VEGETABLES
(Bakmi Goreng)
INDONESIA

Obviously influenced by the Chinese lo mein *stir-fries, this popular Javanese vegetable medley (accented with shrimp and chicken) appears in many guises, all containing plenty of garlic. At the Jakarta Hilton International the dish is accompanied by cucumber, sliced tomato, a flower-cut red chili-pepper, fried shallot flakes (see page 302), puffed shrimp-rice flour crackers* (krupuk *or* kroepek), *and a side of* sambal oelek, *the omnipresent ground chili condiment that fires Indonesian tastebuds.* Salsa picante *from a Latin-American store will do nicely instead, if you like.*

Although the following mix of vegetables is particularly colorful and crunchy, anything goes in this simple-to-make, one-dish meal that is comfortable, easy, but exotic.

½ pound fine egg noodles
7 tablespoons vegetable oil
2 eggs, beaten to blend
1 medium onion, halved and sliced
1½ tablespoons minced garlic
6 ounces peeled raw shrimp (10 medium), cut into 1-inch pieces
1 small boneless, skinless chicken breast (about 5 ounces), cut into thin strips about 2 inches long
2 medium celery ribs, trimmed and cut into 2-inch julienne

4 ounces snow peas, strings removed and cut diagonally into 2–3 pieces
1 medium carrot, cut into 2-inch julienne
1 very small leek, cleaned and cut into 2-inch julienne
8 ounces small bok choy, leaves cut 1 inch wide, stems ½ inch wide
¼ cup plus 1 tablespoon chicken stock
About 2 tablespoons *ketjap manis* (see Note)
Salt and pepper

1. Preheat the oven to 150–200°. Drop the egg noodles into a pot of salted boiling water. Return to a boil and cook for a few minutes until just tender. Drain, rinse in cold water; drain again.

2. Heat an 8-inch nonstick pan with ½ tablespoon oil. Pour in half the egg and tip the pan to coat evenly. Cook over moderately low heat until no longer wet on the surface. With a thin, flexible spatula flip onto a cutting surface. Repeat with the remaining egg and ½ tablespoon oil. Cut both pancakes into thin strips and reserve.

3. Heat a wok over high heat; pour 2 tablespoons oil around the rim. Add the onion and toss for a minute. Add the garlic, shrimp, and chicken and toss until not quite done, about 1 minute. Scoop into a large serving dish and set in the warm oven.

4. Add 1½ tablespoons oil to the wok; add the celery, snow peas, and carrot. Toss over moderately high heat for 1½ minutes, until half-cooked. Add 1½ tablespoons more oil, the leek, and bok choy; toss a moment. Add ¼ cup chicken stock and toss for about 1½ minutes, until just barely tender.

5. Meanwhile, blend together 2 tablespoons of the *ketjap manis* and the remaining 1 tablespoon stock. Raise the heat to high; add the remaining 1 tablespoon oil to the wok, then the noodles; toss. Add the shrimp-chicken mixture, *ketjap manis,* and salt and pepper to taste, tossing vigorously and separating the noodle strands. Taste for additional *ketjap manis.*

6. Scoop into the heated dish. Sprinkle with the egg strips, toss lightly, and serve hot or at room temperature.

Note: Ketjap manis, *a thick, sweet, dark Indonesian soy sauce can be purchased at many Asian markets. If it is impossible to obtain, substitute half Chinese dark soy sauce and half molasses.*
Serving and presentation: *This makes a casual, but special hot main dish; or serve it with additional vegetables as a buffet pasta salad. Do not chill, or the special freshness and balance will be lost.*

4 SERVINGS

SPAGHETTI SAKURA

JAPAN

Sakura is the coffee shop in the Tokyo Hilton International that boasts fast-changing ethnic food promotions, beloved by the adventurous Japanese, who rapidly devour each new subject. A pasta week included this mild, slightly garlickly, creamy hybrid of Italian and Oriental (the shiitake *and* shimeji, *or oyster mushrooms) origin, which became a part of the regular menu in no time.*

5 ounces fresh *shiitake*
3 ounces small oyster mushrooms (*pleurottes*)
3 ounces small button mushrooms
4 tablespoons butter
½ cup minced onion
1–1½ teaspoons minced garlic
⅔ cup very light dry white wine

1 cup heavy (or whipping) cream
2 tablespoons minced parsley
2 teaspoons fresh thyme leaves
2 tablespoons minced basil leaves
1 pound spaghetti
Salt and pepper
Grated Parmesan cheese

1. Wipe the mushrooms clean with a damp towel. Remove the *shiitake* stems; trim the tips of the oyster mushrooms; reserve both for future stock-making. Cut the *shiitake* caps and button mushrooms in thin slices. If the oyster mushrooms are not petite, cut them in small pieces.

2. Heat the butter in a wide skillet over moderate heat. Add the onion and toss for a minute; add the garlic and toss a minute longer. Add all the mushrooms and toss over moderately high heat until some liquid is exuded, about 3 minutes. Turn the heat to high and toss until the juices have nearly evaporated.

3. Add the wine and boil until there are just a few spoonfuls left in the pan. Add the cream and boil until very slightly thickened. Stir in half the herbs, then remove from the heat.

4. Meanwhile, drop the spaghetti into a large pot of boiling salted water. Boil until just tender. Drain well.

5. Add the spaghetti to the skillet; fold together with the sauce over low heat. Add salt and pepper to taste, then sprinkle with the remaining herbs. Serve with the cheese alongside.

4 SERVINGS

Spiced Chick-peas with Fresh White Cheese
(Chana Pindi)

INDIA

Caraway and lime add new dimensions to warming chick-peas tinted tawny by tea. The fresh white cheese is quickly prepared, quite creamy and firm, and turns golden and soft when fried. While Sushil Chugh at the Hilton International Khartoum in the Sudan is the source of this recipe, it is a north Indian dish—which originated in Pindi, once in India, now in Pakistan. A popular street snack, the spicy mixture is served with deep-fried, thick pancake-type breads called bhaturas. *It also makes an unusual main course or side dish to a meat dinner.*

(continued)

2 cups dried chick-peas (1 pound)
1 tablespoon black tea leaves
2 quarts milk
¼ cup lemon juice
2 teaspoons ground coriander
1½ teaspoons caraway seeds
½ teaspoon ground cinnamon
½ teaspoon nutmeg
Black pepper

About 1 teaspoon salt
¼ cup lime juice
½ cup very fine fresh ginger julienne
7 tablespoons vegetable oil
2 medium tomatoes, each cut into 8 wedges and each wedge halved across
¼ cup minced cilantro leaves

1. Bring the chick-peas and 6 cups of water to a boil; boil for 2 minutes. Cover the pot and remove from the heat; let stand for 1 hour. Add the tea leaves, tied in cheesecloth or in a tea ball. Return to a simmer; cook gently, covered, until tender—which can vary from 1–2 hours.

2. Meanwhile, heat the milk in a heavy pot, stirring until it boils. Pour in the lemon juice, stirring constantly. The milk should separate into semi-solid curds and thin, watery whey. Remove from the heat; ladle gently into a sieve lined with several layers of fine-meshed cheesecloth. When most of the liquid has dripped through (about 10 minutes), lift the corners of the cloth and tie to form a bag.

3. Suspend from a faucet to drip for 1–2 hours, as convenient.

4. When the chick-peas are tender, drain off liquid that remains; remove the tea. Add the coriander, caraway, cinnamon, nutmeg, pepper and salt to taste, the lime juice, and 6 tablespoons ginger julienne; mix.

5. Place the ball of cheese on a counter and knead and spread with a dough scraper (or palette knife or sturdy spatula) until the cheese is creamy and fine-textured, about 5 minutes. Press to form a neat 5–6-inch round. Cut into 8 wedges.

6. Heat 4 tablespoons oil in a large saucepan over moderate heat. Toss the chick-peas in this to coat evenly. Add the tomatoes; lower the heat and shake and stir gently for about 5 minutes, until the tomato juices exude slightly.

7. Meanwhile, heat the remaining 3 tablespoons oil in a 9–10-inch black cast-iron skillet or nonstick pan over moderate heat. Brown the cheese wedges on both sides, lowering the heat as necessary to prevent burning. Watch carefully, the cheese colors very quickly.

8. Scoop the chick-peas into a serving dish, then top with the cheese wedges. Sprinkle with cilantro and the remaining 2 tablespoons ginger.

Note: *Alternatively, you can hang the bag of cheese until firm, then chill overnight, without kneading. Unwrap, then gently cut into 8 slices, which will be somewhat irregular-shaped.*
Option: *This is also good as a main course salad, without cheese. Prepare the beans, add the spices, and cool. Toss with tomatoes and lime juice (both increased to taste) and vegetable oil as desired.*
Advance preparation: *The chick-peas and cheese can be prepared in advance, leaving only the browning of the cheese and final assembly.*

4 SERVINGS AS A MAIN COURSE

Perfecting Paradise: Indonesian Nouvelle Cuisine at the Jakarta Hilton International

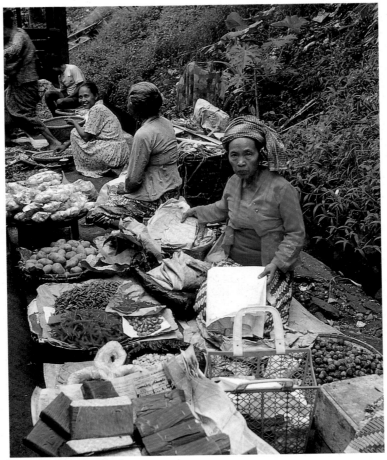

The marketplace in Jakarta

Thirteen thousand six hundred and seventy-seven islands of volcanic origin flung across 3,200 miles in the waters of the Indian and Pacific Oceans and South China and Timor Seas are the gardens and marine storehouse of Indonesia, the world's sixth largest nation. With 169 million inhabitants, more than 100 distinct ethnic groups, and at least 300 languages, its complex composition is further diversified by centuries of foreign rule by Indian, Arab, Portuguese, Dutch, and Chinese, and a few less influential invaders. Unique geologic and climatic conditions have combined to produce an exceptionally rich variety of fruits, vegetables, and spices. Just begin to consider the possibilities for culinary invention!

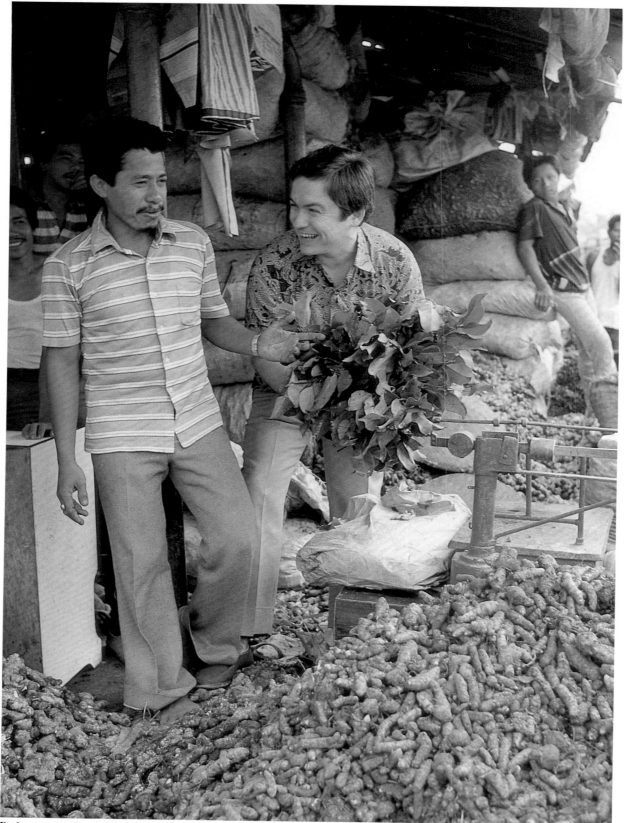

Exuberant executive chef Detlef Skrobanek (right) in the Jakarta market

Like much of Southeast Asia and the Pacific, Indonesia depends heavily upon rice (black and brick red, as well as white) and numerous rice flour products, coconut milk (the milk, cream, and butter of the islands), fermented seafood pastes and sauces, chilis galore, and garlic. But a visit to the market in Jakarta, the capital, on the island of Java, reveals other distinctive mainstays: fresh, dried, pickled, and sugared fruits of every color, texture, and shape; peanuts; intensely sweet-sour tamarind (its sticky prunish flesh liquefied as a common cooking medium); oil-rich nuts that bind and thicken sauces; mountains of pearly-pink shallots; and, of course, the wealth of spices from the Moluccas (the Spice Islands). But what most intrigues a curious cook is the unimaginable array of aromatics in the forms of roots, rhizomes, grasses, and leaves. Citrusy, subtle lemon grass and bright ginger are paramount, but they are only the beginning. Bulbous yellow-orange turmeric and its leaves; *kentjur* and *lengkuas* (also called *laos* or galingale)—assertive members of the ginger clan; a half-dozen varieties of wild and cultivated limes, citrons, and their leaves; and the leaves of pomegranate, papaya, and guava.

At a typical Indonesian meal, such as the one lavishly and lovingly prepared at the Jakarta Hilton International, all dishes (30, in this atypical instance) are offered together in serve-yourself fashion, to be eaten with spoon and fork only. Sauces are principal and omnipresent. They may be thin and fiery, thick and nutty, oily and spicy-sweet— or any combination of the above. Although ingredients reappear in many dishes, each final product is subtle and focused, not repetitious. Food may be hot, warm, or at room temperature, but is usually the latter. Condiments are a must, with soy sauce, chili, shallot, and seafood pastes the main ingredients of the compound sauces, plus a rainbow of raw and pickled fruits and vegetables. Rice, plain-cooked or fancified with aromatics and coconut, appears at all meals.

A few of the savory specialties from this traditional array were *sayur bening,* a colorful soup of fragrant and bitter leaves stirred into a clean, hot stock with bits of sweet corn, tomato, shallot, and garlic; *sayur lodeh,* long beans, jakfruit (or jackfruit, an immense, fleshy tropical fruit), and eggplant braised in a spiced coconut sauce; *ayam tuturuga,* a hot-sweet, lime and chili-sparked chicken stew; *gulai otak,* creamy brains in a thin curry sauce; *ayam goreng padang,* chicken marinated in chili, crushed turmeric and ginger roots, and shallot, half-cooked in stock, then dried and deep-fried; *udang balado,* large chili-marinated shrimps sauced with tamarind, tomato, garlic, and lemon leaves, grass, and roots; *ayam kalio,* chicken simmered in a thick sauce of *laos* and ginger roots, lime leaves, cumin and coriander powders, and coconut; and *nasi kuning,* a golden turmeric and ginger-scented rice.

As if these pleasures were not sufficient to entice even the most jaded palate, a new form of cooking is percolating at the Jakarta Hilton International, where a small team is refining dishes made from these evocative ingredients, honing the flavors, and streamlining the presentation for cosmopolitan connoisseurs. Surprisingly, in a country that appears to be even more nationalistically food-passionate than France or Italy, it is a German-Canadian chef trained in Switzerland, Detlef Skrobanek, who has managed to receive the culinary endorsement of the government through its foreign minister, Dr. Mochtar Kusumaatmadja. The minister, who sadly concedes that the dig-in buffet style of Indonesian meals is little suited to affairs of state and business dinners, but who wishes to present the fare of the country to visiting dignitaries, has encouraged the small revolution in the Hilton International's kitchen.

Nouvelle Indonesian cuisine, with executive chef Skrobanek and Sumatran sous-chef

S. Johan Darussalam in charge, is acquiring a quiet, but devoted audience. Skrobanek (a mastermind of organization and precision, who has systematically studied and deeply absorbed the culture) takes local ingredients and grafts onto them European techniques, without intruding foreign flavors or disturbing the intrinsic balance. He is not creating French menus with Indonesian fillips, but working with the precepts of the native cuisine and adjusting elements that are less desirable to Westerners. For example, foods usually served warm are now either hot or cold. Dishes that have traditionally been over-cooked by Western standards are now cooked *à point*. Dishes that are normally heavily sauced and extremely rich and oily have been lightened. (But the sauces and seasonings that are the roots of the Indonesian cuisine are little touched. Skrobanek is intrigued by the use of leaves, nuts, large quantities of spices, and grated coconut flesh [the soft, immature fruit, not the dry one we know in the United States] and coconut milk as thickeners; no starches are introduced. He is in awe of the brilliant way in which Indonesian cooks invariably balance the complicated mixtures.) Presentation that is festive, but hodgepodge, has been replaced with a personal visual aesthetic that is in keeping with the food, and as graceful as Balinese wood carving or the exquisite (and fleeting) Javanese fresh palm leaf decoration *(janur)* that decorates the dining areas.

A team of eight has also created new dishes using Indonesian ingredients, pure inventions in the style of the country—which are either accepted or rejected summarily by the locals ("fortunately, they are most outspoken," says Skrobanek, "you know at once what they like."). For most Indonesians, the deliberate presentation and comparatively small quantities are reason for hesitation; for Westerners, the mysterious flavors engender ambivalence (what is this? what am I eating?). For those lucky enough to fit somewhere in between, there may be a taste of paradise in their future—such as this exemplary meal of innovative and traditionally based dishes, served in small portions, in the Nouvelle style, and embellished with a centerpiece of weeping jasmine and roses:

—Warm Duck Breast Salad: hot-smoked, spice-marinated duck with a toss of bean sprouts, Chinese black mushrooms, yard-long beans, and tomatoes in a light vinaigrette

—Bird's Nest Soup with Quail Eggs: clarified amber chicken broth made with the world's premiere bird's nests, from Java; the bite of chili and perfume of lemon grass and cilantro dominate, as a confetti of diced carrots, green pepper diamonds, celery strands, and transparent, chewy bird's nest supply textural counterpoints

—Fillets of Sole with Sour Turmeric Sauce: thin fillets sandwiching basil and minced fresh red chili served on a thick, mustard-yellow sweet-sour turmeric sauce, garnished with vegetables and basil leaves

—Cucumber Granita: a bracing *intermezzo* of icy shredded cucumber, ginger slivers, and lime juice

—Beef Tenderloin with Vegetables in Peanut Sauce: beef is marinated in spices, garlic, and shallots, briefly simmered, then roasted until crusty on the outside and cool-rare on the inside; accompanied by a light, hot-sweet sauce and a salad of chili, cucumber, bean sprouts, lime leaves, and baby eggplant with peanut and tamarind dressing served in a nest of braided yard-long beans

—Fruits with Fermented Rice and Cinnamon Sauce: melons, pineapple, and papaya macerated in palm wine, with rough grains of black rice softened and fermented in wine, topped with coconut ice cream, then cloaked in a light sabayon sauce and burnt-glazed under intense heat.

SHRIMP IN COCONUT-CHILI SAUCE
(Sambal Goreng Udang)
INDONESIA

A beginner's guide to the tastes of Indonesia (specifically Sumatra, in this case): Fresh hot red chili-pepper, lemon grass, garlic, shallot, and coconut milk are among the most common flavors and textures to be found, but by no means common in their blending. At the Peacock Café in the Jakarta Hilton International, where this popular (and speedily prepared) dish is featured, it is served with rice topped with fried shallots (see recipe for Hainanese Chicken, page 302) and a dish of bean sprouts.

Because there is tremendous variation in the pungency of lemon grass and chilis, the seasoning may need some adjustment. Stir additional chili into the sauce at the end, if necessary. Coconut milk varies as well, and may be very thick. In Indonesia the sauce is quite thin, but Westerners usually prefer a richer consistency, such as the following. Do not be surprised when the sauce separates slightly, which coconut will do.

2 medium stalks lemon grass
    (see Note)
2 tablespoons vegetable oil
1 tablespoon minced garlic
⅓ cup minced shallots
2–3 teaspoons thinly slivered very
    hot red chili-pepper (such as Cay-
    enne), seeds and ribs removed

2 bay leaves (see Note)
2 cups unsweetened coconut milk
    (see Note)
About ¾ teaspoon salt
1½ pounds shelled raw medium
    shrimp (1¾ pounds in the shell)

1. Cut the heavy, dry upper leaves from the lemon grass and trim off the heavy tip of the base. Unwrap several layers of the coarse leaves. Halve the inner stalks lengthwise. Cut into the very finest slices possible, to equal 3 tablespoons.

2. Heat the oil in a saucepan; stir in the garlic, shallots, 2 teaspoons chili-pepper, bay leaves, and lemon grass; stir for a minute. Cover and cook over lowest heat for 5 minutes.

3. Add the coconut milk and ¾ teaspoon salt; bring to a simmer. Add the shrimp and poach at under a simmer until just cooked through, about 1 minute. Scoop into a wide, heated dish.

Note: *Long stalks of greyish-green fresh lemon grass can be found in some stores that carry foods from Southeast Asia and in some supermarkets. They add a subtle, inimitable lemon pungency.*
   Salam leaves are used in Indonesia instead of bay leaves; substitute these, if they are available to you.
   Coconut milk is available in bottles or cans in stores that carry ingredients from South America and Asia. If you cannot buy it, make your own, following the directions on page 325.
Serving: *This is unquestionably a dish to serve with fluffy, white rice, plenty of it.*
Options: *While testing, we added a sprinkling of fine fresh ginger julienne, which was delicious, if untraditional.*

4 SERVINGS

SHRIMP IN PAPAYA SAUCE

SINGAPORE

The sensitive touch of the chefs at the Hilton International Singapore is evident in this beautiful, simple dish from the Harbour Grill. Lightly sweet, fruity, with a touch of heat, the effect is tropical, but tempered. The deliriously sunset pink papaya of Asia is difficult to come by outside of Hawaii and California, but the easily obtained small, apricot-colored variety will do as nicely—provided you choose one that is yellow-ripe.

**1 ripe papaya (about 1 pound),
  halved and seeded**
**20 medium-large raw shrimp, peeled
  (about 2 pounds in the shell)**
½ cup fish stock (see page 326)
2 tablespoons heavy cream

**¼–1 teaspoon minced hot red chili-
  pepper (seeded, veins removed)**
Lemon juice
Salt, pepper, and sugar
2½ tablespoons butter

1. Preheat the oven to 150–200°. With a 1-inch melon ball cutter, scoop 20 balls of papaya; set aside in a heatproof, shallow serving dish in the warm oven. Scrape the remaining flesh into a blender or processor; puree. (You should have ½ cup.)

2. Set the shrimp on a steaming rack over boiling water; cover and steam for about 1½ minutes, until just cooked through.

3. Meanwhile, combine the papaya puree, fish stock, and cream in a nonaluminum saucepan and bring to a boil, stirring. Simmer for a minute, then remove from the heat. With an electric hand mixer (see Note) beat in the chili and lemon juice, and salt, pepper, and sugar to taste. Gradually beat in the butter.

4. Arrange the shrimp and papaya balls, pour over the sauce, and serve at once.

Note: *If you have one of the handy electric rods with a tiny high-speed blade at the tip that is variously called a hand- or immersion- or stick-blender, place it directly in the sauce pot and whiz to create a light froth.*

4 SERVINGS

FILLET OF SOLE WITH SOUR TURMERIC SAUCE
(Kukus Ikan Sebelah Madura, Saos Acar Kuning)
INDONESIA

A stunning example of an Indonesian dish adapted to Western fine dining-room style by Detlef Skrobanek and S. Johan Darussalam of the Jakarta Hilton International. Fillets that enclose bright shreds of hot pepper, lemon grass, and basil are arranged in graceful slices on a thick, brilliant yellow sauce—pesmol, a classic fish sauce of Indonesian cuisine. The taste is big and exotic, with turmeric, shallots, and vinegar predominating, followed by the sweetness of coconut and citrus-herbal undertone of ginger and lemon grass.

1 tablespoon peanut oil
1 tablespoon finely chopped fresh
   ginger
1 tablespoon finely chopped shallot
1½ teaspoons finely chopped garlic
1 bay leaf
1 stalk lemon grass (see Note)
1 tablespoon ground turmeric
¼ cup roasted macadamia nuts,
   chopped
1 cup coconut milk (see Note)
About 2 tablespoons distilled white
   vinegar

Salt and pepper
About 1 cup fish stock (see page
   326), *or* bottled clam juice
4 lemon sole fillets (each about 7
   ounces)
2 teaspoons very fine julienne-cut
   very hot red chili-pepper (such as
   Cayenne), seeds and ribs removed
1 cup lightly packed basil leaves
   (stems removed), washed and
   dried
Basil sprigs for garnish

1. Heat the peanut oil in a small saucepan over moderately low heat; add the ginger, shallot, garlic, and bay leaf. Trim the tough upper leaves from the lemon grass, then halve the stalk lengthwise, then across. Finely slice the tenderest inner layers from the base of one piece; set this aside. Add the remaining stalks to the pan. Stir for 2 minutes. Add the turmeric and macadamia nuts; continue stirring for 2 minutes. Add the coconut milk and 1½ tablespoons vinegar.

2. Cover the pan and barely simmer for 10 minutes. Uncover and simmer for 5 minutes. Remove the bay leaf and lemon grass. Puree the sauce until smooth in a blender or processor. Season with salt and pepper and additional vinegar to taste. Adjust the consistency with a small amount of hot stock or water, if necessary, to form a smoothly pourable sauce.

3. Halve each fish fillet lengthwise. Sprinkle the sliced lemon grass and 1 teaspoon of the chili-pepper julienne over the 8 strips, dividing equally. Place a layer of basil leaves over each of these pieces to cover completely. Roll each piece tightly and arrange the rolls, seam side down in a wide skillet to fit in one layer.

4. Pour 1 cup of fish stock over them; bring to a simmer. Cover the pan and poach at just under a simmer for 5–6 minutes, until the fish just loses its translucence.

5. With a slotted spoon, transfer the fish to a cutting board. Divide the hot sauce onto 4 heated plates, tipping to form a neat circle. Halve each roll to form 2 equal spirals. Place 4 of these on the sauce. Garnish with a basil sprig and serve immediately.

Note: *Long stalks of greyish-green fresh lemon grass can be found in some Oriental markets and supermarkets. The grass adds a subtle, inimitable lemon pungency.*

   Coconut milk is available in canned or bottled form in stores that carry ingredients from South America and Asia. If you cannot buy it, make your own, following the directions on page 325.

4 SERVINGS

POMPANO WITH GINGER FRAGRANCE

SINGAPORE

When Peter Knipp (now executive chef of the Shanghai Hilton International) was sous-chef in the Harbour Grill of the Hilton International Singapore, he developed this balanced dish, one that still suits his taste: "It's a fine example of ingredients that fit together with no pushing." A garnish of multicolored, fine vegetable julienne with twirls of scallion decorates the snowy, smooth-grained pompano (pomfret is the fish used in the Orient). The sharply gingered cooking stock is much reduced, then considerably mellowed with butter to create the pale yellow "East meets West" sauce that surrounds the fish.

3¼-pound pompano, filleted and skinned, bones and head reserved
½ cup coarsely chopped fresh ginger
1 medium carrot, sliced
1 celery rib, sliced
2 tablespoons parsley stalks
⅓ cup cilantro leaves and stems, sliced
2 medium scallions, sliced
1 teaspoon white peppercorns, crushed
½ teaspoon dried thyme leaves

½ cup dry white wine or dry vermouth
3 cups fish stock (see page 326), *or* 1 cup bottled clam juice mixed with 2 cups water
Salt and pepper
Vegetable garnish (see Note)
⅓ cup very fine fresh ginger julienne
⅓ cup fine celery julienne
⅓ cup fine carrot julienne
⅓ cup thin sliced scallion green
8 tablespoons butter, chilled
Salt and white pepper

1. Remove and discard the gills and innards from the fish skeleton. Rinse the bones and head well and combine in a nonaluminum pot with the chopped ginger, sliced carrot, celery, parsley stalks, cilantro, scallions, peppercorns, thyme, white wine, and fish stock. Barely simmer, uncovered, for 25 minutes. Strain through a cheesecloth-lined sieve. Boil briefly to reduce to ¾ cup.

2. Preheat the oven to 375°. Halve each pompano fillet crosswise; season with salt and pepper. Place in a single layer in a buttered baking dish. Spoon over 2 tablespoons of the stock, distributing evenly. Cover with foil; set in the upper level of the preheated oven until the fish is no longer translucent in the center—about 12 minutes.

3. Meanwhile, spread the julienned vegetables in a 9-inch skillet or saucepan. Pour over the remaining stock. Boil for 2 minutes, until barely tender. On lowest heat, add the butter, a little at a time, stirring vigorously. Season with salt and pepper. Keep over low heat.

4. Transfer the fish to a warmed serving platter. Spoon over the vegetables and sauce.

Note: *It is important to cut the finest julienne of vegetables. The vivid lemony ginger, herbal celery, and sweet carrot should blend, not remain distinct.*

4 SERVINGS

FANCY-CUT SQUID STIR-FRIED WITH ASPARAGUS

TAIWAN

Of Cantonese origin, this light dish hails from the Hilton International Taipei. Scoring the squid tenderizes the flesh and transforms the pieces into patterned twists that look appealing with the orange carrot ovals and diagonally cut jade asparagus. The flavors are natural and unaffected, clear and individualized.

Although cutting the ingredients is comparatively time-consuming, the cooking takes only minutes. Do not skip the squid-blanching, which prevents liquid from seeping into the crisp vegetables.

1½ pounds cleaned squid (or 2¼
  pounds uncleaned; see page 324)
1 pound medium asparagus
2 medium-large carrots, peeled and
  cut into thin diagonal slices
4 medium scallions, cleaned and cut
  into 1-inch diagonal slices
1–2 tablespoons minced garlic

3 tablespoons fine julienne-cut
  fresh ginger
1 teaspoon cornstarch
2 tablespoons rice wine
2 teaspoons rice vinegar
1 teaspoon sesame oil
About 5 tablespoons peanut oil
Salt and pepper

1. Slit the cleaned squid mantles so that they lie flat. With a sharp knife score halfway through the flesh in as small a crosshatch pattern as you can manage, covering the entire surface. Cut the scored squid into bite-size rectangles, triangles, or squares, as convenient. Drop the pieces into a large pot of boiling salted water. Return to a boil over highest heat; drain.

2. Break the woody base from the asparagus. Peel the asparagus, then cut into long diagonal slices about 1/16 inch thick. Prepare the remaining vegetables as indicated. Blend together the cornstarch, rice wine, rice vinegar, and sesame oil in a cup.

3. Heat a wok over high heat; pour 2 tablespoons peanut oil around the rim. Add the carrots and asparagus and toss for 3–4 minutes, until almost cooked through. Transfer to a plate.

4. Add another tablespoon of oil to the wok. Add the squid and toss for about 1 minute. Scoop onto the plate with the vegetables.

5. Add the remaining 2 tablespoons peanut oil to the wok. Toss the scallions, garlic, and ginger for 1 minute. Add the squid and vegetables to the wok and toss for 1 minute. Lower the heat, then stir in the cornstarch mixture. Toss for another minute. Add salt and pepper to taste, then transfer to a heated dish.

Advance preparation: *Although the wok-cooking cannot be done until the last minute, all the cutting can be accomplished ahead of time and the squid scored and blanched.*

4 SERVINGS

SALMON FILLETS WITH VINEGAR SAUCE ON DICED VEGETABLES

SINGAPORE

Graham Cadman, formerly of Gatwick, who then moved on to become executive chef at the Hilton International Singapore, reluctantly admits his personal preferences in food (rather, he loves to please his audience without imposing defined taste limits), but confesses that he much admires the excellent Chinese cooking in Singapore. He favors clean, simple presentations of easily identifiable ingredients ("very British," says Cadman, "but I do use salt") and the taste- and texture-retaining properties of stir-fries—which is what you might be tempted to call the provençal-flavored vegetable mélange beneath the quick-cooked salmon that is barely daubed wih a berry-thickened vinegar.

⅓ cup white wine vinegar
½ cup red currants (cleaned) or raspberries
8 medium dried *shiitake* (Chinese mushrooms, forest mushrooms, black mushrooms)
4½ tablespoons olive oil
¼–½ teaspoon saffron threads
1 small onion, cut into ¼-inch dice
½ yellow bell pepper, cut into ¼-inch dice
½ red bell pepper, cut into ¼-inch dice

½ green bell pepper, cut into ¼-inch dice
1 narrow Japanese or Chinese eggplant (about 4 ounces), unpeeled and cut into ¼-inch dice
1–2 tablespoons capers (preferably the tiny nonpareils)
About 1 tablespoon lemon juice
Salt and pepper
4 skinned salmon fillets (each about 6 ounces)

1. Combine the vinegar and currants or berries (add ½ teaspoon sugar for currants) in a small, nonaluminum pan and bring to a boil. Press through a nonaluminum strainer, squeezing through all the pulp.

2. Preheat the oven to 150–200°. Combine the *shiitake* in a small saucepan with ½ tablespoon oil and water to cover. Bring to a boil, cover, and let stand for at least 15 minutes. Drain and reserve the liquid. Cut off the stems and reserve for stock-making. Cut the caps into ¼-inch dice. Heat 3 tablespoons of the mushroom liquid to boiling, then pour over the saffron.

3. Heat 2 tablespoons oil in a wide skillet over moderately high heat. Add the onion and stir for a minute. Add the *shiitake* and stir another minute. Stir in the peppers and eggplant. Toss until just barely tender, 4–5 minutes. Add the saffron and liquid and toss for a moment. Add the capers and lemon juice to taste; season with salt and pepper. Spread in a heatproof shallow serving dish and set in the warm oven.

4. Sprinkle salt and pepper over the salmon. Heat a nonstick skillet with 1 tablespoon oil over moderate heat. Add 2 of the salmon fillets and cook until golden, about 1½ minutes. Turn the fillets over and do the same. Carefully transfer the salmon to the bed of vegetables and return to the oven.

5. Repeat Step 4 with the remaining 1 tablespoon oil and 2 salmon fillets. Lower the heat in the pan; add the berry vinegar. Bring to a boil, stirring vigorously. Stir for a minute or so, until thickish and reduced to 2–3 tablespoons. Spoon over the salmon fillets and serve at once.

4 SERVINGS

The Best of Both Worlds:
Chef Peter Knipp

"I don't consider myself Western or Asian," says German-born executive chef Peter Knipp, "just plain fortunate." Although barely into his thirties, Mr. Knipp, a 16-year veteran of Hilton International, has worked in the kitchens of West Germany, Canada, Switzerland, Malaysia, Indonesia (where he married his Chinese wife in the Jakarta Hilton), Australia, Japan, Singapore, Taiwan, and now, China. "My cooking has evolved as a natural consequence of the audience I wish to please." At first, a lack of Western produce forced Knipp and his colleagues in Asian countries to fashion local ingredients into forms suitable for a multinational clientele, but now such combinations are sought after. Knipp predicts that during the next 10 years Asian foods will become household words all over the West: "A union of exotic ingredients and European culinary styles is the marriage of the future."

Such an alliance was exemplified in a cross-cultural meal recently created by Knipp:

—A lacquer-skinned tiny *ballottine* of warm, lightly smoked chicken stuffed with ground chicken and pine nuts, sliced into rounds and set on greens in basil vinaigrette

—Pomfret fillets wrapped around blanched scallions, steamed, and served with a ginger butter sauce, slices of luffa gourd stuffed with a puree of fish and chili-peppers, and fennel boats heaped with turmeric rice

—A palate cleanser of barely sugared ginger sorbet

—Rectangles of silken tofu topped with minced veal and *shiitake* drenched with herbal cream sauce and accompanied by baby corn and a fan of *al dente* carrot strips

—Guava compote contained in deep-fried wonton wrappers—hot, crunchy, and sugar-dusted—set between "waves" of custard-soft furled mango slices and a violet sauce of blueberry tofu cream.

Knipp has always felt an affinity with Asian food and culture and is gratified that work as a chef has permitted him to travel in the countries he wished to explore. Despite his remarkable height and youth, his composure, basso voice, and Oriental Vandyke give the impression of an implacable and ageless mandarin. He has learned several Asian languages sufficiently well to communicate in the kitchen and beyond. "Food has a different meaning here, and if you are willing and able to absorb the messages, understanding follows. Food maintains cultural practices and enforces important parts of the life cycle, particularly in Chinese society."

Knipp, whose dedication to Chinese aesthetics is apparent in his work (including photography, his other love), has gathered, through his artistic creations, a bouquet of medals and honors for Hilton International and for the national teams he has headed in Singapore and Taipei. In fact, he may be the one responsible for putting the East

Chef Peter Knipp, fish in hand

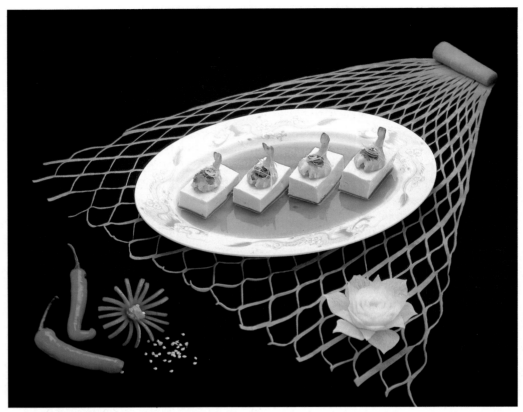

Stuffed Tofu with Shrimp (see page 264 for recipe)

on the map of culinary competitions. As sous-chef in Singapore, Knipp won the overall gold medal in the individual category and the grand prize trophy of the World Culinary Contest (held every 10 years, that time in Osaka) in which 140 European and Japanese chefs participated. Consecutive years of medals followed, including the 1984 gold medal at the prestigious culinary olympics in Frankfurt. With Knipp leading a team of eight chefs from Singapore in a competition of 1,000 professionals, the group culled eight gold medals in as many categories that ran from "pure" Eastern to "pure" Western. Few had even given a thought to an Asian team in the midst of European stars.

Yet no one who knows this chef would be surprised, for he is an inspiring teacher who develops extensive, individualized training programs in each kitchen he oversees, energizing the staff. "Medals are temporary," he declares, "but the stimulating, exhilarating effects of the competition last. These are the most exciting places for cultural exchanges to take place." For many Asian chefs it is a first exposure to the work of their Asian peers and to Western chefs—and for the latter, it can be a stunning eye-opener that leads to awe for the work done in Asia, and to the inclusion of Oriental ingredients and presentation techniques in their food.

At the 1986 Salon Culinaire of Food & Hotel Asia, the panel of judges awarded eight gold medals and two silver to the Taipei International Culinary Team headed by Knipp, whose personal East-West mastery was demonstrated in two entries that stunned the judges. One extravaganza, Eight Divine Diagrams, interpreted the symbols of an octagram devised by Fu-Shi, a primary Chinese saint: earth, heaven, wind, thunder, mountain, fire, water, and swamp were expressed in personal food combinations. In another presentation, tofu, chameleon of the Eastern kitchen, was the medium of the Eight Mythologies, each bearing the name of a god, each perfect as a jewel—and eminently edible. For one mythology, tofu was smoked, then filled with herbs and salmon eggs; for another, it was layered in small cakes with pureed vegetables and black sesame seeds; it appeared rolled with Chinese trout in *nori* and smoked salmon, as a terrine with seaweed, as a canapé with crab mousse and black beans, and enclosed in duck breast with young leeks in a vegetable broth with chilis. Finally, cut in the shapes of ancient Chinese coins, tofu was served on dark bread with a garnish of papaya and herbs. Neither strictly traditional nor culturally or culinarily jarring, the creations might be considered ideograms in a new vocabulary.

A selection of Chinese tidbits (dim sum) in bamboo steamer baskets

BEEF STEAKS WITH MUSTARD CREAM

JAPAN

The exquisite beef from Matsuzaka and Kobe that is offered by executive chef Siegfried Jaeger in the elegant Imari restaurant of the Tokyo Hilton International needs little accompaniment. The lustrous mahogany-hued sauce that surrounds the steak is a meaty classic of reduced veal stock sharpened with mustard, but the dish is given a unique contemporary tone with the addition of a dollop of cold whipped cream enriched with whole-grain mustard. Fresh egg noodles are a must.

4 pounds veal bones, cut or sawed
   into small pieces
1 large onion, cut into chunks
2 medium carrots, cut into chunks
1 celery rib, sliced
6 tablespoons heavy (or whipping)
   cream
3 tablespoons butter

1 teaspoon Dijon mustard
1 teaspoon coarse (whole grain)
   mustard
1 tablespoon vegetable oil
Salt and pepper
4 boneless beef steaks (about 6
   ounces each; see Option)

1. Prepare the veal stock: Preheat the oven to 450°. Spread the bones in a large roasting pan in a single layer. Set in the hot oven until well browned, about 30 minutes, stirring once. Add the onion, carrots, and celery. Reduce the heat to 400° and roast for 10 minutes. Stir and roast for 10 minutes longer. Remove from the oven; tip the pan so the fat runs to one side; let stand briefly. Pour off fat. Dump the contents of the pan into a stockpot; add 2½ quarts water. Bring to a boil, skimming. Meanwhile, add 2 cups water to the roasting pan. Stir over moderate heat to loosen the brown bits. Add to the stockpot. Keep at a bare simmer for 2 hours, or until reduced to about 4 cups.

2. Strain the stock into a saucepan; boil gently until reduced to about ½ cup. Add 2 tablespoons of the cream and bring to a boil. Add 2 tablespoons butter and the Dijon mustard and whisk to just barely blend. Remove from the heat.

3. Combine the remaining 4 tablespoons cream with the whole grain mustard in a small, narrow bowl or measuring cup; beat to form firm peaks. Cover and refrigerate (can be left for at least an hour).

4. Heat the remaining 1 tablespoon butter and the oil in a 9–10-inch skillet. Salt and pepper both sides of the steak and cook to the desired doneness. Place on 4 heated plates.

5. Warm the sauce and divide over the steaks. Scoop neat ovals of the mustard cream with a teaspoon and set one on each steak. Serve at once.

Note: *If you have a supply of veal stock, Step 1 can be skipped.*
Advance preparation: *The sauce can be prepared days ahead and heated. The mustard cream can be made an hour or so ahead.*
Option: *Although tenderloin (fillet) is the cut served in Tokyo, other tender, boneless steaks—such as sirloin or club—are fine.*

4 SERVINGS

BUFFALO FILLETS WITH PUMPKIN SAUCE AND GOAT CHEESE
AUSTRALIA

This most unusual combination of tender, juicy buffalo fillet topped with tart goat cheese set in a pool of sweet pumpkin sauce is adapted from an elaborate presentation devised by chef Herbert Franceschini of the Hilton International Brisbane. As served in the hotel, the buffalo (which is water buffalo in Australia, not bison, and which hails from Kangaroo Island, off the southern coast of Australia) is placed on a caraway-speckled puff pastry trellis and served with shaped beets, carrots, potatoes, rutabaga, and sweet potatoes on sautéed spinach leaves. A simplified version of these flavorful roots and tubers (see page 265) complements colorfully.

---

2 tablespoons butter
1 medium onion, sliced thin
1 pound pumpkin or any hard, orange-fleshed squash, such as butternut or acorn; peeled, seeded, and cut into 1-inch pieces
1 teaspoon sliced garlic
1 cup veal or beef stock
¼ teaspoon dried thyme
1 tablespoon honey

½ cup sweet or semisweet white wine or white port
About ¼ cup heavy (or whipping) cream
Salt and pepper
1 tablespoon vegetable oil
4 buffalo fillets, cut about 2 inches thick (6 ounces each)
2½-ounce cylinder fresh (not aged) goat cheese, cut into 4 slices

---

1. Melt the butter in a medium saucepan over moderately low heat. Add the onion; stir occasionally until browned, about 10 minutes.

2. Add the pumpkin and garlic; stir for about 2 minutes. Add the stock, thyme, honey, and wine. Bring to a boil. Cover, lower the heat, then simmer until very tender (timing can vary from 15–25 minutes, depending upon the variety of squash).

3. Pour the contents of the saucepan into the container of a blender. Puree until very smooth. Add the cream, adjusting to the desired consistency. Add salt and pepper to taste. Scoop into a saucepan.

4. Heat a medium-large skillet over moderate heat. Add the vegetable oil, then the fillets. Brown deeply on both sides, cooking until done to taste—about 8 minutes for rare. (Buffalo needs slightly longer cooking than beef and is particularly luscious when rare.) Just as the meat reaches the desired degree of doneness, place a slice of cheese on top. Remove the pan from the heat.

5. Heat the sauce to simmering. Pour onto a heated serving dish (or onto 4 plates). Set the steaks on top and serve at once.

Advance preparation: *The sauce can be made ahead and reheated.*

4 SERVINGS

SMOKED DUCK BREAST SALAD, JAVANESE-STYLE
(Bebek Asap Lalaban)
INDONESIA

This spicy, beguiling combination, another illustration of the Indonesian nouvelle cuisine of Detlef Skrobanek and his team at the Jakarta Hilton International, was the opener for a spectacular dinner that they developed for the United Nations in New York. It has since become a best-seller at the hotel, although neither smoking, nor duck (with a few exceptions in Sumatra and Bali), is popular in Indonesia.

An adaptation of the dramatically smoky duck breast is surprisingly easy to accomplish at home without a smoker. The mahogany-edged slices are offered with crunchy vegetables in a light vinaigrette and a sweet-hot-sour peanut sauce.

Breasts from two 5-pound ducks
1 teaspoon ground coriander
1 teaspoon ground cumin
1 teaspoon ground cloves
1 teaspoon ground turmeric
2½ teaspoons minced shallot
2 tablespoons vegetable oil
½ cup roasted unsalted peanuts
¼ cup lightly packed brown sugar
About 2 teaspoons minced very hot red chili-pepper, seeds removed
About ⅓ cup lemon juice (see Note)
Salt and pepper

3 tablespoons whole mixed pickling spices
10 dried black Oriental mushrooms (*shiitake*, forest mushrooms, Chinese mushrooms)
4 tablespoons peanut oil
6 ounces string beans, cut into 1½-inch pieces (see Note)
2 tablespoons distilled white vinegar
About 6 ounces mung bean sprouts
Optional: 4 ears baby corn, 4 fresh bay leaves (see Note)

---

1. Bone the breasts; trim each neatly. Combine the coriander, cumin, cloves, turmeric, 1½ teaspoons shallot, and the vegetable oil. Rub over the duck (wear rubber gloves if you will be bothered by a curry-colored temporary stain). Wrap tightly in plastic and refrigerate for about 24 hours. (The marinating may be omitted, if you prefer; simply rub the breasts with the spice mixture; let stand at room temperature as you proceed.)

2. Prepare the sauce: Combine the peanuts, brown sugar, and 1 teaspoon chili-pepper in the container of a blender or processor. Whirl to a medium-fine texture. Add ⅓ cup lemon juice and process to a fine texture. Add salt, pepper, and additional chili and lemon juice to taste.

3. Combine the pickling spices in a small dish with water to cover. Combine the mushrooms, 1 cup water, and 1 tablespoon peanut oil in a small pan. Bring to a boil. Cover and let stand for at least 30 minutes. Trim off the stems (reserve for future stock-making). Cut the caps into thin slices. Boil the beans in salted water until they just lose their raw taste. Drain, refresh in cold water, then pat dry.

(continued)

4. Blend together the vinegar with the remaining 1 teaspoon shallot, salt to taste, and about ½ teaspoon chili-pepper. Blend in the remaining 3 tablespoons peanut oil. Pour over the mushrooms, beans, and bean sprouts. Toss gently, then taste and add salt and/or chili to taste. Cover; refrigerate and chill for at least 30 minutes.

5. Heat a very heavy large cast-iron Dutch oven over moderate heat until very hot, about 10 minutes. Meanwhile, cook the duck breasts, fat side down, in a wide skillet over moderate heat until nicely browned, pouring off the fat as it accumulates. Sear the other side of the breasts to brown.

6. Place the duck breasts, skin side up, on a round cake rack about 9-inches in diameter. Drain the pickling spices and sprinkle quickly and evenly in the cast-iron pot. Immediately set the rack with the duck over the spices; cover at once. Cook for 8 minutes (still over moderate heat). Turn off the heat and let stand 2 minutes longer. Open the pot, remove the ducks directly (quickly pour some water into the pot and cover; the drippings will soak off easily this way). Let the ducks cool on a cutting board for 5–20 minutes before serving.

7. Portion the vegetables onto 4 large serving dishes. Divide the sauce in neat pools alongside. Cut the breasts in thin, lengthwise slices and arrange neatly over the sauce. Sprinkle with the remaining ½ teaspoon or so minced chili. Garnish, if desired, with the baby corn and bay leaves.

Note: *Mr. Skrobanek uses tamarind juice instead of lemon and yard-long beans for the green beans. If these are available to you, do the same, adding the tamarind juice gradually to taste. Cook the beans slightly longer than string beans until tender throughout.*

Ready-to-eat ears of baby corn are sold in jars and cans in Oriental groceries and many supermarkets. If fresh ears of baby corn are obtainable, blanch them.

4 SERVINGS AS LUNCH OR LIGHT SUPPER

Pork Loin with Quince

AUSTRALIA

Chef Gerard Taye of the Hilton International Adelaide created a deep-flavored course of wild boar steeped in brandy, quince, and ginger (a dish that hails back to ancient Rome) for the lavish Ultimate Dinner that is staged annually by the Hilton International Hotels in Australia in conjunction with Penfolds, notable vintners. Because wild boar is extremely difficult to obtain in many areas, pork has been substituted, and the techniques have been simplified for home cooks. The result, an easy-to-prepare melding of tender fruit and meat, is no compromise in taste.

1½ teaspoons peppercorns, crushed
1 medium onion, chopped
About 1 teaspoon salt
¼ cup brandy
¼ cup peeled, thin-sliced
    fresh ginger
4½-pound pork loin roast, boned
    (will equal about 3 pounds);
    bones and trimmings reserved

1 tablespoon vegetable oil
1 tablespoon tomato paste
1 cup chicken stock
1 cup port wine
3 quinces (about 1½ pounds),
    quartered, peeled, and cored
¼ cup (1 ounce) pine nuts (pignolia)
Pepper

1. Combine the pepper, onion, 1 teaspoon salt, brandy, and ginger in a nonaluminum dish large enough to hold the meat. Add the pork; turn to coat. Cover and refrigerate for about 24 hours, turning as convenient.

2. Preheat the oven to 325°. Remove the meat and pat dry; reserve the marinade. Heat the vegetable oil in a heavy 5-quart casserole or Dutch oven (preferably oval, not made of unlined iron or aluminum, which will discolor the quinces). Brown the meat well over high heat, then transfer to a dish. Add the reserved pork bones and trimmings to the pot; brown well. Pour off excessive fat, if necessary.

3. Strain and reserve the liquid from the marinade; add the solids to the pot. Cook over high heat for 5 minutes, stirring occasionally. Add the tomato paste; stir for 1 minute. Add the marinating liquid and ½ cup each of the chicken stock and port.

4. Set the pork on this. Arrange the quinces closely around the pork (set on top of the bones, not immersed in liquid). Roast until the internal temperature of the meat reaches 175°. Timing will vary with the diameter of meat, a thin loin taking only 1¼ hours, a thicker loin somewhat longer. Using a bulb baster, drench the quinces with the cooking liquid every 20 minutes or so during roasting.

5. Meanwhile, spread the pine nuts in a small pan and roast in the oven with the pork for about 10 minutes, until pale golden. Cool.

6. Transfer the meat to a cutting board and cover lightly with foil. Arrange the quince quarters around a platter; set in the turned-off oven. Add the remaining ½ cup each chicken stock and port to the pot. Bring to a boil, stirring to loosen all the brown bits; simmer for 2 minutes. Strain the juices from the pot. Skim off some of the fat. Season to taste with salt, pepper, brandy, and port.

7. Slice the meat; arrange with the quinces. Spoon over a little sauce; serve the rest separately. Sprinkle with pine nuts.

6 SERVINGS

STIR-FRIED PORK AND CASHEW NUTS
(Moo Pad Mamoung Himapan)
THAILAND

This attractive, casual Thai dish (almost Chinese, so direct is the influence) has the quintessential stir-fry look: brown-glazed cashew crescents, onion strips, and pork chunks sprinkled with slivers of red and green chili-peppers. Although the oyster sauce offers a complex undertone, the combination is frankly garlicky, salty, hot, and satisfying.

---

2 medium onions
1 pound boned pork loin
2 tablespoons vegetable oil
2 tablespoons sliced garlic
1 teaspoon sugar
1 cup (¼ pound) roasted unsalted
   cashew nuts

⅓ cup oyster sauce (see Note)
1 large scallion stalk (green part),
   cut into fine julienne
About 1 tablespoon *each* very fine
   julienne of hot red and green
   chili-pepper (such as Cayenne),
   seeds and ribs removed

---

1. Cut the onions into ½–¾-inch squares, separating the layers. Cut the pork crosswise into ½ inch slices. Cut each slice into strips about ¾ inch wide.

2. Heat a wok over moderate heat; pour 1 tablespoon oil around the rim. Toss the onions over moderate heat until lightly browned; add the garlic and toss for a minute. Transfer to a dish.

3. Pour the remaining 1 tablespoon of oil into the heated wok. Add the pork, spreading it out and up the sides in a single layer. Cook over high heat without turning until browned, a few minutes. Sprinkle with the sugar and toss for a minute or so, until browned all over.

4. Add the onion and garlic, cashews, and oyster sauce. Toss for about 2 minutes, until some of the liquid has evaporated and the meat is tender. Scoop into a heated serving dish; sprinkle with the scallions and chili-peppers to taste. Serve at once.

Note: *Bottled oyster sauce, a staple in the East, is available in all stores that carry Oriental ingredients and in many supermarkets.*

4 SERVINGS

Hainanese Chicken-Rice Dinner

SINGAPORE/CHINA/TAIWAN

A traditional specialty of Singapore, this ideal party meal of exotic soup, ginger-flavored rice, poached chicken, three intense sauces, and fried shallot garnish originates in the Hainan Islands of China. When chef Peter Knipp worked at the Singapore Hilton International, he added this version to the coffee shop menu, where it quickly became a fast favorite. When transferred to the Hilton International Taipei, he did the same—with equal success.

While the description and steps appear lengthy, the labor is minimal—and rewards are considerable, with an entire meal the result, not just a single dish.

2 quarts homemade, unsalted
   chicken broth
3 medium scallions, cleaned and
   trimmed
4–5 ounces fresh ginger
3½-pound chicken
1 cup plus 1 tablespoon vegetable oil
8 medium shallots, peeled and sliced
   (about ⅔ cup)
1 tablespoon all-purpose flour
1½ cups long-grain white rice
3 medium (4–5-inch) hot red chili-
   peppers, such as Cayenne
1 teaspoon minced garlic
¼ cup lime juice

1 tablespoon packed brown sugar
2 teaspoons light soy sauce
2 teaspoons Chinese rice wine or
   dry sherry
2 teaspoons Oriental (dark) sesame
   oil
6–8 romaine lettuce leaves
2 medium cucumbers, peeled,
   seeded, and cut into 2–3-inch
   strips about ¼ inch thick
4 teaspoons coarsely chopped
   preserved Chinese vegetable
   (see Note)
⅓ cup dark soy sauce (see Note)

1. Combine the chicken broth, 2 of the scallions, and 4 ginger rounds cut about ½ inch thick in a pot just large enough to hold the chicken. Bring to a boil. Add the chicken; cover, and maintain just below a simmer for 25 minutes.

2. Meanwhile, heat 1 cup of the vegetable oil in a small saucepan over moderate heat. Toss the shallots with the flour. Add to the oil gradually, being careful of bubbling oil; fry until crisp and golden, stirring occasionally, 5–6 minutes. Drain and set aside on paper towels.

3. Carefully transfer the chicken to a platter and cover with wet cheesecloth. When cool enough to handle, cut the leg-thigh sections from the bird and gently twist and cut out the bones. Halve the breast meat and lift from the carcass in 2 sections. Place in a close-fitting skillet and pour over 1 cup of the broth. Cover with cheesecloth. Refrigerate if not heating within an hour.

4. Combine the rice with 2¾ cups of the stock and 4 thin ginger slices in a 2-quart saucepan. Bring to a boil; turn the heat to its lowest point. Cover and cook for 20 minutes; remove from the heat and let stand for 15–30 minutes, covered. Fluff into a warm serving dish. Meanwhile, boil the remaining stock to reduce to 2½ cups.

5. Drop the chilis into boiling water; return to a boil. Mince fine (do not seed). Heat the remaining 1 tablespoon oil in a small pan. Add the chilis and toss for 1 minute over moderate heat. Add the minced garlic, lime juice, and brown sugar; stir for a minute. Set aside.

6. Grate fine enough peeled ginger to equal 3 tablespoons; blend with 4 tablespoons cold water and salt to taste. Blend the light soy, rice wine, and sesame oil. Arrange the lettuce and cucumbers on a platter. *(continued)*

7. Reheat the chicken on low heat. Transfer to a work surface; cut diagonal slices about 1 inch wide. Arrange on the cucumbers. Paint generously with the sesame oil mixture.

8. Slice the remaining scallion into thin rounds. Divide the hot stock into small soup bowls; sprinkle with the scallion, a teaspoon or so of fried shallots, and pickled vegetable. Serve the soup and rice along with tiny dishes of the grated ginger, the chili dip, and the dark soy for each diner.

Note: *Tianjin (Tientsin) pickled vegetable or Sichuanese (Szechuan) preserved mustard greens are among the several tangy members of the cabbage clan available in crocks, bottles, cans, and even sealed in plastic. They can be found in just about all Oriental markets.*

Chinese dark, thick, or black soy sauce is available in all Oriental groceries and many supermarkets.
Serving and presentation: *As much fun to make and serve as a fondue or firepot meal, the progression of dishes begs for company—and all the trimmings: chopsticks, miniature trios of sauceplates for each guest, individual Chinese rice bowls and soup bowls. Also desirable is a sense of play to mix and match the simple but intensely flavorful ingredients, so harmoniously balanced. The usual sequence is to dip a piece of chicken into a sauce, then soup, varying the dips, and drinking the intense brew that results.*
Advance preparation: *Although the chicken will not be just-poached perfect, it is delicious made in advance (but cook only 20 minutes), as is the entire meal. The soup and chili and ginger sauces can be made a day ahead, cooled, and refrigerated. The shallots can be made days in advance, then closed in a tightly sealed jar. Cucumbers and lettuce can be cleaned and cut, then refrigerated in plastic.*

4 SERVINGS

CHICKEN TERRINE WITH COCONUT-CHILI SAUCE
(Sambal Goreng Hati Ayam)
INDONESIA

From the Jakarta Hilton International, another beautiful example of exotic Eastern ingredients fashioned to fit a European mode (but beware of the innocent-looking sauce). The firm, tofu-lightened chicken loaf with its center medallion of cabbage-wrapped liver is complemented by a wildly pungent puree redolent of chilis, garlic, ginger, and citrus, enriched with coconut. The use of cream (which seldom appears in Asian cooking) is due to an Indonesian cook's attendance of a European terrine demonstration. Much impressed, he employed the techniques for creating such a dish, incorporating local ingredients for the main part and adapting the flavors to fit the clientele.

Terrine

1 pound boneless, skinless chicken breast

¾ teaspoon salt

¼ teaspoon white pepper

1 egg

½ cup heavy (or whipping) cream

10 ounces firm tofu (also called Chinese Tofu), well drained and cut into ¾-inch dice

1 tablespoon peanut oil

¼ pound chicken livers, cleaned and halved (see Option)

3 large, smooth Chinese cabbage leaves, about a foot long (choose the narrow, upright kind of cabbage rather than the rounded)

Sauce

1 tablespoon peanut oil

1½ tablespoons minced garlic

1½ tablespoons minced shallots

1 bay leaf

2 tablespoons chopped peeled fresh ginger

1 small stalk lemon grass, halved lengthwise, then cut in 4-inch lengths, or 4-inch strip lemon zest (see Note)

1 teaspoon tamarind paste, or 1 tablespoon lemon juice (see Note)

1 teaspoon brown sugar

1 tomato, peeled, cored, and coarsely chopped

3 tablespoons roasted macadamia nuts (or, preferably, candlenuts if available), crushed with a knife, meat pounder, or heavy pot

1 tablespoon or more Chinese chili sauce (see Note)

1 cup unsweetened coconut milk (see Note)

Garnish: 1 tomato, peeled, seeded, and cut into small dice; a few feathery-cut Chinese cabbage leaf tips

1. Preheat the oven to 350°. Remove and discard all tendons and membranes from the chicken; cut the meat into 1-inch dice. Combine in a processor with the salt and pepper. Work to a smooth paste. Add the egg and cream and whiz just to blend. Scrape into a bowl and mix gently with the tofu.

2. Heat the peanut oil in a small skillet; salt and pepper the livers lightly, then sauté just until they lose their raw look. Drop the Chinese cabbage leaves into boiling salted water; return to a boil. Refresh in cold water, drain; pat dry. Arrange the livers single file along the center of 1 leaf, then enclose with 1 or 2 others to form a neat cylinder. Wrap in a towel to dry and firm.

3. Line a 4½-cup rectangular terrine mold about 3½ by 11 inches with plastic wrap. Spread half the chicken mixture in this. Set the cabbage cylinder on this, then fill with the remaining chicken mixture, packing it tightly against and over the roll so no air holes are left. Bang the terrine against the table a few times to eliminate any other holes. Fold over the plastic wrap. (continued)

4. Set the terrine on a folded dish towel in a roasting pan; half-fill with boiling water. Set in the center of the oven. Bake for 30 minutes. Remove from the water and set on a rack to cool. Chill for 6–24 hours before serving.

5. Make the sauce: Heat the oil in a small saucepan. Add the garlic, shallots, bay leaf, and ginger and stir over low heat until softened, about 3 minutes. Add the lemon grass, tamarind, brown sugar, tomato, macadamia nuts, and 1 tablespoon chili sauce. Stir for 5 minutes over moderately low heat. Add the coconut milk (and lemon juice, if you have not used tamarind). Simmer for 5 minutes, until slightly thickened.

6. Remove the bay leaf and lemon grass (or zest). Puree the sauce in a processor or blender to a fine texture. Season, adding salt, pepper, and chili sauce to taste. Cool, then chill several hours or more.

7. To serve, place 3 tablespoons of sauce (or half this amount, for an appetizer) in the center of each plate. Arrange the garnishes alongside, then place 1 or 2 slices of the terrine on this.

Note: *Lemon grass and tamarind paste (see Clear Shrimp Soup with Lemon Grass for both, page 258) will give the sauce an intense aroma and sweet-tart finish. Substituting lemon zest and juice will result in a delicious, if less concentrated and perfumed mixture.*

Canned or bottled Chinese chili sauce is available in varying thicknesses and pungencies in some super-markets and in all Oriental groceries. It should contain primarily chili-peppers, garlic, sugar, vinegar, and salt.

Coconut milk can be found in Latin American, Caribbean, and Southeast Asian groceries. Or make your own following the instructions on page 325.

Serving and presentation: *Mr. Skrobanek serves the terrine with a palette of colorful, texturally contrasting, decorative garnishes: marbleized quail eggs (for this follow any recipe for tea eggs in a Chinese cookbook, but cut down the cooking and steeping time considerably); yard-long beans cut in small pieces and blanched, and diamond-cut red papaya, water chestnuts, red chili-peppers, and turnips—all blanched and chilled.*

Option: *For a pretty, delicate (non-Indonesian) alternative to the liver, substitute 9 medium, shelled shrimp. Simply season the raw shrimp with salt and pepper and wrap tightly in the cabbage cylinder. Proceed as directed for the livers.*

8 SERVINGS AS A LIGHT SUPPER OR LUNCH; 16 AS AN APPETIZER

CHICKEN STIR-FRIED WITH TREE EARS AND GINGER JULIENNE
(Gai Pad Khing Hed Hoo Noo)
THAILAND

You get an astonishing amount of taste and texture for little effort in this very popular Chinese-influenced dish that was demonstrated by sous-chef Viboon Roongrojpanawan in the busy Thai kitchen of the Hilton International Bangkok. The fresh and bright dish, which is served in the sunlit garden restaurant, Suan Saranrom, is composed of tender white chicken, crisp scallion pieces, a very large quantity of tingly ginger strips, brisk red chili-pepper, and black, crunchy mushrooms—lightly sauced with a bit of garlic and a touch of sweetness.

6 large or 10 medium dried tree ears (see Note)

1 pound boneless chicken breast (3 large breast halves)

3 tablespoons vegetable oil

2 teaspoons minced garlic

1 medium-large Bermuda or Spanish onion, quartered and sliced ¼ inch thick

½ cup peeled julienne-cut fresh ginger (2½ ounces)

1 red chili-pepper (4–5 inches long, such as Cayenne), cut into 1½-inch diagonal slices

¼ cup oyster sauce (see Note)

¼ cup chicken stock

1½ teaspoons sugar

4 small scallions, cut into 1-inch lengths (about ¾ cup)

1 tablespoon distilled white vinegar

¼ cup cilantro leaves

1. Soak the tree ears in about 2 cups warm water until supple, about 15 minutes. Drain and rinse lightly. Cut into 2-inch pieces, trimming off any knotty bits.

2. Trim skin and any tendons or membrane from the chicken. Cut into strips about 2 inches long and ½ inch wide.

3. Have all the other ingredients measured and ready. Heat a wok over moderate heat. Pour the oil around the rim; toss the garlic for a moment until light golden. Add the onion and toss for 30 seconds.

4. Add the chicken and raise the heat to its highest point. Stir-fry until half-cooked, about 1½ minutes. Add the ginger, mushrooms, and chili. Toss for 1 minute.

5. Add the oyster sauce and toss for 30 seconds. Add the stock and toss a moment. Add the sugar and scallions; toss for 15 seconds. Add the vinegar and toss.

6. Transfer to a hot dish. Sprinkle with the cilantro.

Note: *Tree ears, also known as cloud ears,* wood ears, mo-ehr, *black fungus, are readily obtained in most Oriental groceries in many different sizes.*

Bottled oyster sauce, a staple in the East, can be found in all Oriental groceries and many supermarkets. Serving: *If you are not passionate chili-lovers, pick out the peppers and place as garnish.*

4 SERVINGS

OVERLEAF: Chicken Stir-Fried with Tree Ears and Ginger Julienne

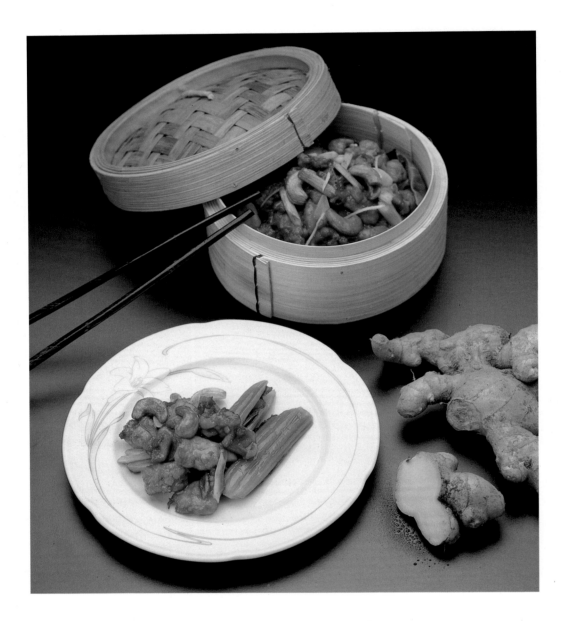

CHICKEN AND CASHEWS WITH CHINESE MUSTARD GREENS

TAIWAN

Yu Wen-Shen and Huang Hsien developed this version of a fine Chinese dish served at the Hilton International Taipei. Simple, attractive, and accessible, it appeals to both Eastern and Western guests. The Chinese mustard greens, furled and channeled like giant seashells, have a radish-cabbage flavor, bitter and cleansing, that is balanced by the sweetness of cashews and tender chicken. Although boldly flavored with garlic and fresh chili-pepper, the egg binding mellows the sauce, making it creamier than most dishes of this kind.

8 medium chicken thighs (about 1½ pounds)
2 tablespoons soy sauce
2¼ teaspoons cornstarch
1 egg
1 medium head Chinese mustard greens (Swatow mustard cabbage, *dai gai choi*; see Note)
4 tablespoons peanut oil
Salt and pepper

1 tablespoon slivered hot red chili-pepper (such as Cayenne), seeds and ribs removed
2 tablespoons Chinese rice wine or dry sherry
1 tablespoon distilled white vinegar
2 large scallions, trimmed and cut into 2-inch lengths
4 medium-large garlic cloves, sliced
½ cup roasted cashew nuts, preferably unsalted

1. Preheat the oven to 150–200°. Remove the skin and bones from the chicken; cut the meat into ½-inch cubes. Stir together 1 tablespoon soy sauce and 2 teaspoons cornstarch. Add the egg and blend. Add the chicken pieces. Cover and let marinate for ½-1 hour.

2. Meanwhile, select 8 of the firmest, prettiest mustard green leaves; trim off most of the ruffly leaf tips and wash the broad ribs. Drop into boiling, salted water; boil for 2–3 minutes, until crisp-tender. Drain, run under cold water. Spread on a towel.

3. Drain the chicken in a sieve, tossing to drip off the excess liquid. Heat a wok over moderate heat. Pour 2 tablespoons peanut oil around the rim. Toss the blanched greens in the oil to heat through. Sprinkle with salt and pepper. Arrange in a heatproof serving dish as a base for the chicken. Set in the low oven.

4. Combine the chili-pepper, rice wine, vinegar, the remaining 1 tablespoon soy, and the remaining ¼ teaspoon cornstarch. Pour the remaining 2 tablespoons oil into the wok. Add the chicken and toss to not quite cook through. With a slotted spoon transfer to a dish.

5. Add the scallions and garlic to the wok; toss until soft. Add the chicken and the rice wine mixture to the pan; toss for a minute. Add the cashews and toss.

6. Scoop into the warm platter lined with the greens. Serve hot.

Note: *Several cultivars of this mustard family member can be found in most Oriental markets. Some are rounded and fairly tightly furled, others long-leafed and loosely bunched. All have pale green midribs with shallow channels or furrows and darker leaf tips (which may be removed). Vaguely resembling a head of long-leafed lettuce, the innocent-seeming vegetable packs a big, bitter, radishy wallop, which is softened by the blanching.*

4 SERVINGS

BRAISED AND GRILLED CHICKEN IN COCONUT AND JAVANESE SPICES
(Ayam Sakang)
INDONESIA

The popular Peacock Café at the Jakarta Hilton International is warmly rose-beige and pink, spacious—and superb for people-watching around the clock. Whether it is 15 French teenagers enjoying a full rijstaffel *buffet, a group of Chinese businessmen downing a mountain of croissants and Danish pastry before an early morning flight, a superbly painted Vietnamese actress and her hairdresser nibbling a salty rice porridge after a night of discos, or the Indonesian family of eight—all members of which were happily eating the following dish—the place is always hopping.*

This informal, curryish Javanese chicken is braised in a rich sauce of coconut milk, ginger, coriander, lemon grass, and chili, thickened and sweetened with roasted nuts and brown sugar, then briefly browned and crisped under the broiler.

6 medium leg-thigh chicken pieces
  (about 3¼ pounds)
3 tablespoons vegetable oil
2 stalks lemon grass (see Note)
4 medium shallots
4 medium-large garlic cloves
2½-inch chunk peeled fresh ginger
3 tablespoons ground coriander
2 teaspoons ground turmeric

4 bay leaves
¾ teaspoon salt
1½ cups unsweetened coconut milk
  (see Note)
¼ cup Chinese chili sauce (see Note)
3 tablespoons brown sugar
⅓ cup roasted macadamia nuts,
  chopped fine
Basil leaves for garnish

1. Trim loose fat from the chicken, then cut apart the legs and thighs.

2. Heat 2 tablespoons of the oil in a 10–11-inch skillet over moderate heat. Add the chicken pieces and brown well on both sides. Remove from the pan and set aside. Pour out all but 2 tablespoons fat from the pan and reserve.

3. Cut the heavy upper leaves from the lemon grass; unwrap the dry green layers until you get to the pale core. Halve lengthwise; cut into 1–2-inch slices (you should have ⅓-½ cup). With the motor running, drop the lemon grass into a food processor. Add the shallots, garlic, and ginger, and grind to a fine texture to make a seasoning paste.

4. Heat the reserved fat over moderately low heat. Scoop in the seasoning paste; stir constantly for 2 minutes. Add the coriander, turmeric, bay leaves, and salt; stir for 1 minute. Add the coconut milk; stir to blend. Add the chili sauce, brown sugar, and macadamia nuts; stir for another minute.

5. Add the chicken; press into the thick sauce. Cook over low heat for 20 minutes, stirring often and moving the chicken around in the pan to cook evenly and prevent sticking.

6. Preheat the broiler. Transfer the chicken pieces to a broiler pan, skin side up. Remove all the fat from the sauce along with the bay leaves. Simmer the sauce, stirring, for about 5 minutes, or until it is pasty. Spoon off any remaining fat. Paint the chicken pieces generously with the sauce (if some remains, save it to use as the base of a curry-type braise).

7. Set the chicken pieces in the middle level of a preheated broiler. Cook until crisped, about 10 minutes.

Note: *Long stalks of greyish-green fresh lemon grass can be found in Southeast Asian groceries and some supermarkets. They add a subtle, inimitable lemon pungency.*

  Coconut milk is available in canned or bottled form in stores that carry ingredients from South America and Asia. If you cannot buy it, make your own, following the directions on page 325.

  Chinese chili sauce (easily obtained in Oriental markets and many specialty stores) has varying pungencies, densities, and flavorings. As long as it is fairly thick but pourable, and contains primarily chili, garlic, salt, sugar, and vinegar, it will do. The bite is considerably tamed by the other ingredients and cooking procedures.

4 SERVINGS

CUCUMBER-GINGER GRANITA
(Ketimun Serut)

INDONESIA

This is not a dessert, but we have no other category into which it might be placed; it is simply in a class by itself. A traditional Indonesian palate-cleanser, served by chef Detlef Skrobanek of the Jakarta Hilton International, this pale-green crushed ice is so sharply refreshing it will wash away the richly pervasive flavors of the Spice Islands—including shallots, garlic, coconut milk, even chili-peppers—to soothe the way for a subtle subsequent course.

---

3 medium-large cucumbers (about 9 ounces each)
¼ cup lime juice

¼ cup sugar
1½ tablespoons finely grated peeled fresh ginger

---

1. Peel, halve, and seed the cucumbers. Shred 2 on the blade of a food processor, pressing very lightly to make fine shreds.

2. Switch to the all-purpose blade and puree the remaining cucumber. Press in a sieve to extract the juice. Add water to make 1 cup.

3. Combine the shredded cucumbers, the cucumber juice, lime juice, sugar, and ginger in a stainless steel bowl; let stand for 2 hours at room temperature.

4. Cover with plastic and place in the coldest part of your freezer. When the mixture is beginning to solidify, (timing varies considerably, depending upon your freezer; begin checking after an hour) stir it up with a fork. Repeat several times during the freezing to break up the crystals and produce a snowy texture. Either serve at once, or close tightly and freeze for up to 24 hours.

5. To serve, soften in the refrigerator for about ½ hour, breaking up the crystals with a fork 3 or 4 times, or until the mixture has a snowy texture—almost on the verge of slushy. Serve at once.

4–6 SERVINGS

Strawberry and Yogurt Mousse with Grand Marnier Sauce

SINGAPORE

A simple-to-make showpiece from the dessert trolley at the Hilton International Singapore: Neat pink mounds of soft, light yogurt mousse inlaid with strawberries are set in pools of golden sauce flecked with mint and garnished with fresh oranges.

Mousse
1 packet unflavored gelatine
¾ cup orange juice
⅓ cup sugar
1 pint medium strawberries, rinsed
    and hulled
¾ cup yogurt
½ cup heavy (or whipping) cream
1 tablespoon rum

Sauce and garnish
1 cup orange juice
3 tablespoons sugar
3 tablespoons Grand Marnier
1–2 teaspoons finely slivered mint
    leaves
3 large navel oranges
Mint sprigs for garnish

(continued)

1. Sprinkle the gelatine over the orange juice in a small nonaluminum saucepan. Add the sugar. Let stand a few minutes to soften.

2. Meanwhile, slice enough berries into crosswise rounds to line the bottom and sides of six ½-cup timbale (dariole) molds (see Note). Do not overlap the slices. Cut enough of the remaining berries into tiny dice to equal ¾ cup.

3. Bring the gelatine mixture to a simmer over low heat, stirring. Add the diced strawberries and stir; remove from the heat.

4. Set the saucepan in ice water. Cool, stirring occasionally, until thickened and partly set. Whisk the yogurt in a mixing bowl to liquefy. Whip the cream in a small bowl to form soft peaks. Pour the gelatine-berry mixture over the yogurt; add the rum. Blend thoroughly with a rubber spatula. Fold in the cream, mixing until few blobs remain visible.

5. Spoon the mixture into the prepared molds. Cover with plastic and refrigerate for 3 hours or longer.

6. While the desserts chill, prepare the sauce: Combine the orange juice and sugar in a small nonaluminum saucepan; bring to a boil to dissolve the sugar. Cool. Add the Grand Marnier and mint to taste. Refrigerate until serving time.

7. Remove all skin and pith from the oranges. Sliver off the membrane, then cut between the partitions to section the oranges closely. Chill.

8. To serve, dip each timbale into warm water for a few seconds; gently unmold onto an individual serving plate (leaving plenty of room for the sauce and fruit). Spoon the sauce onto the plate, arrange 6 orange slices alongside, then garnish with the mint sprigs. Repeat with all the desserts.

Note: *The neat timbale shape looks very stylish and trim, but you can substitute demitasse cups or any other small forms from which the dessert will unmold easily.*

6 SERVINGS

GUAVA FRITTERS AND MANGO WITH BLUEBERRY TOFU CREAM

TAIWAN

Chef Peter Knipp's cross-cultural creations are never predictable. This festive dessert, served at the Hilton International Taipei, looks wild and gaudy: Tart, violet sauce and sweet orange mango are tucked around easy-to-make, extremely delicate fried packets of guava.
(continued)

8 ounces tender ripe guava (or use canned; see Note)
1 tablespoon granulated sugar
1 star anise, broken into 2 sections
¼ teaspoon ground cinnamon
1 lemon slice
Sauce
1 tablespoon granulated sugar
½ cup fresh blueberries
4 ounces silken or silk tofu (about ½ cup; see Note)

About 2 tablespoons half-&-half
About 1 tablespoon lime juice
Final assembly
16 wonton skins, 3½ inches square (see Note)
1 egg yolk blended with 1 teaspoon water
2 medium mangos
Vegetable oil for deep frying
Confectioners' sugar
Sprigs of mint for garnish (optional)

1. Peel, quarter, and seed the guava; cut into ⅛–¼-inch dice. Combine ¼ cup water, the granulated sugar, star anise, cinnamon, and lemon in a small nonaluminum saucepan and bring to a simmer. Add the fruit; stir and cover. Cook over low heat until tender— 5–15 minutes. Uncover; simmer to evaporate any liquid, if necessary. Remove the lemon and star anise. Cool.

2. Prepare the sauce: Combine the granulated sugar, 2 tablespoons water, and the blueberries in a small nonaluminum saucepan. Bring to a boil, stirring. Boil for 30 seconds. Press through a sieve. Chill the puree. Beat the tofu with a whisk to liquefy it. Whisk in the blueberry puree, then the half-and-half, adjusting to the desired consistency. Add the lime juice. Refrigerate.

3. Assembly: Spread the wonton skins on a dry work surface. Place about 1 heaping teaspoon of the guava compote on each; paint the edges with the egg yolk. Fold to form neat triangles.

4. Peel the mangos; cut into thin slices. Arrange on 4 large plates.

5. Pour oil into a deep-fat fryer or electric skillet to a depth of about 2 inches. Heat to 350°. Drop in the wontons, 8 at a time, and fry until light golden, ½–1 minute. Drain on paper towels while you fry the remainder.

6. Spoon blueberry cream onto each plate. Dust confectioners' sugar over the fritters; arrange alongside. Serve warm, garnished with mint.

Note: *If fresh guava is not available to you, substitute a 1-pound can of guava shells in syrup. Drain and rinse the fruit; cut enough into tiny dice to yield ¾ cup. Add 2 tablespoons lime juice and ¼ teaspoon cinnamon. Proceed to Step 2.*

Silken tofu is more delicate and custardlike than soft tofu which may, however, be substituted.

Wonton skins this size are available in all Oriental grocery stores and in many supermarkets, as is the silken tofu.

Advance preparation: *The blueberry sauce improves if made a day in advance. Dumplings made with canned guava can be tightly wrapped in a single layer and refrigerated for 24 hours before frying; ones made from the fresh should wait no longer than 4 hours before being fried.*

Serving and presentation: *Mr. Knipp cuts the mangos in thinnest lengthwise slices and folds them to overlap, like waves. If you have custard-soft, fiberless mangos, do the same.*

4 SERVINGS

A Sip of Australian Wine Country:
The Grange at the
Hilton International Adelaide

Adelaide, in South Australia, a broad, open city that blends aspects of Victorian, Wild West, and state-of-the-art contemporary architecture, is a peaceful place, except during the Grand Prix, which zooms through it. Settled primarily by English, Scottish, and Irish, who had done well in banking, real estate, and mining, the grapevines were first planted in 1838—and 60 percent of the country's wines are now produced there. The Hilton International Adelaide is home to The Grange, an esteemed restaurant named in honor of the Grange Hermitage of Penfolds, one of Australia's most celebrated wines (itself named after the original Grange cottage built by the founder of the vineyard in the mid-nineteenth century). The hotel is within an hour's drive of 120 registered wineries and offers (from a unique walk-in cellar and tasting room) an award-winning wine list of 400 wines, 80 percent of which come from the area.

For a dinner that showcased local foods and wine, Gerard Taye, executive chef, began with Marinated Tasmanian Salmon Roses, a presentation of subtly marinated slices of richly colored raw fish furled into rose forms and served with a piquant and fresh peppercorn sauce. The Atlantic salmon featured has been, until recently, a species found only in northern climes, but is being farmed successfully in Tasmania for the first time. The dish was accompanied by a long-finishing 1984 Orlando St. Hillary Chardonnay, tinged with tropical fruit flavors. There followed an intense consommé of wild Coorong stubble quail which held tiny quenelles—each containing a creamy-soft poached quail egg that burst on the tongue. Matched with the deep amber essence was a like-colored, brilliant special-blend sherry, reminiscent of both amontillado and amoroso, the work of the legendary Master Winemaker of Penfolds, Max Schubert. Smoked loin of kangaroo (surprisingly bland, lean, and tender—and permissible as restaurant fare only in this part of the country) was embellished with black currant sauce, a tiny potato galette, baby carrots and turnips, and perfectly paired with a deeply cassis-flavored Penfolds Bin 389 1982. The complex Gippsland blue cheese and buttery Tasmanian Camembert were complemented by celery bread, pillowy-fat dried muscat raisins, celery sprigs, and the namesake wine of the restaurant, 1980 vintage. Passion fruit, mango, and strawberry sherbets with passion fruit sauce left a clean perfume in the mouth—or one could move on to the multitude of dessert wines offered, if one possibly could survive.

The Hilton International chefs responsible for the annual Ultimate Dinner (from left to right): Jean-Yves Meraud of Sydney; Herbert Franceschini of Brisbane; Gerard Taye of Adelaide; Anton Muhlbock of Perth; Heiner Volkens of Sydney Airport; and Patrick Biddlecomb, of Melbourne. In the center is Max Schubert, the creator of Grange Hermitage, the most celebrated of the wines of Penfolds, the event's co-sponsor.

The Ultimate Dinner

Since 1984, the executive chefs of Hilton International's Australian hotels and the distinguished winery, Penfolds, have created an annual gala known as The Ultimate Dinner, a celebration of native ingredients in elaborate and fanciful guises. In 1986 the event, which took place at the Hilton International Adelaide, progressed from an aspic of hare and kangaroo with a creamy sauce of pureed artichoke bottoms, through pigeon broth garnished with quail eggs and flakes of gold leaf, to a trio of local shellfish (Sydney rock oysters, South Australian green king prawns, Western Australian scallops) with sauces of lobster and mud crabs, to a roast loin of wild boar in quince sauce (see adaptation, page 298), through a cheese course, to a finale of cream-puff pelicans filled with mango and strawberry bavarian creams set in swirled fruit sauce "paintings."

Dried Fruit Bread

AUSTRALIA

Although many of the dishes from The Ultimate Dinner are not ones that can be duplicated at home (unless you live in Australia and have a kitchen staff of vast proportions), part of the meal can be successfully made by the amateur cook. The course dubbed "Cheeses from the Pastoral Lands" was offered with two simple breadstuffs (both recipes follow): long, egg-glazed loaves packed with dried fruits, and pale biscuitish rounds—both unusual complements for the rich cheeses. Outside of Australia, a double cream cheese can be substituted for the King Island cheese, a creamy blue for the Gippsland blue, and Brie for the Jindivick. The three cheeses and two breads were served along with dried muscat grapes or figs and a garnish of celery leaves.

¼-ounce packet of active dry yeast
2 tablespoons warm water
2 tablespoons sugar
1½ cups warm milk
3½ cups (17½ ounces) bread flour, plus about 1 cup for kneading
⅔ cup dried currants
½ cup dark raisins
½ cup golden raisins

⅔ cup mixed glacéed fruit peel, chopped small
1½ cups dried apples, coarse-chopped
1 egg, beaten
1 teaspoon ground nutmeg
2 teaspoons salt
2 tablespoons softened butter
1 egg beaten with 1 tablespoon milk for glaze

---

1. Stir together the yeast, warm water and a pinch of the sugar. Let stand 5 minutes, until slightly fluffy. (If the mixture does not puff, begin again with fresh ingredients.) Add the remaining sugar and ¾ cup warm milk. Stir in 1 cup flour to make a fairly smooth mixture. Sprinkle over ½ cup more flour to coat evenly. Cover with a damp cloth. Let stand until the top has cracked in a marbled pattern, about ½ hour.

2. Meanwhile, combine the currants, raisins, peel, and apples in a bowl. Pour over boiling water to cover.

3. When the dough "sponge" is ready, stir in the flour on top, then beat in the remaining ½ cup milk, the egg, nutmeg, salt, and remaining 2 cups flour. Knead in the soft butter, folding and stirring the dough in the bowl.

4. Spread 1 cup flour on a working surface. Scrape the dough onto this and knead until shiny and supple, about 5 minutes, incorporating only as much flour as needed to prevent the dough from sticking.

5. Drain the fruit thoroughly, then dry on a towel. Gradually knead into the dough, incorporating flour from the board as needed. Cover and let stand for 10 minutes.

(continued)

Dried Fruit Bread (left) and Dampers (right) from the cheese course served at The Ultimate Dinner

6. Cut the dough in half. Roll each piece under your palms to form a cylinder about 15 inches long. With the side of your hand, press a trench lengthwise, down the center of the loaf. Follow this mark to pinch the sides of the dough together and close the seam. Repeat. Turn seam side down and roll to form an even cylinder.

7. With a long spatula gently set the soft loaves well apart on a nonstick or parchment-covered baking sheet. Cover with a towel and let rise until doubled in bulk, about 1½ hours. Preheat the oven to 350°.

8. Brush the loaves with the egg glaze. Set in the center of the oven and bake until the bread is evenly golden brown and sounds hollow when picked up and rapped on the bottom—about 45 minutes.

9. Cool completely on racks.

Advance preparation: *Loaves may be prepared several days ahead and cooled completely, then wrapped in plastic. Unwrap and warm for 10 minutes in a 350° oven before serving.*

2 LOAVES, EACH ABOUT 20 SLICES

DAMPERS

AUSTRALIA

Damper *is a word used in the Australian outback for a primitive pancake made of flour and water that is baked in the coals of a campfire and consumed hot. Although it may be leavened, more often than not it is flat, unseasoned, and tough. By contrast the following so-called dampers are soft-spoken companions for the luxurious cheeses served at the Ultimate Dinner. They are pale, puffy, salty-sweet rounds somewhere between milk crackers and beaten biscuits and are decidedly not campfire fare. Paired with the Dried Fruit Bread (preceding recipe) and cheeses, they make an interesting dessert course. Or serve alongside soups and stews, or for a cheese and wine party.*

3¾ cups (18 ounces) bread flour,
   plus ½ cup for rolling
1 tablespoon sugar
1 teaspoon salt

2 tablespoons baking powder
1 tablespoon butter
⅓ cup heavy (or whipping) cream

1. Place the 3¾ cups flour, the sugar, salt, and baking powder in a mixing bowl. Add 1¾ cups water and mix on low speed for 3 minutes. Add the butter and cream. Mix on medium speed for 3 minutes longer.

2. Cover and let stand for 5–10 minutes. (The dough will be *very* soft and sticky.)

3. Preheat the oven to 375°. Spread ¼ cup of the extra flour on a working surface. Scoop the soft dough onto this. Using a dough scraper or stiff pancake turner, knead the dough briefly to incorporate most of the flour. Sprinkle half the remainder on the board, then pat the dough to form a rectangle. Sprinkle the remaining 2 tablespoons flour over this, then pat to form an even rectangle about 18 × 12 inches.

4. Using a 3-inch round cutter, cut about 20 circles. Lifting carefully with the long side of a spatula, set 14 rounds on one baking sheet, 6 on another. Roll out the remaining dough and cut about 8 more. Place these on the second baking sheet.

5. Set the baking sheets in the middle and lower positions of the oven. Bake for 10 minutes, then switch positions. Bake for about 7 minutes longer, or until the tops are dry and firm and the undersides are lightly golden. Do not bake until browned. Serve freshly baked.

Advance preparation: *Although these soft, doughy dampers are at their best if served warm and fresh, they can be wrapped and stored for a day or so. To revive them, mist with a little water, then reheat for about 5 minutes in a 350° oven.*

ABOUT 28

ABOUT THE INGREDIENTS

Most uncommon ingredients are described within the recipes.

Mail-order sources are provided on page 327 for those foods that travel well and may not be available throughout the country.

Butter is unsalted.

Chili-peppers' heat and intensity are so variable, even within the same variety, that it is impossible to give more than a vague general idea of how much to use. Add gradually, and to taste; remove ribs and seeds for most dishes, but leave in the ribs for passionate heat-lovers.

Cornstarch, cornmeal, and *cocoa* are indicated in ounces (although this is not the American custom) when they occur in relatively large quantities. This ensures accuracy.

Eggs are extra-large.

Flour is all-purpose, unless otherwise specified. It is measured in cups, as is the American custom, except in baking recipes, where the precision of a weight measurement is necessary for accuracy.

Gelatine is the granulated, unflavored type most commonly sold in ¼-ounce packets.

Mussels that are cultivated, generally meatier and cleaner than wild, are available in fine fish stores and some supermarkets. They are well worth the slightly higher price, as there is little waste. To clean, simply rinse the mussels in ice cold water. If any are open, test their freshness by sliding the shells in opposite directions. If there is considerable resistance, and the mussel either closes up or almost closes, keep it. If it stays open, or the shells slide apart, discard it. Remove the byssus threads ("beard").

Soy sauce refers to what is sometimes called "thin" or "regular" soy, such as the Kikkoman brand that is manufactured and available throughout the United States. This is neither as salty as the Chinese soy, nor as sweet as most Japanese brands. If you use either of these others, cut down slightly on the quantity.

Squid cleaning is simple—more so than writing the directions: Holding the body (mantle) with one hand and tentacle part with the other, pull to separate the two: the viscera and ink sac will come out attached to the tentacle section. Cut the tentacle section from the head part and discard the latter. Squeeze the bony beak from the center of tentacles; it will pop out. Cut tentacles into small sections. Pull out the clear plastic-like pen or sword from the mantle section and discard. Peel the purplish membrane from this section, working under running water. Carefully wash the mantle inside and out, emptying it of any remaining material.

Tomatoes, "peeled, seeded, and diced," are treated slightly differently in hotels than most home kitchens. The skin is removed by blanching in the traditional manner; or as we prefer for small quantities, by holding a tomato on a long-handled fork directly in a flame for a few seconds to blister the skin which is easily slipped off. The tomato is then quartered, and the entire soft, seedy section is cut out and discarded, leaving only the firm shell, which is cut into small squares. This presents a more attractive, less unpredictably watery dish (although it wastes the pulp).

COCONUT MILK

1 coconut

1. Preheat the oven to 375°. With clean nail or pick, tap holes in two "eyes" of the coconut; drain and reserve the liquid.

2. Bake for 10 minutes. Holding with a towel, hit around the equator with a hammer until cracked all around. Pry out the flesh and cut into chunks.

3. Add enough water to the reserved coconut juice to make 2 cups; bring to a boil. Combine half the boiling liquid with half the coconut meat in a blender or processor; grind as fine as possible. Pour into a sieve lined with dampened cheesecloth and let drain. Repeat, using the remaining coconut and liquid. Press and twist the cloth to extract all liquid from the coconut shreds.

Note: *For a thinner coconut milk, repeat the process with the ground coconut and an additional 1 cup boiling water. Store for only a day or two in the refrigerator, or for months in the freezer.*

MAKES 2–2½ CUPS

BASIC FISH STOCK

For most stocks, the bones of lean-fleshed, mild fish are preferable, as oily or strong fish may yield an undesirably aggressive flavor. Gauge the oiliness (or assertiveness of taste) by previous eating and cooking experience. Mackerel, herring, sablefish, bluefish, and tuna will be too potent or fatty for most sauces or soups. Fish that contain large quantities of gelatine, such as halibut or cod, should be used in moderation, unless the finished dish will be one with considerable body and some stickiness—such as chowder. Fish that are considered prime candidates for the stockpot might be all types of flounder and sole, whiting, pike, pompano, perch, red snapper, porgy, and sea bass. Before putting any fish into the stockpot, be sure it is completly free of gills and viscera.

4 pounds fish bones and heads, with no innards or gills
2 small onions, quartered
2 celery ribs with leaves, sliced

1 large carrot, sliced
1 bay leaf
Small handful parsley stems

1. Wash the fish heads and bones well in cold water. Combine in a stockpot with 4 quarts water, the onions, celery, carrot, bay leaf, and parsley stems. Bring to a simmer, skimming.

2. Simmer very gently for 20 minutes, skimming as needed. Ladle through a fine sieve.

3. Cool, cover, then refrigerate or freeze until needed.

MAKES ABOUT 3½ QUARTS

MAIL-ORDER SOURCES

Fancy foods:

Maison E. H. Glass Inc.
52 East 58th St.
New York, NY 10022
212-755-3316

Balducci's
424 Sixth Ave.
New York, NY 10011
212-673-2600

Corti Bros.
5770 Freeport Blvd.
Sacramento, CA 95822
916-391-0300

C. Steele & Co.
7303 E. Indian School Rd.
Scottsdale, AZ 85251
602-994-4180

Dean & DeLuca
110 Greene St.
New York, NY 10012
800-221-7714

Todaro Bros.
557 Second Ave.
New York, NY 10016
212-679-7766

Mexican and Southwestern foods:

El Molino Foods
1078 Santa Fe Dr.
Denver, CO 80204
303-623-7870

The Mexican Connection
142 Lincoln Ave.
Santa Fe, NM 87501
505-988-2940

Casados Farms
P.O. Box 852
San Juan Pueble, NM 87566
505-852-2433

Oriental foods:

Kam Man
200 Canal St.
New York, NY 10013
212-571-0330

Katagiri Co.
224 East 59th St.
New York, NY 10022
212-755-3566

Uwajimaya
P.O. Box 3003
Seattle, WA 98114
206-624-6248

Star Market
3349 N. Clark St.
Chicago, IL 60657
312-472-0599

Southeast Asian and Indonesian foods:

DeWildt Imports Inc.
R.D. 3
Bangor, PA 18013
215-588-0600

Uwajimaya
P.O. Box 3003
Seattle, WA 98114
206-624-6248

Middle Eastern foods:

Sultan's Delight
25 Croton Ave.
Staten Island, NY 10301
718-720-1557

Indian foods:

Spice & Sweet Mahal
135 Lexington Ave.
New York, NY 10016
212-683-0900

Bazaar of India Imports
1810 University Ave.
Berkeley, CA 94703
415-548-4110

Antoine's Import Co.
4234 Harry Hines Blvd.
Dallas, TX 75219
214-528-5291

INDEX